CLEOPATRA

CLEOPATRA

LAST QUEEN OF EGYPT

JOYCE TYLDESLEY

BASIC
BOOKS

A Member of the Perseus Books Group
New York

Copyright © 2008 by Joyce Tyldesley
First published in the United States in 2008 by Basic Books,
A Member of the Perseus Books Group
Published in Great Britain in 2008 by Profile Books Ltd

Books published by Basic Books are available at special discounts
for bulk purchases in the United States by corporations, institutions,
and other organizations. For more information, please contact the Special
Markets Department at the Perseus Books Group, 2300 Chestnut Street,
Suite 200, Philadelphia, PA 19103, or call (800) 810-4145, ext. 5000
or e-mail special.markets@perseusbooks.com.

A CIP catalog record for this book is available from the Library of Congress
HC ISBN: 978-0-465-00940-4
PB ISBN: 978-0-465-01892-5
LCCN: 2008921307

British ISBN: 978 1 86197 965 0
10 9 8 7 6 5 4 3 2 1

Dedicated to the memory of my late father,
William Randolph Tyldesley

Contents

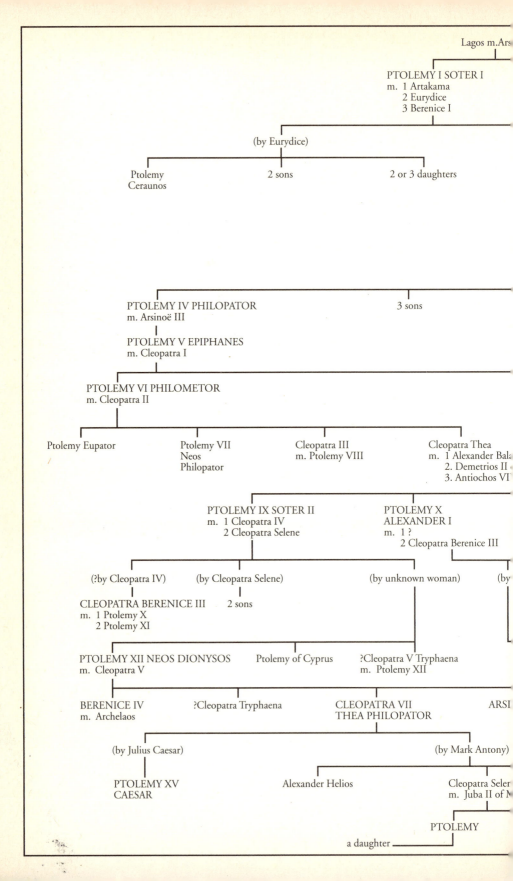

Lagos m.Ars...

PTOLEMY I SOTER I
m. 1 Artakama
2 Eurydice
3 Berenice I

(by Eurydice)

Ptolemy   2 sons   2 or 3 daughters
Ceraunos

PTOLEMY IV PHILOPATOR   3 sons
m. Arsinoë III

PTOLEMY V EPIPHANES
m. Cleopatra I

PTOLEMY VI PHILOMETOR
m. Cleopatra II

Ptolemy Eupator   Ptolemy VII   Cleopatra III   Cleopatra Thea
                     Neos   m. Ptolemy VIII   m. 1 Alexander Bal...
                     Philopator   2. Demetrios II ...
                                                           3. Antiochos VI...

PTOLEMY IX SOTER II   PTOLEMY X
m. 1 Cleopatra IV   ALEXANDER I
2 Cleopatra Selene   m. 1 ?
                                    2 Cleopatra Berenice III

(?by Cleopatra IV)   (by Cleopatra Selene)   (by unknown woman)   (by

CLEOPATRA BERENICE III   2 sons
m. 1 Ptolemy X
2 Ptolemy XI

PTOLEMY XII NEOS DIONYSOS   Ptolemy of Cyprus   ?Cleopatra V Tryphaena
m. Cleopatra V   m. Ptolemy XII

BERENICE IV   ?Cleopatra Tryphaena   CLEOPATRA VII   ARSI
m. Archelaos   THEA PHILOPATOR

(by Julius Caesar)   (by Mark Antony)

PTOLEMY XV   Alexander Helios   Cleopatra Seler
CAESAR   m. Juba II of N

                                             PTOLEMY

a daughter

The Ptolemies of Egypt

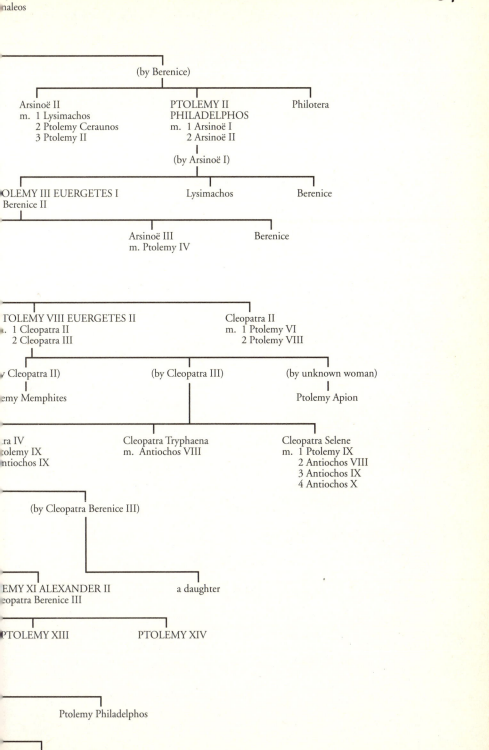

naleos

(by Berenice)

Arsinoë II
m. 1 Lysimachos
    2 Ptolemy Ceraunos
    3 Ptolemy II

PTOLEMY II
PHILADELPHOS
m. 1 Arsinoë I
    2 Arsinoë II

Philotera

(by Arsinoë I)

OLEMY III EUERGETES I
Berenice II

Lysimachos

Berenice

Arsinoë III
m. Ptolemy IV

Berenice

TOLEMY VIII EUERGETES II
. 1 Cleopatra II
    2 Cleopatra III

Cleopatra II
m. 1 Ptolemy VI
    2 Ptolemy VIII

y Cleopatra II)

(by Cleopatra III)

(by unknown woman)

emy Memphites

Ptolemy Apion

ra IV
tolemy IX
ntiochos IX

Cleopatra Tryphaena
m. Antiochos VIII

Cleopatra Selene
m. 1 Ptolemy IX
    2 Antiochos VIII
    3 Antiochos IX
    4 Antiochos X

(by Cleopatra Berenice III)

EMY XI ALEXANDER II
eopatra Berenice III

a daughter

PTOLEMY XIII

PTOLEMY XIV

Ptolemy Philadelphos

a daughter

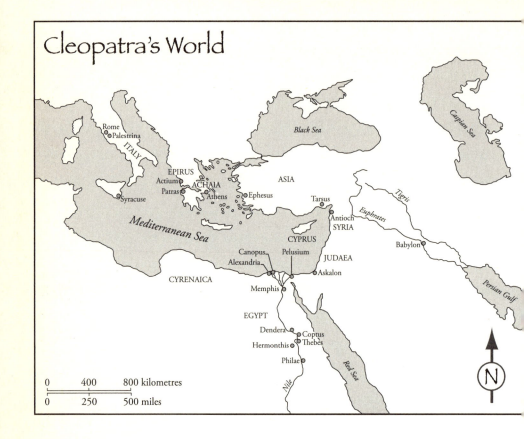

Cleopatra's World

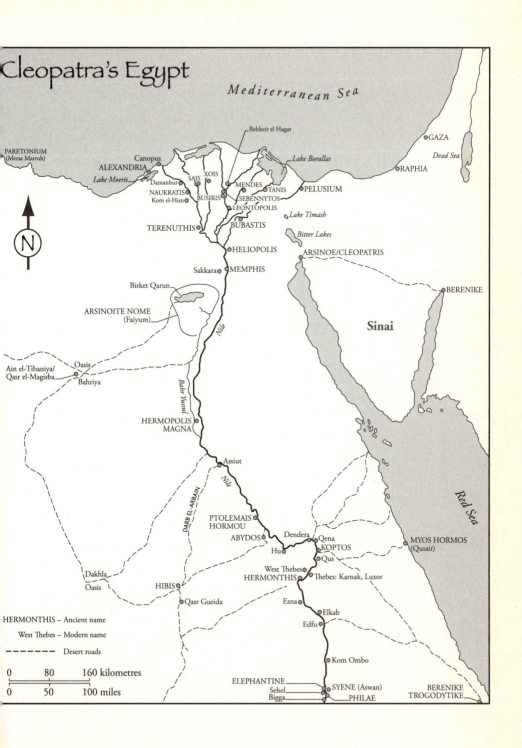

Cleopatra's Egypt

Mediterranean Sea

GAZA

Dead Sea

PARETONIUM
(Mersa Matruh)

Behbeit el Hagar

Lake Borallas

RAPHIA

Canopus

ALEXANDRIA

Lake Moeris

Damanhur

SAIS · XOIS

MENDES

TANIS

PELUSIUM

NAUKRATIS

BUSIRIS

SEBENNYTOS

Kom el-Hisn

LEONTOPOLIS

Lake Timash

TERENUTHIS

BUBASTIS

Bitter Lakes

HELIOPOLIS

ARSINOE/CLEOPATRIS

Sakkara

MEMPHIS

BERENIKE

Birket Qarun

Sinai

ARSINOITE NOME
(Faiyum)

Ain el-Tibaniya/
Qasr el-Magisba

Oasis

Bahriya

Nile

Bahr Yussuf

Red Sea

HERMOPOLIS
MAGNA

Assiut

Nile

DARB EL-ARBAIN

PTOLEMAIS
HORMOU

Dakhla
Oasis

ABYDOS

Dendera

Qena

KOPTOS

MYOS HORMOS
(Qusair)

Hu

Qus

HIBIS

West Thebes

HERMONTHIS

Thebes: Karnak, Luxor

Qasr Gueida

Esna

Elkab

Edfu

Kom Ombo

HERMONTHIS – Ancient name

West Thebes – Modern name

- - - - - Desert roads

| 0 | 80 | 160 kilometres |
| 0 | 50 | 100 miles |

ELEPHANTINE

Sehel

Bigga

SYENE (Aswan)

PHILAE

BERENIKE
TROGODYTIKE

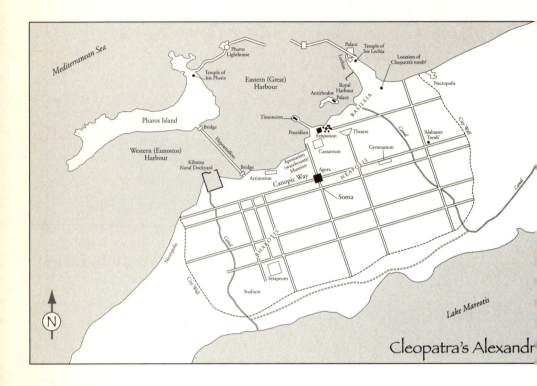

Cleopatra's Alexandr

Author's Note

Personal names are a potential minefield for the student of ancient history. I have aimed at clarity for those new to the Ptolemaic age, and can only apologise in advance to those who may feel that I have made irrational, inconsistent or unscholarly decisions. Throughout the book I have favoured the traditional spelling Cleopatra rather than the more authentic but less widely known Kleopatra. Similarly, when using Roman names I have opted for the more familiar modern variants: Caesar instead of Gaius Julius (Iulius) Caesar, Antony instead of Marcus Antonius, and so on. Octavian was, as Mark Antony so rudely noted, a boy who owed everything to his name. Soon after Cleopatra's suicide, Octavian (initially Gaius Octavius; later Gaius Julius Caesar Octavianus) took the title Imperator and the name Caesar Augustus. To avoid confusion I refer to him as Octavian throughout. As a general rule, I use the '-os' ending for those of Greek heritage, so that, for example, Cleopatra's youngest son becomes Ptolemy Philadelphos rather than the Latinised Ptolemy Philadelphus, but I retain the '-us' ending for those, like Herodotus, who are today widely known by the Latin version of their name.

All dates are BC (BCE) unless otherwise specified. The dynastic Egyptians counted their years by reference to the current king's reign, each new reign requiring the number system to start again at regnal

Year I. The Ptolemies continued this system. The Romans used a lunar calendar of 355 days but neglected to add in the occasional month that would keep the official calendar in line with the seasons. On 1 January 46 Julius Caesar introduced a new Egyptian-inspired calendar of 365.25 days. His Julian calendar remains the basis of our own modern calendar.

Throughout the text I have used the loose term 'dynastic Egypt' to refer to the thirty-one dynasties before the 332 arrival of Alexander the Great.

Introduction

In the case of Cleopatra the biographer may approach his subject from one of several directions. He may, for example, regard the Queen of Egypt as a thoroughly bad woman, or as an irresponsible sinner, or as a moderately good woman in a difficult situation.

Arthur Weigall, *The Life and Times of Cleopatra Queen of Egypt*[1]

In approximately 3100 the independent city-states of the narrow Nile Valley and the broad Nile Delta united to form one long realm. Lines of heroic, semi-divine kings emerged to rule this new land; lines of beautiful queens stood dutifully by their side. If occasionally the kings were less heroic, and the queens less beautiful, than they perhaps could have been, it did not matter overmuch. State propaganda – the convention of presenting all kings as handsome, wise and brave, and all queens as pale, passive and supportive – would ensure that both kings and queens were remembered as they should have been, not as they were. Three thousand years of dynastic rule were to see at least 300 kings claiming sovereignty over the 'Two Lands', the unified Nile Valley and Delta. Those 300 kings were married to several thousand queens, of whom Cleopatra VII was the last.

Included among the thousands of queens were many consorts of immense influence and power, and at least three queens regnant who were accepted by their people as semi-divine female kings.[2] Memories of these queens were embedded in Egypt: in tombs, on temple walls, in palace archives, funerary cults and statuary. But as dynasty succeeded dynasty, century succeeded century, the cults failed, the architecture was destroyed and all understanding of the hieroglyphic script was lost. Egypt's lengthy history was still writ large on her crumbling stone walls, but now no one could read it. Only the Bible and the classical authors, Homer and Herodotus among them, offered western scholars a tantalising, selective and highly confused version of Egypt's past. The dynastic queens were to remain hidden until the nineteenth century saw the development of the modern science of Egyptology.

One group of queens was, however, never forgotten. The Ptolemies, the last dynasty of independent Egypt, enjoyed three centuries of rule sandwiched between the conquest of the Macedonian Alexander the Great (332) and the conquest of the Roman Octavian (30). Their stories, an integral part of Roman history, were recorded not only in Egyptian hieroglyphs, but also in Latin and in Greek. Best remembered of all was Cleopatra VII; certainly not the most successful Ptolemy, nor the longest lived, but the Ptolemy whose decisions and deeds influenced two of Rome's greatest men and, in so doing, affected the development of the Roman Empire. Cleopatra's story did more than survive in dusty official histories. Both Cleopatra and Egypt were seen as sexy in all modern senses of the word, and the thrilling mixture of decadence, lust and unnatural death – the very obvious contrast between the seductive but decaying power of ancient Egypt and the virile, disciplined strength of Rome – captured the imaginations of generations of artists and poets. Told and retold, her tale corrupted and expanded until Cleopatra evolved into a semi-mythological figure recognised throughout the world.

Famous though she undoubtedly is, it is entirely possible to devote a lifetime to the study of ancient Egypt without ever meeting Cleopatra. Paradoxically, the woman whom millions regard as the defining Egyptian queen is more or less ignored by traditional Egyptologists, who confine their studies to the thirty-one dynasties preceding the arrival of Alexander. The Ptolemies are considered peripheral beings and, as such, they have become the preserve of classical and specialised Graeco-Roman scholars, who, naturally enough, set them against a classical rather than an Egyptian background. The Graeco-Roman scholars have, in turn, shied away from Cleopatra VII; maybe because histories emphasising individual rather than national achievement are currently considered somewhat old-fashioned, or perhaps because they feel a reluctance to tackle a subject as obviously popular as Cleopatra.

For a long time this seemed entirely reasonable to me. After all, the Ptolemies were foreigners in Egypt, and relatively modern foreigners at that. They were separated from the true dynastic age by an embarrassing period of Persian rule and, lacking a numbered dynasty of their own, were omitted from many well-respected Egyptian histories that came to a neat end with the reign of the last native pharaoh, Nectanebo II (Nakhthorheb).[3] If that was not enough, they reigned over an Egypt whose pure native culture had been diluted and distorted by Greek and Roman influences: they worshipped curious hybrid gods; they issued coins; they spoke Greek, not Egyptian. But, after many years spent studying Egypt's 'true' queens, I began to realise that placing the Ptolemies in a cultural ghetto was an irrational and unsustainable distinction. The Ptolemies believed themselves to be a valid Egyptian dynasty, and devoted a great deal of time and money to demonstrating that they were the theological continuation of all the dynasties that had gone before. Cleopatra defined herself as an Egyptian queen, and drew on the iconography and cultural references of earlier queens to reinforce her position. Her people and her contemporaries accepted her as such. Could an Egyptian-born woman whose family had controlled Egypt for three centuries really be classed as foreign (and if so, where does this leave the British royal family)? Or as irrelevant to the study and understanding of Egyptian queenship?

I started to grow curious about Cleopatra, and the more I learned about her, the more I grew to respect her as an intelligent and effective monarch who set realistic goals and who very nearly succeeded in creating a dynasty that would have re-established Egypt as a world superpower. 'What if?' speculation is the historian's guilty and ultimately pointless pleasure. But what would have happened if Julius Caesar had avoided the assassins' knives? Or if Mark Antony had triumphed against the Parthian empire? This book is the direct result of my curiosity. Written by an unashamedly traditional Egyptologist, it aims to put Cleopatra back into her own, predominantly Egyptian context. I therefore give only the essential details of the dramatic events occurring in the Roman world – the death of Caesar, the rise and fall of Antony and the triumph of Octavian – but provide more of the archaeological and historical detective work that underpins Cleopatra's story than is perhaps usual in a biography.

The bare bones of her story – Cleopatra's liaisons, children and untimely death – have always been known and cannot be disputed. The flesh that generations of scholars and artists have chosen to cover those bones is a different matter, and each and every account of Cleopatra presents a new version of the same woman. That she was an ambitious and ruthless queen is obvious from even the most superficial examination of her life, although the extent of her ruthlessness tends to be hidden in the more popular histories, which gloss over the murder of her sister and (almost certainly) her brother while concentrating on her 'love life'. That Cleopatra, living in an age of highly unstable governments, chose to form personal alliances with individually powerful Romans should be seen as a sensible (intelligent) rather than a weak (emotional) decision; and 'love', as in any dynastic match, may have had very little to do with it. That Cleopatra never ruled alone perhaps comes as something of a surprise. Cleopatra's 'reign' is in fact a succession of co-regencies with her brother Ptolemy XIII (51–47), her brother Ptolemy XIV (47–44) and her son Ptolemy XV Caesar (44–30). The enormous emphasis that Cleopatra herself placed on her role as a divine mother may be equally surprising. The modern world has grown accustomed to the image of Cleopatra the siren and, sex and motherhood being considered curiously incompatible, has more or less forgotten that she was the mother of four children. But Cleopatra lived at a time when the cults of the Egyptian mother goddess Isis and the mystical Greek deity Dionysos were starting to pose a serious threat to the classical gods of Mount Olympus. Within traditional Egypt the old pantheon and the old priesthood continued much as they had done for thousands of years. But outside the conservative Nile Valley the peoples of the eastern Mediterranean were actively seeking a new religious enlightenment, and there was a growing expectation that a saviour would soon emerge from the east to rule the world. Cleopatra exploited her motherhood with ruthless efficiency. Simultaneously she allowed herself to be celebrated as the mortal mother of the king of Egypt, the divine mother of the young god Horus[4] and the regal mother of her people.

Cleopatra's story is preserved in words rather than objects. The archaeological evidence for her reign has been severely compromised by the loss of Ptolemaic Alexandria, which has either sunk beneath the waters of the Mediterranean Sea or been buried beneath modern building developments. Today, Alexandria can boast several ancient cemeteries, but just one significant non-funereal archaeological site. Kom el-Dik, a small archaeological oasis in a desert of contemporary buildings, provides a tantalising glimpse of the ancient city, including a well-preserved Roman theatre, but offers little to the scholar in search of Cleopatra. Visitors to Alexandria may sit on the corniche and gaze across the wine-dark sea towards Cleopatra's vanished palace. They may scramble through the brambles of the Catholic cemetery to reach the alabaster tomb attributed to Alexander, or may pass a morning in the splendid new library before retiring for a cool beer in the Cecil Hotel, where, if they are so inclined, the tall mirrors might allow them to glimpse the shade of Durrell's incomparable Justine. But they will struggle to find any firm reference to Cleopatra. Within the wider, more Egyptian Egypt beyond Alexandria, the Cleopatra who graces the temple wall at Dendera (Greek Tentyra) appears as just one of a long line of royal women presenting a uniform, age-defying propaganda of immortal queenship. Her face is bland and indistinct, her personality deliberately veiled: the best-known, and most beautiful, portrait of Cleopatra from this temple is a fake. Cleopatra has vanished entirely from Athens, Tarsus, Ephesus and Rome. Looking down on the remains of the Roman temple of Venus Genetrix, the temple where, it is reported, Julius Caesar scandalously erected a golden statue of the mortal queen beside the immortal goddess, it is impossible to conjure up any vision of the woman whose behaviour once shocked the civilised world.[5]

Writings, then, form the basis of our understanding of Cleopatra. But, while many thousands of official inscriptions, formal and informal papyri and ostraca (writings in ink on potsherds or flakes of stone) have survived from Ptolemaic Egypt, the great state and temple libraries, including the renowned Library of Alexandria, are all irretrievably lost. Lost with them are the official histories which may, or may not, have been written about her rule. By an unfortunate quirk of fate, Cleopatra's reign has yielded fewer papyri than the earlier Ptolemaic reigns, while Alexandria's high water table means that there are virtually no Alexandrian papyri. The sole surviving example of Cleopatra's own handwriting – the single Greek word *ginestho*, 'let it be so', scrawled at the end of an official document – if genuinely Cleopatra's hand (and the experts are largely unconvinced), is uninformative to say the least. We cannot read Cleopatra's own version of events and there are no independent, contemporary accounts of her life and deeds. The historian who knew her most intimately, Julius Caesar, accords her scant attention in his works. Nikolaus of Damascus, tutor to Cleopatra's children, adds a few more sentences. Plutarch's *Life of Antony* provides the most complete, most often quoted account of her life; its author even claims to have read the memoirs (now lost) of Cleopatra's physician Olympus. However, Plutarch, writing at the beginning of the second century AD, can hardly be considered an eyewitness, and nor can the alternative Cleopatra 'biographer', Cassius Dio, who wrote his *Roman History* in the years between AD 200 and 222. Later historians, those who have relied on Plutarch and Dio, are even more remote. I have quoted extensively from these secondary texts because they are the texts that have formed the western understanding of Cleopatra's life and times, but they should be read with caution. With an almost complete lack of primary sources we cannot hope to hear Cleopatra's true voice, and are forced to see her through secondary eyes; eyes already coloured by other people's propaganda, prejudices and assumptions. Few of us would wish to be judged in this way.

Given these limitations of evidence it is clearly never going to be possible to write a conventional biography of Cleopatra; there are simply too many important details missing. But it is possible, with goodwill, patience and determination, and without venturing too far into the enticing but ultimately sterile realm of historical romance, to draw some conclusions and, perhaps, to begin to understand something of her motivation. Whether we can also begin to understand something of her personality, the reader must decide. It is certainly unwise and unprofitable to attempt to psychoanalyse the long-dead. But one aspect of Cleopatra's personality is immediately apparent. She is an exceptionally strong individual; a survivor with the power to dominate and diminish those who surround her. Ptolemy XII Auletes, her father, is able to hold his own, as are her Roman contemporaries Julius Caesar, Mark Antony and Octavian. But Flavia, Octavia and Livia, three remarkably capable Roman women, appear as bit parts in her story, while Cleopatra's family, her predecessor Cleopatra V, her two headstrong sisters Berenice IV and Arsinoë IV and her two husband-brothers Ptolemy XIII and Ptolemy XIV, become little more than ciphers. This is compounded by the difficulties inherent in working out precisely which of the identically named Ptolemies (XII, XIII, XIV or XV) is associated with Cleopatra on any particular monument, or which is featured on the many coins marked simply 'of King Ptolemy'. This relegation to the background is unfair, particularly to her spirited sisters, but unavoidable. It means that Cleopatra lacks the detailed family background that would, perhaps, have helped us to understand some of her choices. Had any of her siblings managed to cling on to their thrones Cleopatra herself would have become a footnote in their history. Her more remote ancestors, in contrast, have all the character that her immediate relations seem to lack. Their stories are summarised in the 'Who Was Who' section at the end of this book. They make fascinating reading.

One character does stand out. Alexandria-next-to-Egypt, a Greek enclave in an Egyptian landscape, simultaneously home to a library full of dreaming scholars, a marketplace full of astute merchants, a court of almost unimaginable luxury and an aggressive king-making mob, played a vital role in Cleopatra's story. I make no apology for dedicating an entire chapter to this sparkling, vital city.

Every good story should have a beginning, a middle and an end. But Cleopatra's story has continued to grow with the years, and still lacks a definite ending. My final chapter is therefore a metabiography – an exploration of the development of a cultural afterlife that, over 2,000 years since Cleopatra's own death, shows no sign of dying. Although this chapter briefly considers the many versions of Cleopatra preserved in ancient histories and modern fiction, it is an introduction to, rather than the definitive treatment of, a fascinating topic which is a subject, and one or more books, in its own right.[6] The intention here is to equip the reader with an understanding of the sources which historians have used to piece together Cleopatra's life and, of course, of the biases lurking within those sources.

That the world is still fascinated by Cleopatra – the achingly beautiful Cleopatra of popular culture rather than the real queen – is easily demonstrated. As I finished writing the paragraph above I switched on my radio. On Wednesday 14 February 2007 – appropriately enough St Valentine's Day – Cleopatra was in the news. A silver coin had been 'discovered' in the collection of the Society of Antiquaries at Newcastle. The coin showed a face that would have been instantly recognisable to anyone who had made even the most cursory study of Cleopatra's relatively plentiful currency. It was by no stretch of the imagination an exciting archaeological find. But the discovery made the newspapers, and then the radio and television, and the reporters, steeped in Cleopatra mythology, were all discussing Cleopatra's beauty (or rather her shocking lack of beauty) as if she were a modern celebrity. More than 2,000 years after her death, Cleopatra was still effortlessly making the headlines, even if most of the 'facts' being reported were wrong.[7]

CHAPTER ONE

Princess of Egypt

When everything seemed lost, the heirs of the house of Ptolemy would suddenly have almost put within their grasp a dominion stretching not only over the lost ancestral lands, but over wider territories than Ptolemy I or Ptolemy II or Ptolemy III had ever dreamed of. Those kings, being men, had based their dominion on the power of their arms; but now, when the military power of Egypt had become contemptible beside that of Rome, the sovereign of Egypt would bring to the contest power of a wholly different kind – the power of a fascinating woman.

E. R. Bevan, *The House of Ptolemy*[1]

In 81 the death of Ptolemy IX, king of Egypt, plunged the Ptolemaic dynasty into crisis. Years of vicious family feuds had caused a shortage of legitimate male Ptolemies. With no more obvious heir to the throne, Berenice III, daughter of Ptolemy IX and widow of his brother Ptolemy X, inherited her father's crown and restyled herself Cleopatra Berenice. Soon after, to comply with Ptolemaic tradition, she agreed to marry her young stepson-nephew, Ptolemy XI.

The Romans watched the unfolding royal saga with a proprietorial interest. They believed that they had a valid legal claim to Egypt, which had been gifted to them seven years earlier in a vexatious will drawn up by Ptolemy X. As yet, they had resisted the temptation to annex Egypt, but many believed that it could only be a question of time. Meanwhile, the Roman dictator Sulla gave his gracious approval to the marriage of Berenice and Ptolemy, but the pair were ill-suited and Ptolemy, as the natural son of Ptolemy X, believed that he should rule in his own right. Within three weeks of the wedding the over-eager Ptolemy had murdered his bride and seized her throne. The next day he was snatched by an angry Alexandrian mob, dragged off to the gymnasium, and killed. Egypt was once again in need of a king or queen.

The double murder threw Egypt into crisis. The Alexandrians had dared to kill the king that the Romans had chosen for them; would this provoke the Romans into claiming their property? A new Ptolemy was needed, and quickly. But this was no easy matter. Berenice had been the only surviving child of Ptolemy IX and his consort Cleopatra IV, and she had died childless. Just one legitimate Ptolemy remained. Berenice's aunt, Cleopatra Selene, was the daughter of Ptolemy VIII and Cleopatra III and the ex-wife of Ptolemy IX, but she was also the widow of three kings of Syria[2] and, as the mother of ambitious Syrian sons, she made an unsuitable guardian of Egypt's interests. Bypassing Cleopatra Selene, the crown was offered to the two illegitimate sons of Ptolemy IX: sons born to an unrecorded mother and currently living in Syria. The elder son returned to Egypt and took the throne as Ptolemy Theos Philopator Philadelphos (the Father-Loving, Brother/Sister-Loving God). From 64/3 he was to add Neos Dionysos (the New Dionysos) to his name. In 76 Ptolemy XII was crowned by Pasherenptah III, the newly appointed high priest of the god Ptah, in a traditional Egyptian ceremony held at Memphis. His regnal years were to be counted from the death of his father, Ptolemy IX, a move which stressed continuity in the immediate royal family, but which effectively erased the reign of the ill-fated Berenice III from the official record. As a consolation prize the younger son, also named Ptolemy, was offered the crown of Cyprus. The Romans, irritated by this rapid turn of events, refused to recognise the new kings.

The identification of Ptolemy XII with Dionysos was an astute political move. 'Twice born', once when ripped from his stricken mortal mother, Semele, and again when delivered from the thigh of his divine father, Zeus, the mystical Greek god Dionysos had long been associated with the resurrected Egyptian fertility god-king Osiris. But while the bandaged Osiris promised a calm and ordered afterlife to anyone living a correct earthly existence, Dionysos offered his most enthusiastic followers a lifetime of secret rituals and ecstatic experiences, culminating in the twin promises of union with the god and eternal salvation beyond death. As the austere cult of Osiris retained its popularity with the native Egyptians, the more flamboyant cult of Dionysos flourished both within Egypt and without. In Alexandria, a city where the Greek concept of *tryphe* (endless undisciplined luxury and ostentatious display) underpinned many aspects of official life, Dionysos was considered both a protective deity and a royal ancestor: genealogists had helpfully determined that Arsinoë, mother of Ptolemy I, was a descendant of Heracles and Deianeira, the daughter of Dionysos. So, by identifying himself with Dionysos, Ptolemy was effectively allying himself both with his legitimate Ptolemaic ancestors and with Alexander the Great, who had revered Dionysos as the conqueror of much of the eastern world. At the same time he was distancing himself from the more restrained and conservative Romans who favoured the Olympian gods, and who tended to look upon Ptolemaic excess – indeed, any form of excess – with horror. The stoic philosopher, geographer and historian Strabo, writing some sixty years after Ptolemy's death, was not at all impressed with the Dionysiac royal lifestyle:

Now all the kings after the third Ptolemy, being corrupted by luxurious living, administered the affairs of government badly, but worst of all the fourth, seventh, and the last, Auletes [Ptolemy XII], who, apart from his general licentiousness, practised the accompaniment of choruses with the flute, and upon this he prided himself so much that he would not hesitate to celebrate contests in the royal palace, and at these contests would come forward to vie with the opposing contestants.[3]

Devotees of Dionysos came from all walks of life; they were male and female, rich and poor, free and enslaved, old and young. They drank copious amounts of wine and, in defiance of the taboo against transvestism, challenged the natural order of things by donning diaphanous womanly clothing to perform their mysterious, sex-based rituals. Lucian preserves the story of the staid philosopher Demetrios, who angered Ptolemy XII by drinking only water and refusing to cross-dress during the Dionysiac revels; as punishment he was forced to don a gown, dance and play the cymbals.[4] They also serenaded their god on the *aulos,* or double flute, and from this last association came Ptolemy's irreverent nickname Auletes or 'Flute Player'. Whether this less than flattering sobriquet referred to the king's musical ability, or to his plump cheeks, permanently puffed out like the cheeks of a flautist, or whether it was a snide reference to the well-understood link between male and female *aulos* players and prostitution, is not now clear. More straightforward was Ptolemy's alternative nickname, Nothos or 'Bastard'.

Auletes had inherited the most densely populated land in the Mediterranean world. It is impossible to give precise statistics, but historians have estimated a population of somewhere between two and a half and seven million, while Diodorus Siculus, visiting Egypt in 60, when Cleopatra was about ten years old, suggests a total Egyptian population of about three million. It was a tenuously unified and culturally segregated land. The vast majority of Auletes's subjects were indigenous Egyptians, but over 10 per cent of the population were of Greek extraction, and there was also a sizeable and vociferous Jewish minority. Traditionally, the Egyptians had always made a firm distinction between those who lived in Upper, or southern, Egypt (the Nile Valley) and those who lived in Lower Egypt (the Delta). The southern Egyptians tended to regard themselves as the true guardians of Egypt's heritage, while the northerners tended to regard themselves as superior to the unsophisticated valley dwellers. To further complicate matters, the people of Alexandria, a temperamental, cosmopolitan and racially well-mixed bunch, considered themselves a distinct cultural group, superior in every way to those unfortunate enough to live outside the city.

Tensions between the various factions could run high, and any group was liable to turn against their king at any time. The reigns of Ptolemies III, IV and V had been blighted by southern uprisings, while the reigns of the later Ptolemies had been heavily influenced by the Alexandrians, who considered that they had the right to chose and depose their own king. Ptolemy XII was to suffer rebellions, politically inspired strikes and blatant interference by the Alexandrians. But open warfare was the exception rather than the rule. For most of the time the various cultural groups coexisted in an uneasy truce, leading parallel lives, speaking their own languages, worshipping their own gods and making use of their own, entirely separate, legal systems whereby contracts written in the demotic script used by Egypt's scribes were classified as Egyptian, contracts in Aramaic were considered Jewish and contracts written in Greek fell under the stricter Greek law.[5] Two things unified the various groups: they were all prepared (albeit temporarily) to acknowledge Auletes as king, accepting his edicts as superior to all laws, and they all bitterly resented any form of Roman interference in their land.

The vast majority of Auletes's Egyptian subjects led lives that would have been instantly recognisable to their earliest dynastic fore-bears. The bottom tier of their inflexible social pyramid was made up of the manual workers and peasants, the millions who lived in insignificant mud-brick villages and hamlets dotted along the Nile and the tributaries of the Delta, and who worked the land owned by the king, the temples and the elite. Illiterate and poor, these peasants have left many simple desert graves but few material remains and no writings, so, in consequence, we can say little about their lives and ambitions. We can, however, understand something of their work. Egypt's phenomenal wealth derived from her abundant natural resources: the gold in the deserts, the papyrus in the marshes and, above all, the rich agricultural land. The Ptolemies had made some improvements – there were new iron tools, new crops, new harvesting policies, new methods of irrigation and vast tracts of newly reclaimed land in the Faiyum – but farming life continued much as it had for centuries. The late summer inundation was followed by an autumn sowing. The late spring/early summer harvest was followed by a dry season, when the hot sun baked the fields and sterilised the soil. Then the river burst her banks, the fields flooded and the cycle started all over again. We can get a flavour of this time-honoured, uniquely Egyptian rhythm by looking at the vivid agricultural scenes engraved on the private tomb walls of the Old, Middle and New Kingdoms.

Higher up the social pyramid came the skilled artisans and the educated scribes who lived in the towns and cities, and who made up what can loosely be defined as the middle class. Higher still came the elite: the high-ranking bureaucrats and the hereditary priests who worked closely with the new regime and who, having benefited from Ptolemaic generosity, used their private wealth to maintain Egypt's religious and funerary traditions. Included among this group was the extended family of Egypt's last native king, Nectanebo II, who had fled Egypt in 343.

The royal family occupied the final tier of the social pyramid, with the king standing alone and untouchable at the peak. For 3,000 years the king of Egypt had been recognised as the chief priest of all cults, the head of the civil service and the commander of the army. Only the king could offer to the gods; only the king, through his offerings, could prevent Egypt from being overwhelmed by the sea of chaos that surrounded and constantly threatened his tightly controlled world. Unique and irreplaceable, he was a demigod in his lifetime and a full god at death; Egypt simply could not manage without him. Any king – an infant, a woman, even a foreigner – was considered better than no king at all, and it was understood that the official coronation ceremony could instantly convert a mere mortal into a powerful monarch. Recognising that this belief in the semi-divine kingship did much to keep them in power, and appreciating the need to please the still-powerful and deeply conservative Egyptian priesthood, the Ptolemies were always happy to be seen to be conforming to the royal tradition that distinguished Egypt from the rest of the world. However they dressed, spoke and thought at home, however much they ran Egypt as a profitable business, in public they appeared more traditionally Egyptian – building and restoring temples and reviving long-forgotten rituals – than the Egyptians themselves.

Egypt's most venerable tourist supplies a lively account of this traditional Egyptian way of life. Herodotus of Halicarnassus (modern Bodrum, Turkey) visited northern Egypt some time after 450, at a time when Egypt, temporarily reconciled to Persian rule, was both peaceful and prosperous. An experienced traveller, he could not hide his astonishment at finding himself in a land where everything appeared contrary to the natural order of things:

Not only is the Egyptian climate peculiar to that country, and the Nile different in its behaviour from other rivers elsewhere, but the Egyptians themselves in their manners and customs seem to have reversed the ordinary practices of mankind. For instance, women attend markets and are employed in trade, while men stay at home and do the weaving. In weaving the normal way is to work the threads of the weft upwards, but the Egyptians work them downwards. Men in Egypt carry loads on their heads, women on their shoulders; women urinate standing up, men sitting down. To ease themselves they go indoors, but eat outside in the streets, on the theory that what is unseemly but necessary should be done in private, and what is not unseemly should be done openly. No woman holds priestly office, either in the service of goddess or god; only men are priests in both cases. Sons are under no compulsion to support their parents if they do not wish to do so, but daughters must, whether they wish it or not ... Men in Egypt have two garments each, women only one.[6]

Herodotus is by no means an infallible source. Culturally, he is unashamedly anti-Persian, pro-Greek and, up to a point, pro-Egyptian. He is prone to believing what he is told, no matter how unlikely, and he is attracted to tales of the strange and unexpected. Far from keeping an open mind, he contrasts all his experiences with the proper (i.e. Greek) way of doing things. Yet there is clearly more than a grain of truth in his writing. Egypt's rainless climate was peculiar, and the river was undeniably strange; it flooded in summer, whereas normal rivers, as everyone knew, flooded in winter. And Egypt's women, however they might choose to urinate, were definitely unusual when compared to the women in Herodotus's own family. Egyptian women were free to live alone, and to own, inherit, buy and sell property. They could choose their own husbands, initiate a divorce and raise children without male interference. In marked contrast, Greek custom decreed that women should play a non-conspicuous role in society, living permanently under the protection of a male guardian. As Greek women never formally came of age they could never become legally competent; they had no independent political or social rights, no right to choose a husband and no rights over their own children. Family circumstances permitting, Greek women were expected to remain indoors, providing for the family, guarding their chastity and weaving wool.

As an educated Greek, Herodotus would have arrived in Egypt with an inbuilt admiration for its ancient traditions, its scientific, magical and medical knowledge, and its gods. The Egyptians were barbarians, it was true, but unlike the Persians they were cultured barbarians worthy of respect, and Herodotus would have felt quite at home in a land where, even before the arrival of the Ptolemies, so many people were of Greek heritage. There were Greek mercenaries in the Egyptian army and navy, a sizeable Greek population in the northern cities, and one specifically Greek city, or *polis,* run on entirely Greek lines in the western Nile Delta. The city-port of Naukratis (modern Kom Ge'if) had been specifically developed to handle trade between Egypt and Greece; Herodotus tells us that the site was given to the Greeks by the 26th Dynasty king Ahmose II (570–526), although archaeological evidence shows Greek settlement at the site dating to at least sixty years earlier. As the only legal outlet for Greek merchandise in Egypt, Naukratis flourished, surviving the political and international upheavals that characterised the later dynasties and outliving the Ptolemies to serve as a trading centre throughout the Roman era.

Ptolemy I had encouraged large-scale Greek immigration, a policy that continued until the reign of Ptolemy V, when almost overnight the stream of new arrivals slowed to a trickle. In consequence, by the time Auletes took his throne Naukratis had been joined by a further two Greek cities. Alexandria, founded by Alexander the Great soon after the Macedonian conquest of Egypt, lay on the Mediterranean coast and was home to some 300,000 people, including the largest Jewish community outside Jerusalem. Ptolemais Hormou (modern el-Mansha, near Sohag), founded by Ptolemy I, lay near the ancient city of Thinis in Upper Egypt and served as a Greek regional capital that might, it was hoped, provide a check to the notorious hot-headed nationalism of the southern Egyptians.

The early Ptolemies, who were by no means averse to imposing Greek-style rule on their colonies, had recognised the Egyptian bureaucratic system as one of the most competent in the world. Leaving the basic structure in place, they had 'improved' it by adding several more tiers of officials to the scribes and tax collectors already in place. An extract from an official document concerning an army enlistment, written in Memphis in February 157, shows just how unwieldy the bureaucracy had become:

> ... *I received back the decree from Ptolemaios the memorandum-drafter and the letter from Epimenides. And I conveyed them to Isidoros ... and from him I carried them to Philoxenos and from him to Artemon and from him to Lykos, and he made a rough draft, and I brought that to Sarapion in the office of the secretary and from him to Eubios and from him to Dorion, and he made a rough draft, and then back again to Sarapion. And they were handed in to be read to the chancellor and I received them back from Epimenides and I carried them to Sarapion and he wrote to Nicanor...*[7]

Egypt was still divided into approximately forty traditional *nomoi* or nomes (administrative districts) run by local officials, but the nomes now had Greek rather than Egyptian names, so that the Middle Egyptian Hare nome, for example, became the Hermopolite nome.[8] Each nome had been under the authority of a nomarch, or local governor; the role of the nomarch was now taken over by a Greek *strategos* (literally 'general') appointed by the king. The *strategoi* themselves reported to an *epistrategos*.

As increasing numbers of educated Greeks arrived in Egypt, they started to take over the more important administrative posts, while the indigenous Egyptians retained the bulk of the menial and unpleasant jobs, including all the jobs that in Greece would have been assigned to slaves. The king himself – an absolute ruler – was advised by official 'friends', who bore honorific kinship titles designed to stress their personal ties to the royal family, and by high-ranking hand-picked bureaucrats who were, of course, of Greek extraction. He was protected by a Macedonian bodyguard. This institutional racism rankled with the Egyptians, who recognised that they were quickly becoming second-class citizens in their own land. While many elite Egyptians retained their inherited positions, Greek gradually became the language of public life. Ambitious Egyptians were forced to become bilingual; Greeks, on the other hand rarely bothered to learn the notoriously difficult demotic Egyptian script. The decree issued by the priesthood at Memphis on 27 March 196, in honour of the anniversary of the accession of Ptolemy V, had to be published both in the Egyptian language (in two scripts) and in Greek so that all the king's literate subjects could read it. A copy of this bilingual decree, engraved on the so-called Rosetta Stone, was to prove instrumental in Champollion's AD 1822 deciphering of the hieroglyphic script.

Many of the new arrivals chose to live insular, colonial lives in the self-governing Greek cities, where they hoped to maintain Greek traditions, marry fellow Greeks and avoid mixing with the Egyptians, whom, on the whole, they considered their social inferiors. Despite their self-imposed segregation, the city dwellers gradually succumbed to the influence of their adopted land, and we find increasing numbers of Greeks worshipping Egyptian gods, consulting skilled Egyptian doctors and abandoning cremation in favour of mummification. But by no means all the immigrants headed for the cities. The astute Ptolemy I, intent on extracting the maximum profit from his new land, encouraged Egypt-wide settlement by rewarding his loyal soldiers and senior civil servants with plots of land in the countryside (*chora*), spread throughout the valley, the Delta and the fertile Faiyum Oasis, which he gave either at a nominal rent or rent-free. This tradition was continued until as many as 100,000 ex- and serving soldiers, plus unknown numbers of male civilians and accompanying women, were settled in the Egyptian countryside and in the reclaimed agricultural lands of the Faiyum (now known as the Arsinoite nome), where there was a thriving Greek culture.[9] This system, superficially generous, ensured a maximum return from the land. The settlers enjoyed the right to cultivate their own fields; the state then levied a heavy tax on their produce and Egypt's granaries filled with the wheat that underpinned the economy. Taxes – paid by everyone in Ptolemaic Egypt, be they producer, consumer or importer – were invariably high, and a constant cause of complaint. So much so that Ptolemy II had been forced to issue a decree forbidding lawyers to represent clients disputing their tax bill.[10] Meanwhile, hand in hand with the development of a punitive tax regime went the development of state monopolies in the textile, papyrus and oil industries, the development of a centralised banking system and the development of a specific Egyptian coinage that replaced the traditional barter system and allowed the Ptolemies to make a profit on every foreign coin exchange. While most taxes were still collected in kind, those who offered services rather than goods could now look forward to paying monetary taxes on their income.

Mixed Greek-Egyptian marriages were forbidden in the Greek cities. But there were no restrictions in the *chora* and, as time went by, Greek settler families started to intermarry with the local Egyptians. Graeco-Egyptian families experienced a fusion of cultures: marriages were conducted along either Greek or Egyptian lines (often utilising a comfortable mixture of the two), and parents were happy to give their children a seemingly random mixture of names, making it almost impossible for modern Egyptologists to judge ethnicity on the basis of a personal name alone. Indeed, many Egyptians found it convenient to have two names, an Egyptian name that they used at home and a Greek name that they used at work. We now find some astute Greek women making absolutely sure of their rights by employing the more 'liberated' Egyptian legal system, which allowed them all the privileges and responsibilities accorded to Egyptian women.

Strict Greek law relating to women was becoming unsustainable in a rapidly expanding world where respectable single women were starting to travel far from the shelter of their city-states, and where growing numbers of Greek men were settling with non-Greek women. Legal papyri, written in Greek, introduce us to independent, strong-minded women who act as guardians for their children, arrange their own and their children's marriages, and initiate divorces. Some women own houses, slaves, orchards or vineyards; others own large boats – important possessions in Nile-centred Egypt, where the river acted as the main highway and where barges were used for transporting grain. The poet Theocritos writes about elite Greek women who feel free to walk in the streets of Alexandria, and who consider it perfectly acceptable both to talk to unrelated men and to grumble loudly about the 'rascally' Egyptians who surround them.[11] As educational opportunities for elite women gradually increase throughout the Mediterranean world, we find occasional female musicians, poets, artists, philosophers, doctors and lawyers. Some women, wealthy in their own right, are invited to play a part in civic affairs. Many who stay at home are able to read the novels that are now being published with a female readership in mind. Others, as this letter of complaint shows, are expected to contribute to the family finances:

> To King Ptolemy [Ptolemy III], greetings from Ctesicles. I am being wronged by Dionysos and my daughter Nike. For though I had nurtured my daughter, and educated her and raised her to womanhood, when I was stricken with bodily infirmity and my eyesight grew feeble she would not provide me with any of the necessities of life. And when I wished to obtain justice from her in Alexandria she begged my pardon, and in Year 18 she gave me in the temple of Arsinoë a written

oath by the king that she would pay me 20 drachmae every month from her earnings. If she failed to do so, or transgressed any of the terms of her bond, she was to pay me 500 drachmae or incur the penalties of her oath. Now however, corrupted by Dionysos, who is a comic actor, she is not keeping any of her promises …[12]

The story of the well-brought-up daughter who runs away with an unsuitable boyfriend – in this case the comic actor Dionysos – is one familiar to parents of all ages.

In spite of the new air of freedom, the overwhelming majority of women living in Egypt, be they Greek, Egyptian or Jew, were denied a formal education. We can see from the surviving papyri that some women could sign their own names, but the extent to which women were taught to read and write is unclear and many more women required a scribe to both write and sign on their behalf. Taught at home, women studied the household skills that they would need to care for their husband and children. Those who, for economic reasons, had to work outside the home took unimportant and archaeologically invisible jobs; none expected to enjoy a career beyond that of wife and mother.

Cleopatra V Tryphaena (the Opulent One), wife of Auletes, is a shadowy figure whose parentage is never mentioned. But it is possible to hazard a guess at her origins. Her first and only confirmed child, Berenice IV, was born during the 70s. This suggests that Cleopatra married Auletes after his assumption of the throne in 80. She must, therefore, have been chosen to be queen consort of Egypt, a role of such overwhelming political and religious importance that it was only awarded to women of impeccable social standing. Given the Ptolemaic penchant for incestuous unions, it is likely that Auletes would have preferred to marry a close relative. His wife's name tends to support this assumption. The Macedonian name Cleopatra – literally 'Renowned in her Ancestry' or 'Famous in her Father' – had been favoured by the Ptolemies for six generations, but was not particularly popular outside royal circles. Names, of course, can easily be changed, and we cannot assume that the queen was born Cleopatra Tryphaena. Nevertheless, we may tentatively deduce that Cleopatra V was either a daughter born to Ptolemy IX by an unknown woman (and therefore full or half-sister to her husband) or, perhaps, a previously unidentified daughter born to the unfortunate Berenice III and her first husband, Ptolemy X (and therefore her husband's cousin). If the latter was the case we should perhaps reinterpret the post-Berenice III succession, and see Berenice's crown passing directly to her daughter and indirectly to her daughter's husband.

Incest had been an occasional feature of earlier dynasties, when some of Egypt's kings married their sisters or half-sisters. In a land happily oblivious to the perils of inbreeding, these incestuous marriages brought definite practical benefits. They kept non-royals at arm's length, restricted the number of potential claimants to the throne, provided a suitably royal husband for princesses who could not be allowed to marry foreigners or men of low social status, and ensured that a future queen could be trained from birth to understand her demanding role. On a more theoretical level, but perhaps of equal importance, they allowed the royal family to differentiate themselves both from their subjects, who favoured cousin–cousin or uncle–niece unions, and from other, more conventional royal families. The kings and queens of Egypt allied themselves with the gods, who, at the very beginning of time, had been more than happy to marry their sisters. Those who studied Egypt's ancient mythologies knew that Shu, the dry god of the air, had married his damp sister Tefnut, goddess of moisture. Their son Geb, the green earth god, then married his sister Nut, goddess of the sky, and their children Osiris and Isis, Seth and Nephthys also wed each other. Royal brother–sister marriages were, however, by no means compulsory, and by the end of the New Kingdom the tradition had more or less died out.

The Greek gods, too, had not been averse to incest, and Zeus had happily married his quarrelsome sister Hera. But in Greece full-sibling incest was discouraged, and the Macedonians had mocked the 'inbred' Persian royal family for their brother–sister unions. It was considered acceptable for Arsinoë II to marry her half-brother Ptolemy Ceraunos, but her marriage to her full-brother Ptolemy II, which took place some time between 279 and 274, was seen as scandalous perversion outside Egypt. Just how it was perceived in Alexandria is not clear, as few cared to make public comment. Sotades the Obscene, inventor of the palindrome and celebrated author of many fine and filthy poems, was foolish enough to pen some humorous verses about the royal union; he was rewarded by a long period of imprisonment and, having fled Alexandria, was eventually captured, sealed in a lead chest and thrown into the sea. The far wiser Theocritos recorded the incestuous marriage with approval. Ptolemy II, who was not averse to associating himself with Zeus, would have been pleased to read how:

> … *no better wife embraces her young husband in the halls, loving with all her heart her brother and her husband. In this manner too was accomplished the sacred marriage of the immortals whom Queen Rhea bore as kings of Olympus: it is one bed that Iris, to this day a virgin, prepares for Zeus and Hera, when she has cleansed her hands with perfumes.*[13]

Perversion or not, the marriage was perceived as beneficial to the royal family – it had all the advantages of the earlier royal incestuous marriages, and the additional benefit of linking the *nouveaux* Ptolemies to the earlier Egyptian kings – and it set a precedent that subsequent monarchs would follow with increasing enthusiasm so that only Berenice II (daughter of Magas of Cyrene; cousin and wife of Ptolemy III) and Cleopatra I (daughter of Antiochos III of Syria; wife of the sisterless Ptolemy V) subsequently married into the royal family. Outside the royal circle full-sibling incest would remain rare until the Roman period, when it became a popular means of avoiding inheritance disputes. Roman census returns from the Faiyum suggest that an astonishing 25 per cent of the population adopted the practice. Egypt's queens now found that they were expected to provide not only an heir to the throne plus a spare, but also a sister for the king to marry. It perhaps comes as no surprise to find the Ptolemaic sister-queens assuming an increasingly prominent role in both politics and religion. The queens develop their own regalia and are well represented in the surviving statuary. They also, for the first time, have their own title. While ancient Egypt had no word for queen – all royal women were classified by their relationship to the king, so we find many 'king's wives' (queens), 'king's great wives' (queen consorts), 'king's mothers' (dowager queens) and 'king's daughters' (princesses), plus a handful of 'female kings' (queens regnant) – Greek had the word *basilissa*, or queen.

While some of the dynastic kings of Egypt enjoyed incestuous unions, all of them enjoyed polygamous marriages. In this respect they differed from both their people and their gods. Kings maintained one 'king's great wife'; the consort who played a well-defined role in state and religious ceremonial, who was featured in official writings and art, and whose son, gods willing, would inherit his father's crown. At the same time there were many secondary wives condemned to live sheltered, dull lives in harem palaces away from the court. All these harem wives could be classed as queens, or 'king's wives', but they were by no means wives of equal status and all ranked far below the great wife. As all the harem queens were wives, there could be no illegitimate royal children. Each and every child was a potential future king, his or her chances of succeeding being determined by gender, age and, most important of all, their mother's status. Just occasionally, when the queen consort failed to produce an heir, a harem-born son acceded to the throne, allowing his mother to shed her obscurity and become a 'king's mother'.

The kings of Macedon had also been polygamous. Their multiple marriages and their oft-repeated failures to nominate a successor from among their many children caused endless familial strife, which was made worse by the fiercely ambitious Macedonian queens, all too many of whom were prepared to lie, cheat and kill to place their own favoured son on the throne. But the Ptolemies, like their people, practised serial monogamy, taking one partner at a time, remarrying after death or divorce and, in many cases, maintaining an unofficial harem of mistresses whose children were not considered legitimate. Thus Auletes the Bastard, son of an unknown and we assume insignificant mother, was in the curious position of being completely acceptable to his Egyptian subjects, who recognised both his paternity and the validity of his coronation, but less acceptable to the Greeks and Romans, who consistently questioned his right to the throne.

We know that Auletes had either five or six children – three or four daughters, (Berenice IV, the ephemeral Cleopatra VI, Cleopatra VII, born 70/69, and Arsinoë, born some time between 68 and 65), followed by two sons (Ptolemy XIII, born 61, and Ptolemy XIV, born 59) – but, with the exception of Berenice, we cannot with certainty name their mother or mothers. The natural assumption is that Cleopatra V bore all five (or six) and, in the absence of any evidence to the contrary, this is the view that many modern historians take. But, as the archaeologist's mantra reminds us, absence of evidence can never be equated with evidence of absence, and Strabo specifically tells us that just one child, the first-born Berenice, was legitimate. The unspoken implication is that the other children were not legitimate to Graeco-Roman eyes, and therefore not born to the queen consort. We may justifiably choose not to believe Strabo, who, writing half a century after Octavian's conquest of Egypt, was keen to belittle the Ptolemies as a means of flattering the Romans. The suggestion that Cleopatra VII was innately, irredeemably flawed – a bastard like her father – even before she came to the throne was perhaps his means of prejudicing his readers against her from the start, and it is curious that no contemporary historians mention her illegitimacy. But maybe Strabo is correct, and maybe some or all of the younger children were born to a variety of different mothers. The large age gaps between the children – with a possible twenty years between the eldest and the youngest – combined with the fact that Cleopatra V vanishes from royal documents during 69, perhaps indicate that Auletes had more than one wife. We can then further speculate that Cleopatra V either died (perhaps in childbirth) or for some reason retired from public life before the birth of Cleopatra VII. Auletes, a still-vigorous king without a son, would naturally seek to replace her.

The birth of Cleopatra VII in the winter of 70/69 is nowhere recorded. To calculate her birth year we have to work backwards from Plutarch's account of her death, which is known to have occurred on 12 August 30, when, he tells us, she was thirty-nine years old. The name of Cleopatra's mother, as we have already seen, is similarly unrecorded. Given that Auletes openly acknowledged Cleopatra as his daughter, do we really care who this missing mother was? That depends very much on our viewpoint. The royal family, Cleopatra included, would certainly have cared, both at a personal level and when considering the succession. It is highly unlikely that a daughter born to a slave would have been mentioned in the king's will; the fact that Cleopatra was classed as a princess is a strong indication that her mother was a woman worthy of respect. The Egyptian people – including the all-important priesthood – would not have cared at all: as Cleopatra was an acknowledged king's daughter, her mother was an irrelevance. Contemporary Greeks and Romans may have cared, as they held strong views on legitimacy, but the Egyptian Greeks very much took the view that any Ptolemy was better than none. Later classical historians, Strabo included, demonstrably did care.

And what of people today? Yes, we care. Not because we care overmuch about illegitimacy, but because we care perhaps too much about race and appearance and, with Cleopatra's paternal line firmly rooted in the Macedonian Ptolemaic family tree, Cleopatra's mother and grandmother(s) hold the key to her ethnicity. Two thousand years after her death Cleopatra still has political relevance, and arguments over her racial heritage – was Cleopatra black or white? – inspire fierce debate, with 'black' variously defined as meaning of Egyptian origin, or a person from non-Mediterranean Africa, or any person of colour, and 'white' usually being equated with Greek. These definitions in themselves, of course, are open to charges of Eurocentrism and Afrocentrism – can we not have black Greeks? Or non-black Africans? Is white not a colour? In the USA in particular, the recognition that traditional history has too often been written by a male, Eurocentric elite who, consciously or not, have promoted their own agenda and cultural expectations has led to the development of the theory – sincerely held by many – that Cleopatra was a black Egyptian queen whose achievements have been reallocated to a white proto-European.[14] Scholarly discussions and heated Internet arguments abound between the 'black' and 'white' camps. It is easy, but lazy, to ignore this popular debate, classify Cleopatra and her family as Greek and move swiftly on, tacitly dismissing any claim that Cleopatra may have a mixed-race heritage. So, who exactly was Cleopatra VII?

We know that Cleopatra was a direct descendant of Ptolemy I, and we know that Ptolemy I was a Macedonian. Whether he was of 'pure' Macedonian descent we will never know – can anyone, anywhere in the world, swear that they are of pure descent, with all the compatibility of race, nationality and religious belief that this emotive term involves? Was he then a 'Greek'? The kingdom of Macedon stretched across northern Greece, an anomaly topping a land of oligarchic and democratic city-states. The Macedonian people spoke a distinctive, almost unintelligible dialect, they drank their wine undiluted with water, worshipped their own gods and buried their dead under tumuli as well as cremating them. But Macedon was by no means culturally isolated and by the time of Ptolemy's birth there were many true Greeks living within her borders. The Macedonian elite certainly regarded themselves as true Greeks, or Hellenes, and after a certain amount of argument they had, during the reign of Alexander I (c. 495–450), been permitted to compete in the Olympic Games – a sure and certain measure of 'Greekness'. But not everyone was convinced. Macedon's non-elite regarded non-Macedonians with the habitual suspicion reserved for all foreigners, while the true Greeks tended to regard all the Macedonians at best as uncouth quasi-foreigners.

Ptolemy and his descendants belong to the Hellenistic Age, the three centuries between Alexander's accession to the Macedonian throne in 336 and the death of Cleopatra in 30, when an evolved form of classical Greek (or Hellenic) culture spread throughout the eastern Mediterranean world. Culturally, then, the Ptolemies were Hellenistic Macedonians who had, by the time of Cleopatra's birth, lived in Egypt for long enough to have acquired at least some Egyptian habits. But what of Cleopatra's racial heritage? Her mother is, of course, unknown, although we suspect that she was Cleopatra V, who in turn we suspect of being closely related to Cleopatra's father, Auletes. If this assumption is wrong, if Cleopatra's mother was not a Ptolemy, then she could have been an elite woman from anywhere in the Hellenistic world, although it seems most likely that she was either Egyptian or Greek. Auletes is known to have had a close working relationship with Pasherenptah III, high priest of Ptah at Memphis, and it is not impossible that this relationship was sealed with a diplomatic marriage. An Egyptian mother might, perhaps, explain Cleopatra's reported proficiency in the Egyptian language.

But again, to assume that an Egyptian mother would be 'pure' Egyptian is perhaps an assumption too far. For almost 3,000 years tradition, theology and ideology had taught the Egyptian elite that they lived at the heart of the controlled, civilised world. Other, non-

Egyptian lands were places of unrestrained chaos occupied by ill-favoured peoples destined to be denied eternal life. It followed that those who lived and died by Egyptian custom within Egypt were Egyptian: the most blessed people in the world. 'Egyptianness', like 'Greekness', was very much a matter of culture. Colour – both skin tone and racial heritage – was an irrelevance. The well-known Greek tale of the xenophobic King Busiris, who habitually slaughtered any foreigner who set foot in Egypt until Heracles put an end to his cruelty, was quite simply a myth. Egypt had always been open to immigrants. Libyans, Nubians, Asiatics and others had settled beside the Nile and there had never been any problem with individual Egyptians marrying people who looked or spoke differently. As a result, the Egyptian people showed a diverse range of racial characteristics, with red-headed, light-skinned Egyptians living alongside curly haired, darker-skinned neighbours. Problems only came when too many people attempted to settle at once, bringing their own cultures with them. This willingness to accept, and the willingness of foreigners to assimilate, make it difficult to estimate just how many 'Egyptians' were actually of non-Egyptian origin.

If we step back one generation, our problems grow worse. Cleopatra's paternal grandfather was Ptolemy IX, but her paternal grandmother, who may have been her sole grandmother, is again unknown. She could have been a Ptolemy but, as her children are regarded as illegitimate, she is more likely to have been an outsider from Egypt, Syria, Greece, Rome, Nubia or somewhere else entirely. Her maternal grandmother and grandfather are equally unknown. Moving back in time again, we get a further dilution of the 'pure' Macedonian blood with the introduction of Berenice I, Berenice II and the part-Persian Cleopatra I into the incestuous family tree. All we can conclude from this survey of just two generations is that, in the crudest of statistical terms, Cleopatra was somewhere between 25 per cent and 100 per cent of Macedonian extraction, and that she possibly had some Egyptian genes. And, although there are blond Macedonians (Ptolemy II was apparently fair-haired) and red-headed Egyptians (the mummy of Ramesses II the Great confirms his fiery hair), this suggests that Cleopatra is most likely to have had dark hair and an olive or light brown complexion.

Roman historians did not subscribe to the theory that childhood experiences help to shape the adult and so rarely showed any interest in their subjects' early years. In consequence, we know very little about Cleopatra's infancy and childhood in (we assume) Alexandria. But we do know that no one expected Ptolemaic princesses to confine themselves to the palace or to weave wool. Raised to stand alongside their brothers as queens, the Ptolemaic women participated both covertly and overtly in state affairs, with Arsinoë II, Cleopatras I, II and III, and Berenices III and IV all proving themselves effective, and occasionally ruthless, queens. They were women of substance, owning land, property, barges and bank accounts. Many controlled sizeable estates that they leased out to generate additional income. The extent to which these highly professional businesswomen were formally educated is unclear. To be effective they had not only to be able to read, write and do arithmetic, but to understand the laws, history and traditions of Greece, Egypt and the wider Mediterranean world. Cleopatra VII must have had one or more private tutors borrowed, we might reasonably assume, from the Museion, home to the world-famous scholars of Alexandria: we know the names of Ptolemy XIII's tutor-guardian (Theodotos of Chios) and of Arsinoë's tutor-guardian (the eunuch Ganymede), but Cleopatra's tutor, like most of her personal advisers, goes unrecorded. Cicero, who met and took an instant dislike to Cleopatra, confirms that she had academic leanings – 'Her promises were all things to do with learning, and not derogatory to my dignity …' – while Appian tells us that she tried to interest Mark Antony in education and learned discussion.[15] Plutarch was impressed by her unusual (some might say unbelievable) command of the barbarian tongues, although he omits Latin from his list, possibly because he assumes that every well-educated person will be able to speak it:

> *She could readily turn to whichever language she pleased, so that there were few foreigners she had to deal with through an interpreter, and to most she herself gave her replies without an intermediary – to the Ethiopians, Troglodytes, Hebrews, Arabs, Syrians, Medes and Parthians. It is said that she knew the language of many other peoples also, although the preceding kings of Egypt had not tried to master even the Egyptian tongue, and some had indeed ceased to speak the Macedonian dialect.*[16]

This tradition of Cleopatra the intellectual would persist, and long after her death medieval Arab historians would revere Cleopatra as 'the virtuous scholar': a philosopher, alchemist, mathematician and physician with a special interest in gynaecology. However, we have no confirmation of any scientific training, and the only evidence for her interest in medicine is the fact that she supported the temple of Hathor at Dendera, a temple associated with female health and healing. It is perhaps more telling that Cleopatra herself employed the distinguished scholar Nikolaos of Damascus to educate her twins Alexander Helios and Cleopatra Selene. Clearly, Cleopatra regarded education as an important matter for both boys and girls.

Auletes understood that Egypt's future was bound up with the future of Rome. Unfortunately, he was incapable of persuading his people – the kingmakers of Alexandria – to accept the situation. With the benefit of hindsight, it all seems terribly obvious. Egypt was a fertile and ill-defended land ripe for the taking, while Rome was a greedy, ever-expanding military nation with a constant need for grain and a legal claim, however dubious, over Egypt. Now, as Auletes's reign progressed, Egypt's position was deteriorating from bad to worse.

In 65 the Roman censor Marcus Licinius Crassus proposed the annexation of Egypt; two years later the tribune Publius Servillius Rullus proposed an agrarian reform that would give Romans a right to Egyptian land. Both proposals were defeated, but Egypt's days of independence were clearly numbered. Only by increasing his cooperation with Rome did Auletes have any hope of keeping his kingdom. And so, very much against the wishes of the Alexandrians, he bent over backwards to cooperate. In 63 the influential Roman general Gnaeus Pompeius (Pompey the Great) graciously accepted a golden crown, the lavish gift of Auletes and Egypt. Later that same year Egyptian soldiers were sent to fight alongside Pompey's troops in Palestine. Meanwhile, back in Rome, senators of all political factions received copious bribes; bribes which Auletes, impoverished after years of bad management and overspending, had borrowed from Roman moneylenders, and which he could only hope to repay by raising the taxes that were already causing his people much suffering.

In 60 Pompey, Crassus and Gaius Julius Caesar united to form the 'first triumvirate'.[17] Essentially, the three now ruled Rome. Seizing his moment, Auletes offered Pompey and Caesar 6,000 silver talents, an almost unimaginable sum, the equivalent of half of Egypt's entire annual revenue, in exchange for recognition as Egypt's true king. They accepted and Auletes, having borrowed the money from the Roman moneylender Gaius Rabirius Postumus, was confirmed in his position as 'friend and ally of the Roman people' (*amicus et socius populi Romani*), a specific legal phrase that conferred obligations on both parties. Auletes had sacrificed his dignity, saved his crown and bought Egypt a few more years of independence; his achievement had little to do with his persuasive diplomatic powers and generous bribes, and much to do with Rome's reluctance to reduce Egypt to the status of a province. The senators feared, with some justification, that this would allow the ambitious Caesar too much power.

Auletes had been recognised as a friend and ally but his brother had not. And, as Cyprus as well as Egypt had been gifted to Rome in the will of Ptolemy X, this left the younger Ptolemy in a precarious position. In 58 the Romans decided to claim their property. Cyprus was annexed by Marcus Porcius Cato (Cato the Younger) and King Ptolemy, declining the offer of an honourable retirement as high priest of Aphrodite at Paphos, swallowed poison. As the people of Alexandria took to the streets to protest against their king's apparent indifference to his brother's fate, Auletes fled to Cato in Rhodes. His visit was conspicuously unsuccessful: he arrived soon after Cato had taken a laxative, and was forced to plead his case as Cato sat on the toilet. From Cato's latrine he moved on to Pompey's villa in Rome. Few fathers choose to take young children on business trips, and it is generally assumed that Auletes left all his children behind in Alexandria. However, an undated dedication made in Athens at about this time by a 'king's daughter from Libya' has led some historians to suggest that perhaps the twelve-year-old Cleopatra accompanied her father at least as far as Greece. The confusion between Egypt and Libya is, however, an odd one and, with no precise date for the dedication, the Libyan princess is far more likely to be a daughter or granddaughter of Juba II of Mauretania, and therefore Cleopatra's granddaughter or great-granddaughter.

With her unpopular father indefinitely absent, Berenice IV proclaimed herself queen. She was associated in her early reign with a 'Cleopatra Tryphaena'; whether this is Berenice's ephemeral sister or her mother, who has been missing from our history for over a decade, is not clear. Just one historian, Porphyrius of Tyre, writing three centuries after the event, specifies that this Cleopatra, who is by convention numbered Cleopatra VI, is a daughter of Auletes. Porphyrius's somewhat confused and occasionally incorrect Ptolemaic history is today lost, but fragments have been absorbed into the works of later historians, including Eusebius's *Chronicle,* where we read how:

In the reign of the New Dionysos, a three year period was ascribed to the rule of his daughters Cleopatra Tryphaena and Berenice, one year as a joint reign and the following two years, after the death of Cleopatra Tryphaena, as the reign of Berenice on her own.[18]

If Porphyrius is wrong, and his Cleopatra VI Tryphaena is to be equated with Cleopatra V, this brief joint rule offers further indirect proof that Cleopatra V was born a member of the Ptolemaic dynasty with an inherited right to rule Egypt. Whoever she was, Cleopatra VI Tryphaena vanished before the end of 57 and, in the absence of any evidence to the contrary, is presumed to have died a natural death.

History had started to repeat itself. Berenice, now renamed Cleopatra Berenice, was a female ruler in need of a husband. Ideally she would have married one of her younger brothers, but as the elder was just three years old she chose an insignificant cousin, Seleucos, instead. This time it was the bride who took a violent dislike to the bridegroom: according to Strabo, the refined Berenice was unable to bear her husband's 'coarseness and vulgarity', while his crude and unappealing personality and perhaps his low standards of personal hygiene inspired the Alexandrians to rename him Cybiosactes, or 'salt-fish monger'. The unfortunately vulgar Seleucos was strangled within a week of his wedding and a replacement husband was hastily recruited. Berenice's second choice, Archelaos, self-appointed son of Rome's great enemy Mithridates VI of Pontus (and actual son of Mithridates's general, Achelaos), proved more satisfactory and the couple ruled for two years with the full support of the people of Alexandria.

The Alexandrians may have been happy; Auletes and his Roman hosts were not. The influential Pompey offered his support to Auletes; a demonstrably weak king but one who had proved his loyalty to Rome and who, of course, owed such a large debt to Roman bankers that it seemed prudent to help him regain both his throne and his treasury. However, Auletes could not return to Alexandria without aid, and the Romans were hesitant, consulting oracles and failing to decide Egypt's fate. Meanwhile, realising that she needed Roman approval if she was to retain her crown, Berenice dispatched a 100-strong delegation, headed by the brilliant academic and philosopher Dion of Alexandria, to plead her case. Auletes reacted with brutal efficiency, and a shameful combination of murder, coercion and bribery prevented the delegation from speaking. The resulting scandal, which threatened to involve the prominent bankers who were backing Auletes, was quickly brushed behind the official arras. Disgraced, Auletes borrowed yet more money and fled to the temple of Artemis at Ephesus.

Auletes's exile continued until, early in 55, he managed to bribe Aulus Gabinius, governor of Syria, to give him military support. As Plutarch delicately puts it, 'Gabinius himself felt a certain dread of the war, although he was completely captivated by the ten thousand talents'.[19] Later that same year Gabinius's mercenary army marched across Sinai and into the eastern Delta. Pelusium, Egypt's easternmost city, fell and Archelaos was killed in battle; although a traitor, he was given an honourable burial by Gabinius's cavalry officer, Marcus Antonius (Mark Antony). Auletes returned home in triumph to find Alexandria suffering under a fairly brutal foreign occupation. His vengeance was swift and uncompromising, tempered only by Mark Antony's generous pleading on behalf of the ordinary citizens. Berenice and her most prominent supporters were executed and their confiscated property was used to repay some of Auletes's ever-increasing debt to Rabirius, who, for one extortionate year, became Egypt's finance minister.

Rabirius brought havoc to the bureaucracy and poverty to the countryside. Stripping the Egyptian civil servants from their hereditary positions, he introduced his own ruthless men. Soon there were civil disturbances in Alexandria, the Faiyum, Oxyrhynchus and Heracleopolis as the farmers threatened to withhold their labour unless they received protection from the avaricious tax collectors. Ousted from power, Rabirius returned to Rome, where he was tried, and acquitted, for financial improprieties. Pleading poverty, he agreed that Julius Caesar should take over the collection of his outstanding Egyptian debt. Gabinius, too, was to be tried in Rome for financial irregularities; less fortunate than Rabirius, he was sent into exile. However, long after the danger had passed the 'Gabinians', the major part of Gabinius's army, which included many Germans and Gauls, remained in Egypt, ostensibly to support the restored Auletes. Gradually these soldiers married local women and fathered Egyptian children, adding yet another cultural and racial strand to an already well-mixed Egypt.

Auletes emerged from the bloodshed a poverty-stricken king whose family had been torn apart by treachery and whose country was suffering from erratic Nile floods and unacceptably high taxation. Egypt had stopped minting gold coins during the reign of Ptolemy VIII. Now, to make his money go further, Auletes debased the silver content of his coins to just 84 per cent. This sparked a dramatic rise in inflation but did little to improve the economy. To protect the succession, and pre-empt any further family squabbles, Auletes united his four surviving children within the royal cult as the rather optimistically named Theoi Neoi Philadelphoi, (New Sibling-Loving Gods). Traditionally, Egypt's living kings had been semi-divine beings who acquired full divinity with death. The distinction between the gods, the semi-divine king and his mortal subjects had been theologically clear, but not always obvious to the masses, who, faced with a temple decorated with colossal images of their king, may well have been confused over who exactly was, and who was not, a god. Ptolemy II had swept away any confusion by establishing the royal cults. All Ptolemaic rulers now routinely became a part of the dynastic cult during their lifetime, their group divinity frequently being supplemented by a personal divinity either at death (during the earlier part of the Ptolemaic age) or during their own lifetime (during the later part of the Ptolemaic age).

Auletes was a pharaoh without a queen. This is extremely rare. The precise role of the traditional Egyptian queen consort is as yet ill-understood, but it seems that she offered the king a vital female element that would complement his maleness and make him a whole, perfect ruler. Egypt's priest would have considered that Auletes needed a queen to be able to perform the religious rituals that pleased the gods and kept the ever-threatening chaos at bay. Kings whose consorts died – and this itself was unusual; in contrast to the situation in non-royal Egypt, where women often died as a result of pregnancy-induced illness, queens tended to outlive their husbands – acquired a replacement consort quickly. The 19th Dynasty monarch Ramesses II, blessed (or cursed) with an extremely long reign, outlived two Egyptian-born consorts and eventually promoted, and married, at least three of his daughters.[20] The Ptolemies were inclined to emulate the Ramesside kings; it therefore would not have been unexpected if Auletes, given the shortage of Ptolemaic brides, had used his eldest surviving daughter as his consort and partner in religious rituals. Inscriptions in the crypts of the Dendera temple of Hathor add some support to this theory by linking the king's name with the cartouche of a 'Cleopatra', and with an unnamed woman who is described as the 'eldest daughter of the king'. As work on this temple did not start until 54, after the assumed death of Cleopatra V, it is likely that this is Cleopatra VII acting as her father's consort. There is, however, no suggestion that Auletes married Cleopatra: father–daughter incest was not acceptable in the Hellenistic world, even at the louche court of Auletes.

When, in 51, Auletes died an apparently natural death (Strabo emphasises that he 'died of disease'), the throne passed as he had planned to the eighteen-year-old Cleopatra and her eldest brother, the ten-year-old Ptolemy. Auletes's will appointed the people of Rome guardians of Egypt's new king and queen and protectors of the Ptolemaic dynasty. One copy of this will was lodged in the Library of Alexandria, a second was sent for safe-keeping to Pompey in Rome.

(Auletes had intended that it be lodged in the public record office, but Rome was a city teetering on the brink of disaster and, for reasons of his own, Pompey chose to keep the will at his house.) Few Alexandrians grieved for Auletes, yet Cleopatra chose to highlight her unswerving loyalty to her dead father by immediately adopting the name Philopator (Father Loving). Her slightly later assumption of the epithet Thea (Goddess), and later still Nea Isis (the New Isis), signals her continuing devotion to the Neos Dionysos Theos Philopator Auletes, as does her determination to complete many of Auletes's unfinished building projects.

It is easy for us to underestimate Auletes. Classical authors like Strabo, quoted earlier in this chapter, were happy to spread the propaganda of the last and most corrupt king of a decaying line; a king chosen by a mob, with a reign that was characterised by uncertainty, dissipation, economic hardship and civil unrest. We are left with the unpleasant image of the impotent Auletes frittering away his days throwing sumptuous banquets, drinking to excess and blowing his *aulos* with the palace dancing girls and, or so it was rumoured, boys. However, impotent or not, Auletes did manage to preserve his throne and, whatever the Romans and the Alexandrians thought about him, the Egyptian priesthood respected him as a pharaoh prepared to invest in traditional temple building schemes.[21]

So Cleopatra VII Philopator and her brother Ptolemy XIII came to the throne with the blessing of the people of Alexandria and the qualified support of the Romans. They inherited an insecure land suffering from high inflation and unreliable Nile floods, and their father's extensive debts.

CHAPTER TWO

Queen of Egypt

Cleopatra was an Egyptian woman who became an object of gossip for the whole world ... She came to rule through crime. She gained glory for almost nothing else than her beauty while on the other hand she became known throughout the world for her greed, cruelty and lustfulness ...

Boccaccio, *On the Lives of Famous Women*[1]

For many hundreds of years the sacred Bakhu or Buchis bull had been worshipped as a living god in the Theban region. During his lifetime the bull was associated with the warrior god Montu and, to a lesser extent, with the fertility god Osiris and the sun god Re. He received offerings, delivered oracles and cured the sick (specialising in eye diseases), and he occasionally fought with other bulls in a dedicated bullring. In death he was mummified and buried, with all the pomp and ceremony due to a deceased god, in a vast bull cemetery known as the Bucheion, at Armant (ancient Iuni-Montu; Greek Hermonthis), on the west bank of the Nile to the south-west of Thebes. A funerary stela recovered from this cemetery details the enthronement of a Buchis bull on Phamenoth 19 (22 March 51):

... He reached Thebes, his place of installation, which came into existence aforetime, beside his father, Nun the Old. He was installed by the King himself in year 1, Phamenoth 19. The Queen, the Lady of the Two Lands, the Goddess Philopator, rowed him in the boat of Amen, together with the boats of the king, all the inhabitants of Thebes and Hermonthis and priests being with him. He reached Hermonthis, his dwelling place on Mechir 22 ...[2]

The precise date of Auletes's demise is unknown: all we can say for certain is that some time during 51 Auletes's Year 30 became 'Year 30 which is become Year 1' (i.e. the first year of the new regime), and by August of that same year news of his death had reached Rome. But the Bucheion stela tells us that the installation ceremony occurred at a time when Egypt was ruled by a king and a queen, the 'Lady of the Two Lands, the Goddess Philopator'. The names within the text are left blank – something that frequently happens in later Ptolemaic inscriptions – and therefore both king and queen are unnamed. However, given the date of the stela, it seems that they are more than likely to be Ptolemy XIII and Cleopatra VII. The stela therefore offers a *terminus ante quem* for Auletes's death, which is likely to have occurred in late February or early March 51. The only alternative is that the unnamed king is Auletes rather than Ptolemy XIII. If this is the case, it may be that Auletes did not die until as late as June or July 51, and the wording of the stela may be read as an indication that Cleopatra was indeed her father's co-regent.

The image is a standard view of a king making an offering to the Buchis bull, and the text is a version of a standard Bucheion text found on three other late Ptolemaic stelae:

He was installed by the King himself. Going on the boat of Amen, together with the boats of the king, all the inhabitants of Thebes and Hermonthis, prophets and priests being with him. He reached Hermonthis, his dwelling place.

The fact that the priests felt the need to adapt a standard text to include the queen confirms Cleopatra's political importance immediately after her father's death. The Ptolemies observed the rites of the native religion, and developed a strong interest in the cult of the Apis bull (celebrated at Memphis, cult centre of the creator god Ptah, where the Apis was worshipped as the physical manifestation of Ptah) and the cult of the Mnevis bull (celebrated at Heliopolis, cult centre of the sun god Re, where the Mnevis was considered to be the physical manifestation of the sun god). However, given the Egyptian fondness for formulaic texts, and given that the Bucheion text was inscribed in 29, after Cleopatra's death, the stela does not prove beyond all reasonable doubt that Cleopatra actually attended the ceremony in person.

Although Ptolemaic tradition suggests that Cleopatra is likely to have married her brother soon after their father's death, their marriage is nowhere recorded. An inscription on the barque or boat shrine of the earth god Geb in the Koptos temple, dedicated by Cleopatra, shows the queen offering to the divine triad of Min, Isis and Horus, and describes her as 'Mistress of the Two Lands, Cleopatra Philopator, Beloved of Min-Re of Koptos, King's Wife, King's Daughter', but the husband-king is unnamed, and could be either Ptolemy XIII or Ptolemy XIV.[3] If it did occur, and a marriage between his eldest surviving daughter and son may well have been a condition of Auletes's will, it is likely to have been, in 51, a marriage in name only. The age gap between sister and brother was unfortunate. The eighteen-year-old Cleopatra was rather too old to remain unwed, while Ptolemy, at just ten years old, was a little too young to consummate a marriage. There are no known legal age limits for marriage in Ptolemaic Egypt, but archaeological evidence indicates that most women married in their mid- or late teens, acquiring husbands older rather than younger than themselves. Tayimhotep, wife of the high priest of Ptah Pasherenptah III, whom we last met at Auletes's coronation, would not have been unusual in marrying, aged fourteen, a husband eighteen years older than herself.[4] This left Cleopatra in an awkward position. As a queen of marriageable age she needed to start producing the children who would continue her dynastic line.

Husband or brother, Ptolemy, as king, should have been the dominant partner in the relationship. But he was a minor, ruling via a regency council, and for the first year and a half of their joint reign Cleopatra became the effective monarch, while her brother was pushed into the background. The earliest documents from this period suggest that Cleopatra ruled alone, although it is important to view documents dated to the first year of the solo queen 'Cleopatra Philopator' with a degree of caution, as Berenice III had also been a Cleopatra Philopator. The most intriguing of these documents is a unique limestone stela, of unknown provenance but probably from the Faiyum, which is now housed in the Louvre, Paris. The piece is a fusion of Egyptian and Greek traditions, with a conventional Egyptian religious image topping a text written in Greek. It shows a slightly damaged 'Cleopatra', dressed in the kilt and double crown of a traditional pharaoh, making an offering to the goddess Isis, who is sitting on a throne and suckling her infant son. The somewhat confusing inscription, which details the dedication of a 'seat' (*topos*) by the priest Omnophris, president of the association of the devotees of Isis, reads:

> *For Queen Cleopatra Thea Philopator [is dedicated] the seat of the association [of Isis] Snonais, the president of which is the chief priest Omnophris. July 2 51.*

Cleopatra, on this stela, appears entirely male; the inscription, which makes it clear that she is in fact a woman, implies that she is the sole ruler of Egypt. This, the only surviving image of Cleopatra as a female king, recalls the Theban artwork of the early New Kingdom female pharaoh Hatshepsut. Hatshepsut (reigned 1473–1458) struggled with the convention decreeing that a king of Egypt should be a young and healthy male. Soon after her coronation she abandoned the customary woman's sheath dress and queen's crowns, and started to appear in the traditional king's regalia of short kilt, bare chest, crown or head-cloth, broad collar and false beard. Very occasionally, towards the beginning of her reign, Hatshepsut was depicted as a woman dressed in this male clothing, but more usually she was shown performing male actions with a man's body.[5] It would be easy to suggest that Cleopatra is here deliberately emulating Egypt's most successful female monarch, as in many ways Hatshepsut, who effectively usurped the throne from a weaker and much younger male co-regent, makes an appropriate role model for Cleopatra.[6] But Hatshepsut was forced to battle against a system which could not cope with the idea of female rule, while Cleopatra, living in an age which had already experienced the vigorous rule of Cleopatras I, II and III, encountered no such problem. Indeed, it seems unlikely that Cleopatra would have known much about Hatshepsut's history, art or propaganda, as the majority of Hatshepsut's images were defaced within thirty years of her death, and her name was omitted from Egypt's official King List. Today Hatshepsut's Red Chapel, decorated with multiple images of the female king performing traditionally male actions, is the highlight of any tour of Karnak temple, but the chapel is a modern reconstruction, painstakingly compiled from the demolished remains of the original building, which would have been invisible to Cleopatra.

A re-reading of the text on Cleopatra's stela indicates that, although it features Cleopatra, she did not commission it. The image of the female king cannot therefore be taken as official propaganda. The text is not all it seems. The Greek letters are uncomfortably squashed into the space available, and it seems likely that it is a later addition, cut over an earlier text. This suggests that the stela was first cut for Cleopatra's father and then changed, rather ineptly, when he died. Nevertheless, the important fact remains that Cleopatra is featured as a sole ruler, while Ptolemy's name is excluded from the stela.

When, over two centuries earlier, the intelligent and experienced Arsinoë II married her younger, weaker brother Ptolemy II, she determined to work with him. In so doing, she strengthened the Ptolemaic hold on the Egyptian throne. Cleopatra, intelligent and ambitious and not one to suffer fools gladly, would have done well to heed this precedent. Her sidelining of her brother was to prove a tactical mistake, as it left Ptolemy vulnerable to a group of manipulative and ambitious Alexandrian courtiers, including his tutor Theodotos, the soldier Achillas and the eunuch Pothinos, who was soon to become Egypt's chief minister. All three were to use the young king to further their own political ambitions. By the time Ptolemy was old enough to embark on a full married life, his relationship with his sister had irretrievably broken down and Egypt was teetering on the brink of civil war.

On 27 October 50 we find the first decree to be issued with Ptolemy's name preceding Cleopatra's. Egypt, usually so fertile, was suffering the effects of years of unreliable Nile floods. The decree, issued after a second disappointing inundation, directed that all surplus grain and legumes grown in Upper and Middle Egypt should be sent straight to Alexandria – and nowhere else. The penalty for contravening the decree 'by order of the king and queen' was death, those who informed on rogue traders were to receive a specified reward dependent on their social status.[7] The crisis was severe enough to unite the royal couple, who recognised that, at a time of national shortage, the volatile citizens of Alexandria must be their primary concern. But, as the Alexandrians ate their grain supplies, the people outside Alexandria suffered from shortages, high inflation and high taxation. And, as the Nile continued to under-perform, the workers began to desert their hamlets, taxes went unpaid and the cities started to fill with hungry peasants. As wheat prices reached an all-time high, the priests of the Faiyum village of Hiera Nesos grew worried; their hungry villagers had mysteriously vanished, leaving them unable to complete the temple rituals.[8]

Rome was temporarily distracted from Egyptian affairs. In 54 Julia, the only acknowledged child of Julius Caesar and the beloved wife of Pompey, had died, severing the personal link between the two men. The following year Crassus perished in a disastrous campaign fighting the Parthians at Carrhae (modern Harran, Turkey). A wave of unease rippled through the Mediterranean world; it was assumed, quite rightly, that the Parthians would now attempt to take Syria. In late 51 Marcus Calpurnius Bibulus, the new Roman governor of Syria, sent his two sons to Egypt to plead with the Gabinians, Gabinius's now Egyptianised army, to return home and protect his land against Parthian attack. The Gabinians, however, had grown comfortable serving as a mercenary Ptolemaic army and were reluctant to uproot themselves to fight. Rather than negotiate, they killed the two sons of Bibulus. This left the king and queen of Egypt in a difficult situation. Risking the anger of the Gabinians, Cleopatra and Ptolemy had the murderers arrested and sent in chains to Syria.

In January 49 Caesar and his army of veterans crossed the Rubicon, the official boundary between Italy and Cisalpine Gaul. As Roman law forbade any general from crossing the river with an army, this was treason. The die was cast: Caesar had effectively declared war on Pompey and Rome. Soon after, Gnaeus Pompey, Pompey's son, arrived in Alexandria to beg for military aid on his father's behalf. His request could not be honourably refused. Pompey had been Auletes's host and patron in Rome, and he was entitled to call upon the Ptolemies for support. Egypt supplied Gnaeus with a large quantity of wheat, 500 Gabinians and sixty warships that were to play a key role in his father's subsequent campaigns. The decision to grant this aid was taken by

Ptolemy (or, more likely, his ministers), with Cleopatra's name recorded second. It was a decision that angered the people of Alexandria, who blamed Cleopatra for the whole affair. Her apparent eagerness to please the Romans, first in the matter of the Bibulus murderers and then by giving arms to Pompey, reminded them too much of her father's reign. Later there would come a rumour, preserved for us by Plutarch, that the sexually voracious Cleopatra had seduced Gnaeus during his Egyptian sojourn. Much later still, due to a misreading of his sources by William Shakespeare, would come the fiction that Cleopatra had had an affair with Gnaeus's father.

Cleopatra's obvious and growing unpopularity in Alexandria may in part explain why Ptolemy's advisers chose this time to act against his co-regent. In 49 we find the development of a new regnal-year numbering system. 'Year 1 which is also Year 3' equates the third year of nominally joint rule following the death of Auletes with a new Year 1; presumably Ptolemy's first year as a solo king. In the summer of 49 Cleopatra's name disappears from all official documents and the new 'Year 1' dating system is dropped. Ptolemy is backdating his reign, erasing the memory of his sister and retrospectively claiming sole rule from the time of his father's death. Cleopatra and her supporters had been forced to flee Alexandria, travelling first perhaps south to Thebes – a city notoriously prone to rebellion, but one that may have been inclined to support Auletes's daughter against the Alexandrians – then eastwards to Syria.[9] Here she set to work raising the mercenary army that would allow her to reclaim her throne. Quite how Cleopatra managed to raise an effective army at a time when the Roman civil war was causing massive disruption across the Mediterranean world is nowhere explained; the fact that she was able to achieve this in a very short space of time confirms that, outside Alexandria, she was considered a viable candidate for the Egyptian throne. It is likely that the majority of her troops came from the Philistine coastal city of Ashkelon (near the modern Israeli city of the same name), which owed a long-standing debt of loyalty to the Ptolemies and which issued coins bearing Cleopatra's image in 50/49 and, perhaps, 49/8. Meanwhile, in Thessalonica (Salonica), the Roman counter-senate recognised Pompey as high commander and, in direct contravention of Auletes's will, Ptolemy XIII as sole king of Egypt with Pompey as his legal guardian. Ptolemy, like his father before him, had become a 'friend and ally' of Rome.

On 9 August, 48 armies loyal to Pompey and Caesar met at Pharsalus in Thessaly, central mainland Greece. Pompey had the advantage of numbers – his 47,000 men outnumbered Caesar's by two to one – but he was the weaker general, his advisers were inexperienced, and Caesar had Mars, god of war, and Venus, his divine ancestress, on his side. Caesar won the battle and, magnanimous in victory, pardoned his enemies, including Marcus Junius Brutus, the son of his long-term mistress Servilia. Defeated but by no means inclined to give up the fight, Pompey fled with the remnants of his army to the island of Lesbos, where he was reunited with his younger son, Sextus, and his fifth wife, Cornelia, the widowed daughter-in-law of Crassus. From Lesbos Pompey sailed to Cilicia, thence to Cyprus and finally, after some hesitation, to his old ally, Egypt. Confident of a warm welcome from Auletes's son, he sailed to Pelusium and dropped anchor in sight of the beach. The 'eyewitness' accounts of what happened next are provided by Plutarch and Dio; neither, of course, a true witness, but both capable of telling a moving story calculated to touch even the most stony of hearts.[10]

Having established camp outside Pelusium, in the foothills of Mount Casius (Ras Baron), Ptolemy and his army of Gabinians were nervously awaiting Cleopatra's army, which was known to be marching from the east. Messengers came to announce Pompey's arrival and to ask for an audience with the king. Panicking, Pothinos called a meeting of Ptolemy's most trusted advisers so that each could suggest a course of action. Some argued that Pompey should be welcomed as an honoured guest; others that he was a troublemaker who should be driven away from the shore. But Theodotos could see flaws in both arguments, and he argued his case with all the skills of an experienced teacher. If Pompey was welcomed as a friend, Caesar would automatically become Egypt's enemy. But if Pompey was driven away, he would become Egypt's enemy and Caesar would blame Ptolemy for allowing him to escape. Furthermore, Pompey already had links with Cleopatra through his son Gnaeus; it was more than likely that he would support the queen in her battle for the throne. It seemed to Theodotos, perhaps correctly, that Pompey's cause was already irretrievably lost. Wishing to ingratiate his king with Caesar, and worried that Egypt might become Rome's battleground, he argued that the vulnerable Pompey should be killed before he landed. After all, as everyone knew, 'A dead man does not bite.'

It was agreed. Ptolemy's army marched to the beach and formed themselves in ranks facing the sea. Commandeering a fishing boat, Achillas rowed out to Pompey's flagship with two of the Gabinians, the tribune Lucius Septimus and the centurion Salvius. Pompey's followers, worried that a lone, undignified fishing boat was an inappropriate vessel for their master, urged him not to leave the safety of his ship. Indeed, they argued, it might be prudent to row away from the shore, at least until they were out of missile range. But Septimus, speaking in Latin, gave Pompey a courteous welcome: 'Hail, Imperator [commander]'. And Achillas, speaking in Greek, explained that the undignified transport was an unfortunate necessity, the harbour at Pelusium being too shallow to accommodate Pompey's fine ship. Reassured, Pompey embraced his wife and transferred to the fishing boat with two bodyguards, his freedman Philip and a slave. Once on board he busied himself reading through the speech he meant to make to King Ptolemy.

As the boat bumped on the beach Pompey held out his hand so that Philip might help him to rise with dignity. Then, far too late, he realised his danger. 'He uttered not a word and made no complaint, but as soon as he perceived their plot and recognised that he would not be able to ward them off or escape, he veiled his face.' Cornelia, watching from the ship, screamed as the treacherous Septimus ran her husband through with a sword, and Salvius and Achillas stabbed him in the back with their daggers. Pompey's head was hacked from his body, his corpse thrown into the sea. It was the day before his fifty-eighth birthday. Ptolemy, sitting on his throne on the shore, turned a blind eye to the murder of his father's friend. For this callousness Dante would consign him to circle nine, the circle reserved for those who betray their guests, in his *Inferno*.[11]

The loyal Philip retrieved Pompey's body from the sea and cremated him on a pyre of discarded ship's timbers on the beach. His ashes were eventually returned to the grieving Cornelia, who buried him in Italy. A few weeks later Egypt experienced the lowest Nile flooding ever recorded and the already depleted food supplies became perilously low. Divine retribution, some said, for the murder of Pompey.

Four days later Caesar, chasing Pompey with a small fleet of ten warships and some 4,000 men, arrived in the great harbour of Alexandria. Pothinos and Theodotos hurried from Pelusium to meet him, eager to tell their tale before Caesar heard it from others less sympathetic to their cause. They took with them, as macabre greeting gifts, Pompey's severed (and in some accounts pickled) head and his signet ring. Caesar must have had mixed feelings when viewing these grizzly trophies. In many ways Ptolemy and his advisers had done him a huge favour: it was far better that the disruptive Pompey be killed by foreigners than by a fellow Roman. But the manner of his death was appalling, and Caesar could not be seen to condone the murder of a Roman citizen conducted so blatantly before so many witnesses. He therefore averted his eyes from Pompey's head and wept ostentatious tears over his ring. Then he donned his purple-edged toga and left his ship to process with his twelve lictors carrying the *fasces* – the bundle of rods and an axe bound with red tape and laurel, which signified his office – through the city. The people of Alexandria watched this miniature Roman invasion with incredulity and a well-vocalised resentment that soon turned to rioting. By nightfall Caesar had commandeered the royal palace, and there had been several deaths.

Although Pompey was dead, the Roman civil war was far from over and Caesar's own position was far from secure. The bulk of his army was still stationed in Greece. Nevertheless, he chose to make an extended stay in hostile Alexandria, where, or so he tells us, he soon found himself stranded by adverse northerly winds. This curious decision is nowhere explained. Authors of a romantic disposition have suggested that Caesar lingered in Egypt because of his deep love for Cleopatra, but he had not yet met the queen, who was still camped with her army to the east of Pelusium. It seems instead that Caesar stayed for the most practical of reasons: he wished to tax the wealthy Alexandrians in order to recover some of the money lent by Rabirius to Auletes. Settling in for a long visit, and turning a blind eye to the local resentment, Caesar sent for reinforcements and spent his days writing his memoirs and sightseeing. He was particularly impressed by a visit to the tomb of his great hero Alexander the Great.

Egypt was a land trembling on the brink of civil war. Perhaps Caesar calculated that increased stability would bring increased wealth, and that increased wealth would allow increased taxation. Perhaps he understood that a grateful Egyptian king and/or queen might be of some use to him in the future. Maybe he was simply bored. Whatever his reasoning, Caesar took it upon himself to settle the dispute between Cleopatra and Ptolemy, and he ordered both to appear before him at Alexandria. Ptolemy did as he was bidden, leaving his troops at Pelusium under the command of Achillas. In Alexandria he moved into the palace district with Pothinos, who, acting as a negotiator between the Romans and the Alexandrians, did all he could to foster bad feeling between the two sides. Thanks to Pothinos, the Romans were fed rotten grain while Ptolemy's supporters were misfed information, and dined off crude pottery under the mistaken impression that the Romans had confiscated the valuable royal plate. No one was happy and the city was fast approaching boiling point.

Superficially, Ptolemy held all the cards. He had the military support of the Gabinians and the vocal support of the people of Alexandria. He was here, on the spot, in Alexandria. Caesar's easiest, most obvious option was surely to award him the crown, with Arsinoë replacing her sister as queen. But Cleopatra, too, had something to offer. That she was older and more experienced was obvious: Ptolemy, still only thirteen years old, was controlled by a clique of advisers and had, as yet, made no independent decisions. That she had the support of the native Egyptians was perhaps an irrelevance; far more important was the fact that she could display an impressive track record of loyalty to Rome. If Caesar was hoping to recover Rabirius's debt, Cleopatra might be inclined to help him. But this was not necessarily an argument that Cleopatra wanted to plead in a public meeting in Alexandria. A preliminary, private meeting with Caesar would better suit her needs.

Cleopatra too set off for Alexandria. With Achillas and his army blocking her route through Pelusium, and Pothinos guarding the harbour at Alexandria, hers was a secret, undignified journey. Abandoning her troops, she was able to slip past Achillas and make her way in a small boat along the coast. She landed in the Palaces district at nightfall. The story of how Cleopatra had herself smuggled into the palace by the Sicilian merchant Apollodorus, who hid her in a bedroll or a bundle of linen sheets, has grown in the telling so that in modern versions of her tale we find Cleopatra being unrolled from an exotic, anachronistic Persian rug to tumble, alluringly dishevelled and breathless, at Caesar's feet. This is a romantic story that really does not hold up to detailed scrutiny, and it stems in its entirety from the fluent pen of Plutarch. Was this truly the only means by which Cleopatra could make her way into Caesar's presence? Having gained the security of the palace, could she not have abandoned her bedroll to make a more conventional entry? It is hard to imagine that Caesar would allow an unknown Sicilian to bring a potentially dangerous package into his suite without having it searched. Was Caesar then expecting Cleopatra's arrival? Dio tells us that they had already been in correspondence; had Caesar been warned to turn a blind eye to strangers bearing bundles? Or did Cleopatra deliberately plan to arrive as the ultimate gift-wrapped package? Was this in fact a carefully stage-managed production designed to appeal to Caesar's notoriously susceptible nature? It would certainly be naïve to assume that Cleopatra – whose later history confirms that she shared the Ptolemaic love of elaborate spectacle – was unaware of the impact of her unorthodox arrival. Plutarch for one believed that her entry was well planned:

> *It was by this device of Cleopatra's, it is said, that Caesar was first captivated, for she showed herself to be a bold coquette, and succumbing to the charm of further intercourse with her, he reconciled her to her brother ...*[12]

What did Caesar see when Apollodorus dropped his bundle and revealed his queen? If we are imagining the scene as described by Plutarch we should probably indulge our wildest fantasies and picture a dark room, flickering torchlight, high stone walls, gilded furniture, a mosaic floor and a dark-haired, olive-skinned young woman dressed in Greek rather than Egyptian garments. Cleopatra is likely to have been short by modern standards and she probably, like almost everyone of her time, suffered from bad teeth. Her coins, unflattering to modern eyes, suggest a prominent nose and chin and a rather thick neck. It is hard for us to be more precise in our imaginings, as we have no real idea what Cleopatra looked like. No contemporary descriptions and few contemporary illustrations have survived.

So much for Cleopatra's appearance. What did she see when she tumbled from her bedding roll to lie at Caesar's feet? A man thirty years older than herself. Well built, tall by Roman standards, with dark eyes, a pale, rounded face, receding fair hair and a bad 'comb-over': Caesar was notoriously self-conscious about his baldness and insisted that his statues be topped with youthful mops of curly hair. He liked to be well groomed; his biographer, Suetonius, gives us perhaps more information than we would like, telling us:

> *he was something of a dandy, always keeping his head carefully trimmed and shaved; and has been accused of having certain other hairy parts of his body depilated by tweezers.*[13]

His clothes were the height of fashion: Suetonius mentions wrist-length sleeves with fringes on his striped senatorial robe and a daringly loose belt. Clearly Caesar appreciated luxury. But he was no hedonist. Unusually for a Roman, he drank sparingly, and he ate anything that was put in front of him, seemingly unable to distinguish good food from bad.

Caesar was the supreme celebrity of his age, known by reputation throughout the civilised world. Cleopatra would have understood that she was facing a man with exceptional drive and ambition. An excellent politician, orator and author, a superb horseman, and an extremely successful though by no means infallible general, Caesar was known to be both good-humoured and amusing. And he had a reputation for sexual excess that his legionaries repeated with awe and pride: he was 'every woman's man and every man's woman'.[14] Stories of his same-sex alliances are likely to have been greatly exaggerated, although there was a persistent rumour, potentially politically damaging but impossible to quash, that he had enjoyed a youthful fling with King Nicomedes of Bithynia. Cicero certainly believed that there was no smoke without fire:

Caesar was led by Nicomedes's attendants to the royal bedchamber, where he lay on a golden couch, dressed in a purple shift ... So this descendant of Venus lost his virginity in Bithynia.[15]

In classical Greece, where men and 'decent' women lived very separate lives, and where men of all ages routinely spent many hours naked at the gymnasium, it was expected that an older man might feel a tenderness, or more, for a young boy. The Romans, who were on the whole tolerant of homosexuality, took the view, as did the Egyptians, that to be sodomised was to betray weakness. Roman masters might bugger their slaves and Egyptian soldiers might rape a defeated enemy, but no one would willingly submit to this perceived humiliation. If Caesar had really been Nicomedes's lover, he had been devalued by the experience. His enemies never let the matter drop.

Perhaps to compensate, Caesar's heterosexual alliances were many, varied and well documented. He had been married three times, to Cornelia the mother of Julia (dead), Pompeia (divorced after an allegation of adultery) and Calpurnia (current wife). He had a long-term mistress, Servilia, who was widely acknowledged to be the most beautiful woman in Rome, and an impressive list of casual conquests, including the wives of Gabinius, Crassus and Pompey, and Servilia's own daughter Tertia. After leaving Cleopatra he was to have a torrid affair with Eunoe, wife of King Bogudes of Mauretania. We could reasonably expect that he also had insignificant, unrecorded liaisons with prostitutes and slaves. No wonder his marching soldiers sang with pride:

Home we bring our bald whoremonger; Romans, lock your wives away!
All the bags of gold you lent him, went his Gallic tarts to pay.

And, far more provocatively:

Gaul was brought to shame by Caesar;
By King Nicomedes, he.
Here comes Caesar, wreathed in triumph
For his Gallic victory!
Nicomedes wears no laurels
Though the greatest of the three.[16]

Caesar was older and more experienced in all aspects of life than Cleopatra, but the two nevertheless had much in common. Both were ruthlessly ambitious and both were prepared to take prodigious risks to achieve their ambitions. Both had a vested interest in ensuring that Egypt did not succumb to civil war. Both had the knack of persuading the ordinary people to love them, yet both were to a certain extent lonely and insecure. Caesar had lost his only daughter and suffered from terrible nightmares; Cleopatra, estranged from her younger siblings, had lost her mother, two sisters and the father who had taught her his politics. From her uncle Ptolemy she had learned that defiance of Rome meant certain death. From Auletes she had learned that Rome, and Rome alone, could protect the Ptolemaic dynasty, and that Romans could be bought. Caesar needed Egypt's wealth, while Cleopatra needed Rome's protection. So who seduced whom? If we accept that Cleopatra planned her unorthodox entrance to entice Caesar, we should probably also accept that she planned to seduce him. For a queen in need of both an ally and a son, this would have been a sensible diplomatic move. But, as most cultures believe that 'nice girls' don't plan to sleep with a blind date at their first meeting, this seemingly wanton behaviour has stigmatised Cleopatra as little more than a high-class whore.

Ptolemy XIII had gone to bed that night a happy lad, secure in the knowledge that his sister, trapped at Pelusium, would be unable to plead her case before Caesar. With the Gabinians and the people of Alexandria on his side, it could only be a matter of time before he, a recognised friend and ally of the Roman people, was confirmed sole ruler of Egypt. He woke up the next morning to find that his sister had somehow arrived at the palace. She was already on the most intimate of terms with Caesar and had managed to persuade him to support her cause. It was all too much for a thirteen-year-old boy to bear. Rushing from the palace, he ripped off his diadem and, in a well-orchestrated public display of anger, the crowd surged forward, intent on mobbing the palace. But Caesar would not be intimidated. Before a formal assembly he read out Auletes's will, making it clear that he expected the elder brother and sister to rule Egypt together. Meanwhile, and most unexpectedly, the younger siblings, Arsinoë and Ptolemy XIV, were to become king and queen of Cyprus, which, after ten years as Roman property, Caesar was now returning to Egypt.

Soon after Cleopatra's death her victorious rival Octavian ordered that all images of Cleopatra be destroyed. As Cleopatra was, at the time, perceived as public enemy number one, his Roman subjects were happy to comply: it is, in any case, unlikely that there were many Roman Cleopatras to be destroyed. But in Egypt, where Cleopatra's images were cult images connected with the worship of the goddess Isis and with Cleopatra's own personal cult, this order caused great offence. Plutarch tells us that some of her Egyptian statues were saved by the priest Archibios, who, acting either as Cleopatra's friend or as a representative of the native priesthood, offered Octavian an irresistible 2,000 talents to preserve them. Her two-dimensional images carved high on the temple walls were difficult to destroy and so remained untouched, but the majority of her statues were indeed lost.

Those images that do survive may be divided into two very different groups which can, if considered out of context, give Cleopatra the semblance of a severely split personality. There are images composed in the classical or Hellenistic style (but not necessarily by non-Egyptian artists) which show Cleopatra dressed as an elite Hellenistic woman, and images composed in the Egyptian style which present her as a traditional Egyptian queen bearing the time-honoured regalia designed to express political and religious power. When viewed side by side, the two styles convey a strikingly mixed message. To modern, western eyes the Hellenistic Cleopatra looks relaxed and natural, while the Egyptian Cleopatra seems stiff and artificial; there is therefore a great temptation to interpret the Hellenistic Cleopatras as true-to-life representations. This is wishful thinking. Classical portraiture was intended to convey an idealised, recognisable, often heroic representation of its subject rather than a warts-and-all snapshot. In the case of the Ptolemies, artists often included attributes intended to hint at the subject's divinity, so that it can be difficult to distinguish a fragmentary queen from a fragmentary goddess. Hellenistic images of Cleopatra might therefore be expected to look alike because they are the official image of Cleopatra; it does not necessarily follow that they look particularly like the flesh-and-blood queen. It is highly unlikely that Cleopatra sat for each and every formal portrait, so we must assume that the majority of her images were carved from artists' models and sketches. The standard practice of creating statue heads and bodies separately, maybe even in different workshops (the head of marble finished, perhaps, with plaster, then painted; the body of stone, wood or metal), makes accuracy of the composite whole even less certain, and accounts for the disproportionate number of recovered Ptolemaic heads.

For over 2,000 years non-experts have habitually identified any and every classical-style statue of a woman holding a snake, or standing next to a snake, or wearing a snake bracelet, as 'Cleopatra'. This has gone hand in hand with a predictable tendency for enterprising masons to reach for their chisels and add snakes to classical statues, instantly turning bland Aphrodites into exciting and far more valuable Cleopat-ras. It is only in the past century that art historians have been able to discard the fake and, or so they hope, identify genuine contemporary or near-contemporary Hellenistic Cleopatra statuary on the grounds of date and style. The identification of genuine Cleopatras is, of course, a matter of personal conviction as well as scientific proof, and a room full of expert art historians would undoubtedly produce different opinions on different pieces. Today just one Hellenistic head is more or less universally accepted as an authentic Cleopatra, with a further three heads being championed by various experts.[17]

The one undisputed Cleopatra was recovered from the Villa of the Quintilii, on the Via Appia, Rome, in the late eighteenth century. Today it is housed in the Vatican Museum. Originally the head was displayed on the body of a statue of a priestess of the Roman goddess Ceres recovered from the same villa; it was not until 1933 that art his-torian Ludwig Curtius recognised that the head and body were not a true pair. The head has a broken nose (an over-delicate late eighteenth-century 'restoration' has recently been removed). It was designed to be inserted into a now-lost body, and a rough patch on one cheek and a curious stone knob on the head suggest that it was originally part of a larger statue group. Cleopatra appears as a mature woman whose hair is dressed in the 'melon coiffure' (sectioned and braided hair drawn back into a low bun; the name reflects the supposed resemblance to a melon segmented lengthways) worn by many upper-class Hellenistic women. Royal women topped this hairstyle with a broad diadem whose ribbons tied beneath or underneath the bun. Cleopatra has large heavy-lidded eyes, a small mouth, badly made ears, a long face, a broad forehead and a curled fringe. This fringe of kiss curls, often described as snail curls, is a defining characteristic of Cleopatra's Hel-lenistic portraits and appears in a more exaggerated form on her coins.

All of Cleopatra's coin portraits are in the Hellenistic style. These are generally taken to be her most lifelike portraits, purely because they are the least obviously flattering. Almost sixty silver and bronze coin types have been identified, issued in Egypt, Cyprus, the cities of Syrio-Palestine, and perhaps in parts of Italy and Greece. The coins may be divided into two broad types.[18] The vast majority, minted in Egypt and Cyprus throughout her reign, show Cleopatra as a typical Ptolemaic queen, although a bronze coin minted in Cyprus that shows her nursing her infant son Caesarion, apparently represents Cleopatra as the mother goddess Isis. The reverse of these coins show Egyptian symbols. Her Romanised coins, minted late in her reign outside Egypt, show Cleopatra with Mark Antony. Here the queen appears in a slightly diminished light, not as an independent ruler, but as a client-queen of Rome and, perhaps, as part of a married couple.

Silver tetradrachm of Cleopatra VII from Askalon, dating to 50–49 when Cleopatra was feuding with her brother Ptolemy XIII.

All the coins reveal the same woman in profile: a woman whose prominent nose and pronounced chin do not suggest, to modern western eyes, a great beauty. These features tend to become more pronounced with age, so that Cleopatra appears 'softer' or more conventionally attractive in the earliest coins issued in Alexandria when she was nineteen years old, while the later coins, shared with Mark Antony, show a more defined, slightly hooked aquiline nose, a strong chin and mouth and enough fat folds (politely known as Venus rings) on the neck to allow some observers to suggest that she suffered from a goitre. This older Cleopatra looks like a slightly feminised version of Mark Antony, and both resemble Auletes. Comparing statues and coins, we can see that Cleopatra inherited more than her nose from her father. Both share deep-set eyes and a firm, slightly bulbous chin; both, in fact, bear a passing and presumably deliberate resemblance to Ptolemy I. The strong nose can be traced back to Ptolemy VIII, suggesting that Cleopatra may have deliberately chosen to emphasise the one trait that unequivocally identified her as a genuine Ptolemy.

Cleopatra's coins reflect, to a greater or lesser extent, the skills and traditions of their makers. Allowing for this, it seems entirely understandable that Cleopatra might not have wanted to appear soft and feminine on the tokens that represented her sovereignty both within Egypt and in the wider Mediterranean world. Both Cleopatra Thea (queen of Syria, and great-great-aunt to our Cleopatra) and Cleopatra III (great-grandmother to Cleopatra VII) issued coins that gave them strong, almost masculine faces and, in the absence of an accepted Hellenistic iconography representative of politically powerful femininity, Cleopatra VII might have chosen to follow their example. This tendency to an increasingly masculine appearance is obvious in the statuary of Cleopatras I–III; as the queens grow more powerful their images become less feminine, climaxing in a basalt Egyptian-style statue of Cleopatra III now housed in Vienna Museum which gives the elderly queen the appearance of an old man in an incongruously frivolous curly wig.

Modern observers have not been slow to comment on Cleopatra's perceived lack of beauty and, in particular, on her nose, which has been the subject of learned discussion and many jokes, culminating in Lord Berners's 1941 novel *The Romance of the Nose*.[19] The kindest comment is perhaps that she was 'a *belle laide* with a rather large mouth and, on some specimens, a long hooked nose which she had inherited from her father'.[20] The unspoken question hovers – how did Cleopatra manage to captivate two of Rome's greatest men if it was not by her looks? Beauty is, of course, in the eye of the beholder, and standards of beauty vary from time to time, culture to culture and person to person. Most would in any case agree that beauty, pure and stark, is far removed from sexual allure. There is general agreement that another of Egypt's queens, the 18th Dynasty Nefertiti, possessed a beauty that appeals to every age, race and gender, but although many have marvelled before Nefertiti's world-famous Berlin bust, few have found her in any way sexy.[21] The real question here is not whether we find Cleopatra beautiful, but whether Caesar found her attractive enough to sleep with. And the answer is that clearly he did. Plutarch, who of course never met her, tells us that Cleopatra's charm lay in her demeanour, and in particular in her voice:

> … *Her beauty, as we are told, was in itself not altogether incomparable, nor such as to strike those who saw her; but converse with her had an irresistible charm, and her presence, combined with the persuasiveness of her discourse and the character which was somehow diffused about her behaviour towards others, had something stimulating about it. There was sweetness also in the tones of her voice; and her tongue, like an instrument of many strings, she could readily turn to whatever language she pleased …*[22]

Dio, writing a century after Plutarch, begs to differ. His Cleopatra is beautiful, and all too well aware of the effects of her beauty. The whole private meeting has therefore been planned so that she might seduce the susceptible Caesar:

Cleopatra, it seems, had at first urged with Caesar her claim against her brother by means of agents, but as soon as she discovered his disposition (which was very susceptible, to such an extent that he had his intrigues with ever so many other women – with all, doubtless, who chanced to come in his way) she sent word to him that she was being betrayed by her friends and asked that she be allowed to plead her case in person. For she was a woman of surpassing beauty, and at that time, when she was in the prime of her youth, she was most striking; she also possessed a most charming voice and a knowledge of how to make herself agreeable to every one. Being brilliant to look upon and to listen to, with the power to subjugate every one, even a love-sated man already past his prime, she thought that it would be in keeping with her rôle to meet Caesar, and she reposed in her beauty all her claims to the throne. She asked therefore for admission to his presence, and on obtaining permission adorned and beautified herself so as to appear before him in the most majestic and at the same time pity-inspiring guise.[23]

Presumably the fact that Cleopatra was queen of Egypt, the last of an ancient and semi-divine line, precociously intelligent, politically powerful and extraordinarily rich, simply added to her charms.

If the Hellenistic Cleopatra is a woman of doubtful physical appeal, the Egyptian Cleopatra has all the beauty and serenity of a goddess. This is exactly what we would expect. Like their Greek and Roman contemporaries, Egypt's official artists never set out to create true-to-life portraits. Nor did they manufacture 'art for art's sake'. Invariably, they created symbolic or idealised representations of an individual at a particular stage of his or her life, usually for a specific religious purpose. In this respect, royal art may be considered as the ultimate extension of the hieroglyphic writing system, where every word is a picture and every picture can be read as a word. A statue or a two-dimensional image can be read, just as a papyrus scroll can be read.

A quick glance through any illustrated book of Egyptian art will reveal ranks of near-identical kings smiting foreigners, near-identical scribes sitting with a papyrus roll across their lap, and near-identical sons and daughters standing naked with fingers in their mouths beside their much larger parents. This tradition continued for over 3,000 years, so that the 1st Dynasty King Den, who wields a mace to smite an enemy on an ivory label in c. 3000 appears scarcely different from Auletes smiting an enemy on the pylon of the Edfu temple of Horus in 57. As the office of the king continued unchanging from reign to reign, irrespective of the office holder, this similarity was a good and desirable thing; a reinforcement of the cyclical continuity of Egyptian life. And, in case anyone really wanted to know which king was being shown, the artists invariably added a name.[24] The Egyptian-style art of the Ptolemies was essentially propaganda, designed to allow the Ptolemies to appeal to their Egyptian people and their Egyptian gods by reflecting and fuelling their political and religious beliefs.[25] With pose, material, scale and placement all predetermined, it seems impossible that these images can tell us anything of Cleopatra's appearance. They do, however, tell us quite a lot about her perceived role. Egypt had a long tradition of highlighting powerful women using a combination of religious and political symbols, and Cleopatra exploited this tradition to the full. The two-dimensional Cleopatra standing larger than life at each end of the rear wall of the Hathor temple at Dendera is an uncompromisingly traditional Egyptian queen. The bewigged, crowned, beautiful and eternally young Cleopatra can barely be differentiated from the queens who lived thousands of years before her, and she can barely be differentiated from the goddesses Isis and Hathor. The confusion is deliberate and convincing.

Again, however, we have to be careful when approaching Cleopatra's Egyptian art. Cleopatra has long been recognised as a brand name, with strong selling power, and canny antiquities dealers have found it all too easy to add a cartouche to an insignificant ancient statue, instantly tripling its value. As a result, many of the 'Cleopatras' that made their way into western collections during the nineteenth and early twentieth centuries are now recognised (recognised, often, by their ill-written and badly copied hieroglyphs) as forgeries. Cleopatra's genuine Egyptian-style three-dimensional images are all relatively small; we do not have any colossal Cleopatras, although the ongoing reclamation of Ptolemaic statuary from the sea at Alexandria offers a glimmer of hope that one day this situation might change. In the meantime, it seems likely that all her surviving statues are cult images, manufactured for the temples and shrines dedicated to her personal cult. They show Cleopatra as a healthy woman in the prime of life; again, this to be expected. Women rarely grow old in Egyptian art.[26] Although conforming to the same general pattern, the statues show a degree of flexibility and individuality; the overall appearance is typically Egyptian, with traditional postures, wigs and clothing, but Hellenistic accessories occasionally appear, there are classical noses and eyes, and we can sometimes glimpse Hellenistic curls beneath the formal Egyptian wigs.

The best example of this art style is a black basalt statue of unknown provenance, now housed in the Hermitage, St Petersburg. It shows a young queen standing tall and slender against a back pillar, her left foot slightly advanced. Her tight linen sheath dress – impossible to walk in without the benefit of Lycra – clings to the curves of her breasts, stomach, hips and thighs. Her navel is a dimple beneath the fine cloth. In her right hand she holds the *ankh*, the Egyptian symbol of life; on her head she wears a heavy tripartite wig (a wig which divides into three parts; one falling on each side of the face and one falling behind). She wears the triple uraeus (triple snake) on her brow. Her oval face has the prominent ears and exaggerated almond-shaped eyes seen in earlier Ptolemaic statuary. Her mouth turns downwards and her chin is square. The only dissonant note is the double cornucopia that she carries in the left hand. For the cornucopia, or horn of plenty, is a Greek symbol. Firmly associated with queens, it first appears in Egyptian royal art during the reign of Ptolemy II, when it is added to images of the deified Arsinoë II. This statue is unlabelled and, on the basis of the double cornucopia, was for a long time identified as Arsinoë II. But Cleopatra, too, favours the cornucopia, and the presence of the unusual triple uraeus strongly suggests that this is a representation of Cleopatra VII.

The uraeus is the rearing cobra worn on the forehead by kings and queens from the Old Kingdom onwards. Wadjyt, 'The Green One', the snake goddess of Lower Egypt and the Nile Delta, decorates and protects the royal crown and its wearer. To understand the symbolism of the uraeus, we need to understand the ancient creation myth told by the priests of the sun god Re at Heliopolis. This explains how the first god, Atum, lived on the island of creation with his twin children, Shu and Tefnut. One terrible day Atum's children fell into the sea of chaos surrounding the island. Devastated, Atum sent his Eye (a form of the goddess Hathor) to search for his missing children. But when the Eye returned with the children she found that the sun had replaced her. Enraged by this betrayal, she transformed herself into a cobra, and Atum, first king of Egypt, placed her on his brow.

Most of Egypt's dynastic queens wore a single or a double uraeus on the brow. Many also wore the short *modius* or platform crown, surrounded by multiple uraei and often topped by a more elaborate crown. But the triple uraeus – three cobras worn on the brow – is rare and has, in recent years, come to be associated with Cleopatra VII.[27] The symbolism of the three snakes is difficult to assess. It may be that the triple uraeus is to be read as a rebus – a visual pun – that translates from Ptolemaic Egyptian as either 'queen of kings' or 'goddess of goddesses'. Alternatively, it could represent three individuals: Isis, Osiris and Horus perhaps, or a queen's triple title of king's daughter, king's sister and king's wife.[28] It may even be a simple misunderstanding of dynastic symbolism, with the more traditional double uraeus plus central vulture head worn on the brow by earlier queens being transformed into three snakes by the Ptolemaic artists.

The use of the triple uraeus as a diagnostic tool to identify otherwise unidentifiable Cleopatra images remains contentious. A limestone crown, part of a broken statue recovered from the temple of Geb at Koptos and now in the Petrie Museum of Egyptian Archaeology, London, is a good example of this type of reasoning. The inscription recorded on the crown refers to a 'hereditary noble, great of praise, mistress of Upper and Lower Egypt, contented … king's daughter, king's sister, great royal wife who satisfies the heart of Horus', but omits to name names. The crown, which is made up of double plumes (two tall feathers associated with the cult of the Theban god Amen), a sun disc (associated with solar cults), cow horns (associated with the goddesses Hathor and Isis) and triple uraeus, was originally identified as belonging to a statue of Arsinoë II, who is known to have been active in this region; the Koptos Isis temple was associated with the Iseion at the central northern Delta site of Behbeit el-Haga, which was patronised by her husband Ptolemy II. But Arsinoë tends to wear her own, specific crown and, as Cleopatra is now strongly associated with the triple uraeus, historians have started to wonder whether the anonymous husband could be either Ptolemy XIII or his brother Ptolemy XIV. Similarly, a pale blue glass intaglio with a portrait of a Ptolemaic woman of unknown provenance (now in the British Museum) is identified as Cleopatra on the basis of the hairstyle, broad diadem and a peculiarly prominent triple uraeus, which virtually sits on top of the queen's head.

Just one sculpted 'Cleopatra' appears to straddle the gulf between the Hellenistic and Egyptian art styles. A Parian marble head, recovered from the wall of the Church of San Pietro e Marcellino in the Via Labicana, not far from the sanctuary of Isis in Rome, is today housed in the Capitoline Museum. The head was originally part of a composite statue. It has no Egyptian-style back pillar, yet the face is unmistakably Egyptian in appearance. The head wears a tripartite wig and a vulture crown or headdress. This headdress, as its name suggests, has the appearance of a limp bird draped over the head, with the wings falling either side of the face, the tail hanging down the back and the vulture's head and neck rising from the wearer's forehead. In this case the vulture's delicate head has been lost, as have the queen's inlaid eyes and the tall crown that she originally wore on top of her headdress. The vulture headdress was originally worn by Nekhbet, goddess of southern Egypt and, in some tales, mother of the king. Other goddesses subsequently adopted it, as did dynastic queens; the earliest example of a vulture headdress, worn by a now-anonymous queen, comes from Giza and dates to the 4th Dynasty. Nekhbet's northern counterpart, the snake goddess Wadjyt, introduced a variant by replacing the bird's head with a snake; as vultures and snakes were regarded as good mothers, this modified vulture headdress emphasised the link between queens and motherhood. By the Ptolemaic age the headdress had become closely associated with goddesses and divine or dead queens. Experts are divided over the subject of this head: it has been variously identified as Cleopatra VII, Berenice II and the goddess Isis.

CHAPTER THREE

Alexandria-next-to-Egypt

We were still two or three hours' steaming distance before land could possibly be in sight, when suddenly we saw, inverted in the sky, a perfect miragic reproduction of Alexandria, in which Pharos Light, Ras-el-Tin Palace, and other prominent features were easily distinguishable. The illusion continued for a considerable time, and eventually as suddenly disappeared, when, an hour or two later, the real city slowly appeared above the horizon! A good augury, surely, of the wonders I hoped to discover on landing!

R. T. Kelly, *Egypt*[1]

The pharaohs of old had founded many capital cities. The northern city of Memphis, situated at the junction of the Nile Valley and the Nile Delta, just a few miles to the south of modern Cairo, was the first and most ancient. Here the thoughtful creator god Ptah dwelt in his extensive stone temple, and here the kings of the Old Kingdom raised their pyramids in the desert cemeteries of Sakkara and Giza. Cosmopolitan Memphis would remain the administrative centre of

Egypt for much of the dynastic age. Four hundred miles to the south lay proud Thebes, home of the warrior god Amen-Re and, during the New Kingdom, home and burial place of the elite whose rock-cut tombs honeycombed the east-bank Valleys of the Kings and Queens. Shorter-lived were Itj-Tawi (built by the Middle Kingdom pharaohs and now entirely lost), Akhetaten (Amarna: Akhenaten's Middle Egyptian city of the sun god) and the Delta cities of Per-Ramesses (Tell ed Daba), Tanis (San el-Hagar) and Sais (Sa el-Hagar). All these cities were built at a time when inward-looking Egypt was able to flourish in splendid isolation, and none allowed easy access to the outside world.

Silver tetradrachm of Alexander the Great who appears as Heracles dressed in a lion skin.

In 332, when Alexander the Great arrived in Egypt, Memphis was again serving as the capital city. Realising Egypt's need for a modern, outward-looking city-seaport, Alexander sailed along the Mediterranean coast, inspected various sites, consulted his architects and was on the verge of making a decision. Then, as Plutarch tells us, he had a vivid dream:

… in the night, as he lay asleep, he saw a wonderful vision. A man with very hoary locks and of a venerable aspect appeared to stand by his side and recite these verses: 'Now, there is an island in the much-dashing sea, in front of Egypt; Pharos is what men call it.' Accordingly, he rose up at once and went to Pharos, which at that time was still an island, a little above the Canopic mouth of the Nile, but now it has been joined to the mainland by a causeway. And when he saw a site of surpassing natural advantages (for it is a strip of land like enough to a broad isthmus, extending between a great lagoon and a stretch of sea which terminates in a large harbour), he said he saw now that Homer was not only admirable in other ways, but also a very wise architect, and ordered the plan of the city to be drawn in conformity with this site.[2]

The wise old man of the night was Alexander's great hero Homer, and the lines that he quoted were from Book 4 of his *Odyssey*, a part of the tale where Menelaos finds himself stranded in Egypt. Such exalted advice could not be ignored, and Alexander hastily revised his plans. Pharos island was clearly too small to house a great city. But on the mainland, opposite Pharos, was Rakhotis, an old and undistinguished fishing village which in better days had served as a pharaonic customs post and a Persian fortress.[3] Alexander made up his mind. His new city, Alexandria, was to be built around Rakhotis (Ra-Kedet), on a limestone spur running between the Mediterranean to the north and the freshwater Lake Moeris (Lake Canopus) to the south. The sea would allow easy contact with the Hellenistic world; canals running into the lake would allow contact with the River Nile, southern Egypt and Africa beyond Egypt. The omens were propitious: as the architects marked out the city boundaries in barley flour, flocks of birds swooped down to feed. Clearly, Alexandria would soon be fertile enough to feed the world.

The Greek historian Arrian tells a less romantic, more practical, but essentially similar story. Alexander again chooses the city site himself and is involved in its planning:

And it seemed to him that the site was the very best in which to found a city, and that the city would prosper. A longing for the task seized him, and he personally established the main points of the city – where the agora should be constructed, and how many temples there should be, and of which gods, those of the Greek gods and of Egyptian Isis … [4]

The Alexander Romance, a legendary account of Alexander's life collated 500 years after his death, adds further details: the architect of the new city is Deinocrates of Rhodes and he is assisted by the financier Cleomenes of Naukratis. [5]

Having founded his city, Alexander left Egypt in 331, intending to return. But on the evening of 10 June 323 he died of a fever in Nebuchadnezzar's palace in Babylon. The ancient doctors were baffled: modern historians have suggested that Alexander may have contracted malaria or typhus, that he drank himself to death or that he was poisoned. As his generals started to wrangle over the succession a magnificent funerary chariot was commissioned and Egyptian embalmers, the best in the world, were summoned to prepare the dead god for his last journey. Alexander was to lie in a golden coffin, possibly an Egyptian-style anthropoid coffin, filled with aromatic spices. His shield and armour were to be displayed on a richly embroidered purple sheet draped over the coffin lid. The chariot, effectively a mobile temple, was to have a high canopy supported by columns, and was to be decorated with a painted frieze depicting scenes from Alexander's life. A golden olive wreath was to hang above the coffin. The chariot would be pulled by sixty-four mules, each, like the dead Alexander, wearing a golden crown.

Two years after his death, the slow cortège left Babylon for the royal Macedonian burial ground of Aegae (modern Vergina). It drew vast crowds wherever it passed. But it had travelled no further than Damascus when it was diverted. Ptolemy, son of Lagos, Egypt's new and highly ambitious governor, had recognised the high propaganda value of heroic mortal remains and had decided that his 'brother' Alexander should enjoy permanent rest in Egypt. Officially it was announced that Ptolemy was merely fulfilling Alexander's own death-bed wishes: a whispered desire (heard by Ptolemy alone) to be buried at the temple of Jupiter-Ammon in the Siwa Oasis. But Siwa was too remote for Ptolemy's purpose. Alexander's body was first interred in Memphis, then, probably during the reign of Ptolemy II, transferred to Alexandria. An alabaster chamber within a tumulus – today an open alabaster box half-hidden in the Catholic cemetery of Terra Santa – may have served as the antechamber to Alexander's first Alex-andrian tomb. Later, probably during the reign of Ptolemy IV, he was reinterred in a magnificent mausoleum in the Soma, the Ptolemaic royal cemetery. Here, in a testament to the skill of the Egyptian embalmers, Alexander's body was housed for 300 years, first in the original gold coffin and then, after the poverty-stricken Ptolemy X had scandalously seized the gold to pay his rebellious troops, in a translucent alabaster replacement.

Alexander's tomb, the centre of the cult of the deified Alexan-der, naturally became a place of pilgrimage. Julius Caesar visited his hero while trapped in Alexandria in 47. Octavian visited in 30, soon after Cleopatra's suicide. Suetonius records his encounter with the god:

> *... he had the sarcophagus containing Alexander the Great's mummy removed from its shrine and, after a long look at its features, showed his veneration by crowning the head with a golden diadem and strewing flowers on the trunk. When asked, 'would you now like to visit the mausoleum of the Ptolemies? He relied: 'I came to see a king, not a row of corpses.'* [6]

An element of humour creeps into Dio's account of the same visit as he describes how Octavian, over-eager to touch the god, accidentally snapped off a piece of his mummified nose.[7]

The Roman emperor Caracalla visited Alexander in 215, then we hear no more. The Soma, Alexander's tomb and Alexander's body were lost during the late third or early fourth centuries AD, at a time when Alexandria, now a Christian city, was suffering civil unrest and rioting. But archaeologists, scholars and Alexander enthusiasts have not given up hope. Today the search for the lost tomb of Alexander has become a mission with more than a passing similarity – abundant theories, counter-theories and intricate conspiracy theories – to the quest for the Holy Grail.[8]

In 304 General Ptolemy, son of Lagos, officially assumed the throne of Egypt, vacant since the murder of the young Alexander IV, posthumous son of Alexander the Great. He became King Ptolemy I

Silver tetradrachm of Ptolemy I.

Soter (the Saviour), and Alexandria became Egypt's capital city. It was, at first sight, a curious choice. Lying on the very edge of the western Delta, Alexandria was far from the Nile Valley and far from the Sinai land bridge that formed Egypt's busy north-eastern border. But Alexandria's ports allowed her ships to participate in the valuable Mediterranean trade routes, while the city itself had the distinct advantage of being young and unsullied, with a new population and no lingering loyalties to earlier regimes or gods. Alexandria attracted residents from many parts of the world. From the earliest times there were three main cultural groups: the Egyptians, the Greeks and the Jews. Although historians have tended to regard Alexandria as the supreme 'melting pot', a city where all races and creeds mingled happily together, there is growing evidence to suggest that, as happened outside the city, these three main factions tended to keep themselves to themselves.

The majority of the original Egyptian Alexandrians arrived under duress. Faced with the problem of populating an empty city, the astute Cleomenes simply gathered a ready-made workforce from neighbouring towns and villages, and relocated it in the old Rhakotis district. Those unwilling to move to Alexandria had to pay a large bribe to gain exemption.

Educated Greeks were tempted to Alexandria with offers of a new and prosperous life; a sensible policy of recruiting throughout Greece and Macedon ensured that Alexandria was not tied to the traditions of one mother city. The Greeks were the only Alexandrians allowed to become full citizens and it seems likely that (in theory at least) Greeks and Egyptians were forbidden to intermarry.

Egypt had a significant Jewish population long before the arrival of the Ptolemies. Late Period papyri written in Aramaic and recovered from the island of Elephantine (by modern Aswan) confirm the existence of a well-established Jewish colony at Egypt's southern border. The Jews of Elephantine retained their traditional names, laws and religious beliefs while, occasionally, marrying into the native Egyptian community. In 410 their temple was destroyed by Egyptians loyal to the local cult of the ram-headed creator god Khnum: the Egyptians had been angered by the Jews' friendly attitude towards the Persians and, perhaps, by what may have been interpreted as their anti-Egyptian celebration of the Passover, a festival which included the sacrifice of the Paschal Lamb. The Elephantine temple was eventually rebuilt, but the community had already started to disintegrate. Now, under the Ptolemies, Jews were being encouraged to settle in Egypt. Two major phases of Jewish immigration can be distinguished, one during the empire-expanding reign of Ptolemy I, when prisoners captured at Jerusalem were relocated in Egypt, and one during the reign of Ptolemy IV, when Egypt received a wave of political refugees following the revolt of Judas Maccabaeus against the Seleucid empire. Eventually Ptolemy VI would celebrate decades of peaceful coexistence by allowing the construction of a magnificent Jewish temple in the Delta town of Leontopolis (modern Tell el Yahudeyeh), and by granting the Alexandrian Jews a form of demi-citizenship. In return, Jewish support would help keep first his widow, Cleopatra II, and then his daughter, Cleopatra III, on their thrones. This did not please everyone, and Josephus tells a chilling tale of Ptolemy VIII rounding up the Alexandrian Jews, stripping them naked and chaining them up to be trampled by drunken elephants. Happily, a miracle occurred, and the elephants turned instead on Ptolemy's soldiers. Ptolemy VIII was well aware that the people of Alexandria could make or break a king, and was prone to take drastic action against anyone perceived as supporting his estranged sister-wife Cleopatra II. In one notorious incident he even sent his troops to a busy gymnasium with orders to kill anyone inside. Nevertheless, the story of the murderous elephants is highly unlikely to be true.[9]

Ptolemy I, his son and grandson ploughed money into developing Alexandria, which quickly became the largest city in the Mediterranean world, with an estimated population of between a quarter and half a million inhabitants by 200. But, despite its dazzling facilities, the links to Lake Moeris and the Nile beyond, and the constant influx of traders, Alexandria ad Aegyptum or Alexandria-next-to-Egypt was always seen as a city somehow apart from Egypt proper. The old pharaohs, recognising the dangers of isolation, had spent many months travelling up and down their long, thin land, visiting temples, administering justice and generally reminding their people of their presence. The Ptolemies, seemingly content to live apart from the majority of their people, did not. In consequence, while the people of the Nile Valley gradually lost any sense of personal connection with their monarchs, the people of Alexandria developed an abnormally close relationship with their kings, and a fine disregard for anyone who lived outside their city. Initially this was a blessing: the Alexandrians of the third century were, broadly speaking, prepared to work with their royal family and to respect their policies. But the Alexandrians of the second and first centuries considered themselves to be kingmakers.[10] Volatile and prone to riot, they murdered the supporters of Ptolemy IV, drove out Ptolemies IX and XII, and killed Ptolemy XI. Ultimately, in their determination to reject any form of Roman interference, the Alexandrians drove their kings further into the Roman embrace.

An Egyptian visitor to Alexandria would have felt that he or she had stepped into another world. Egyptian cities invariably lay inland, sandwiched between the Nile and the desert, but long, thin Alexandria had two wide fronts, one opening on to Lake Moeris and one opening on to the Mediterranean Sea. While Thebes and Memphis were hot, dry and dusty, Alexandria had salty sea breezes, a cooler climate and winter rains, and, unlike the rest of Egypt, Alexandria did not flood in the summer. Traditionally the Egyptians built their houses and palaces from mud brick and their temples and tombs from stone. With mud brick plentiful and cheap, towns and cities grew organically, sprawling along rivers and canals without any overall plan. But walled Alexandria was a planned city of straight, wide streets and gleaming white stone buildings (the local limestone plus, perhaps, some imported marble) decorated with elegant touches of pink and grey granite. As the water in Lake Moeris was not suitable for human consumption, drinking water was supplied by a canal that, stretching from the Canopic branch of the Nile, emptied into over 700 vast underground cisterns connecting directly to the elite houses.

Alexandria's main thoroughfare, 'Canopus Street', was a colonnaded processional way covered with awnings, running west to east from the Necropic Gate to the Canopic Gate. At right angles to Canopus Street ran 'Soma Street'. The grid system allowed the city to be divided into five districts named after the first five letters of the Greek alphabet (Alpha, Beta, Gamma, Delta, Epsilon); this in turn gave the residents of Alexandria easily comprehensible addresses. The precise boundaries of these districts are now unclear, although Josephus quotes Apion in asserting that the Delta district, the Jewish quarter, lay in the eastern part of the city near the Palaces, and it seems that there were also substantial numbers of Jews living in Beta. The Greeks lived in the city centre, while the Egyptians lived in the western quarter in the area of the old Rhakotis.

Strabo lived intermittently in Alexandria from *c.* 25–20. His *Geography* therefore provides us with a near-eyewitness view of Cleopatra's city, and is worth quoting at length:

> … *the city has very fine public sanctuaries and 'The Palaces', which form a quarter or even a third of the entire enclosure [the city]. For each of the kings added some adornment to the public dedications [shrines and statues] and also added privately further residential blocks to those already existing, so that now, in the words of the poet, 'From others grow'; but all are continuous to each other and to the harbour and what lies outside it. Within 'The Palaces' lies the Museion, which has a covered walk and an exedra and a block in which are the refectory and mess of the scholars who belong to the Museion … The monument known as the Sema [Soma] is also part*

of 'The Palaces'. This was an enclosure containing the tombs of the kings and of Alexander ...[11]

From this regrettably vague description we may develop a tentative plan of Ptolemaic Alexandria. 'The Palaces' (Bruchion), effectively an extensive elite town within the city, occupied the north-east sector, and included the now sunken peninsula of Lochias and island of Antirrhodos. Here were the spacious villas of the Greek upper classes, interspersed by temples and public gardens, and here too were the 'Inner Palaces', an even more exclusive area incorporating the Museion (or Museum: a research centre inspired by Aristotle's Athenian Lyceum and dedicated to the nine Muses), the Soma, and the private residences and harbour of the kings. If Strabo is correct in his assertion that each Ptolemy built a new palace, creating a larger and more luxurious residence than those of his predecessors, this area must have been a warren of under-used royal buildings, colonnades and gardens. Alexandria suffered a devastating series of earthquakes in AD 365, 447 and 535. At roughly the same time – no one is quite sure when it occurred – subsidence estimated at between thirteen and twenty-three feet removed the ancient coastline and submerged much of the ancient city. Today all the palaces and Ptolemaic royal tombs, Cleopatra's included, lie under the waters of the harbour.

Strabo's description of Alexandria outside the Palaces is even less precise, but we can deduce that the public facilities – the gymnasium, law courts and agora or marketplace – lay in the centre of the city, while the main theatre lay between the agora and the Palaces, with the hippodrome just outside the city walls. Alexandria's working and middle classes lived in suburbs in the south and west of the city, and on the island of Pharos. Beyond the city walls there were cemeteries to the east and west. Here too was the Nemeseion, a temple dedicated to Nemesis, the Greek goddess of divine retribution, built by Julius Caesar to honour Pompey's severed head.

The Heptastadion, a man-made causeway seven stades long (a stade was approximately 600 feet in length), ran from the city to Pharos Island, dividing the Eastern or Great Harbour (Megas Limen) from the less important Western Harbour (Eunostos or 'Harbour of Happy Returns') and the naval dockyard (Kibotos or 'The Box'). Two arched bridges punctuated the causeway and allowed ships to pass from one harbour to the other. Offshore, on Pharos Island, shone the great white stone lighthouse that was included among the Seven Wonders of the Ancient World. Standing over 330 feet tall, the lighthouse tower was 'dedicated' – either designed or financed – by Sostratos of Knidos, working initially for Ptolemy I and then for his son. Strabo tells us that the tower was made of marble and had many tiers, although the shortage of local marble suggests that it is more likely to have been made from polished limestone, while contemporary illustrations suggest that it had just three tiers: a rectangular tower, topped by an octagonal tower, topped by a cylindrical tower. On the uppermost tower stood a statue of Zeus Soter (Zeus the Saviour) and a beacon whose ever-blazing light was focused by gigantic polished bronze mirrors. However, although we have several descriptions of the lighthouse, the precise arrangement of the top tower, the all-important beacon, the statue(s) and the mirrors or lenses is not yet understood. We do know that the lighthouse was completed in *c.* 280 and stood firm until the Middle Ages. In AD 796 the ruined uppermost tower collapsed; a century later a mosque was built on top of the second tower. In AD 1303 Alexandria was hit by another series of major earthquakes that inflicted further damage on the lighthouse. In AD 1326 the traveller and scholar Ibn Battuta visited Pharos and noted that the lighthouse was damaged but more or less intact. Returning twenty-three years later: 'I visited the lighthouse again, and found that it had fallen into so ruinous a condition that it was not possible to enter it or climb up to the door'.[12] Today the fort of Sultan Qait Bey, built in AD 1477, stands in its place.

Strabo makes it clear that the Museion was a part of the wider Palaces complex. Included within the Museion was the world-famous library: an institution that could boast every book ever written in Greek, plus many foreign books in translation. The library even included a unique Greek version of the Jewish Torah, which was known as the Septuagint after the seventy Jewish scholars who had been summoned to Alexandria to work on the translation. To ensure that the library kept up to date, all visitors to Alexandria were required to hand over their own scrolls to the library copyists; the library then kept the original scroll, while its owner was presented with a hasty copy. This relentless collecting explains how, in its heyday, the library came to house upwards of half a million papyrus scrolls.

Within the precincts of the Museion the Hellenistic world's finest scholars, many of them in receipt of government salaries, slept in dormitories, ate in dining halls and strolled through communal pleasure gardens. Relieved of the tiresome obligation to earn a crust, they were free to concentrate on the work that brought glory to Alexandria and the Ptolemies. This freedom came at a price – the scholars were expected to offer their services as and when required to the royal family, and Timon of Phleius perhaps spoke for many when he described them as 'cloistered bookworms, endlessly arguing in the bird cage of the Muses' – but many thought this the price worth paying. The writers of the Museion made important advances in Greek literature and language: from Alexandria came the pastoral mode (Theocritus: *Idylls*); a reinvention of the epic (Appollonius: *Argonautica*); and the development of literary theory and criticism (Callimachos, Zenodotus and Aristarchus). The Alexandrian doctors Herophilus and Erasistratus dissected and even, so it was whispered, vivisected condemned prisoners supplied by the Ptolemies, and in so doing developed a new understanding of anatomy and the workings of the brain and the pulse. Euclid wrote his thirteen-volume *Elements*, Eratosthenes drew maps and calculated the circumference of the earth, Aristarchus tentatively

1. Alexander the Great: this marble head, supposedly recovered from Alexandria and probably carved after his death, originally formed part of a larger composite statue. Although king of Egypt, Alexander appears as a Classical rather than an Egyptian monarch.

2. Ptolemy XII 'The New Dionysos'. Father of Cleopatra VII. This marble head, again part of a larger statue is probably re-carved from the portrait of an earlier Ptolemy.

3. The mystical god Dionysos; a threat to the Classical gods of Mount Olympus, and an inspiration to Ptolemy XII.

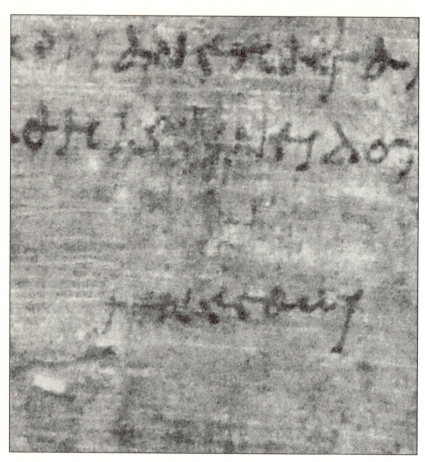

4. *A late Ptolemaic papyrus detailing privileges to be granted to Publius Candidus. Some scholars have argued that the scribbled word 'ginestho', 'let it be so', at the end of the document is written in Cleopatra's own hand.*

5. Limestone stela showing
Cleopatra dressed in the kilt and
crown of a male king of Egypt,
offering to the goddess Isis and her
infant son. Below, written in
Greek, we can read the queen's
name.

6. Portrait head of unknown
provenance, believed to be
Cleopatra VII. The queen wears
a melon hairstyle, a curled fringe
and a broad diadem.

7. *Most experts accept this marble portrait as Cleopatra VII. The queen again wears a 'melon' hairstyle and diadem; a curious stone lump on the forehead may be the remains of a crown or uraeus.*

8. *'Cleopatra restored'; two very different statues have been joined together to make one queen.*

9. *Originally identified as Arsinoë II, this unlabelled black basalt statue of unknown provenance is today more widely accepted, because of the triple uraeus, as an Egyptian-style Cleopatra VII.*

10. *Faience head of a Ptolemaic queen recovered from Naukratis, often identified as the powerful Arsinoë II, inspiration to Cleopatra VII.*

11. *Cleopatra II or Cleopatra III? This restored portrait demonstrates that Ptolemaic women were not afraid to present a forceful, even masculine, face to the world.*

12. Romans relaxing on the Nile: fragment of mosaic recovered from Palestrina, Italy.

13. Ptolemy II, his face wiped blank by the waters of the Mediterranean Sea, stands beside the new Library of Alexandria.

14. Mosaic once believed to depict Berenice II as the personification of Alexandria. The city-queen wears a ship on her head.

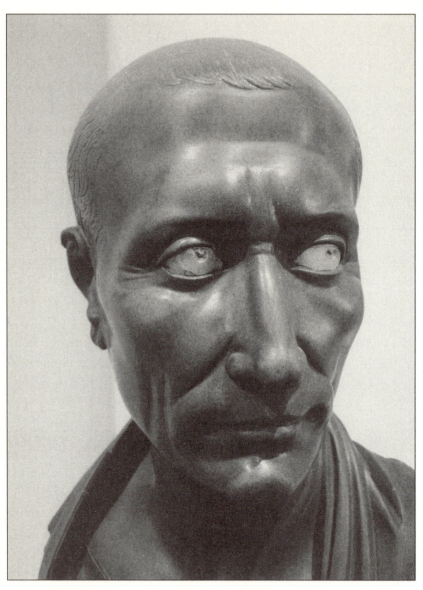

15. Julius Caesar: a green basanite bust with modern eye inlays carved after Caesar's death from Egyptian stone. Note the thinning hair.

suggested that the earth might revolve around the sun, and Ctesibius developed the art of ballistics. And so it continued, with just one major hiccup. In *c.* 145–44, during the turbulent reign of Ptolemy VIII, the scholars were unceremoniously expelled from Alexandria, and Alexandria's reputation as a centre of learning plummeted.

The Ptolemies valued the Museion as an obvious and internationally acknowledged manifestation of their city's superiority. But it would be a mistake to imagine ancient Alexandria as a dull city dedicated to dry scholarship and reading. It was first and foremost a port, and the harbours and the marketplaces were hives of activity as Egypt's own products (wheat, papyrus, linen, stone, glass, perfumes, drugs and spices) were joined with exotic goods from Africa, Asia and India, to be loaded on to large merchant ships and relatively small state-, temple- and privately-owned sailing boats. Away from the ports the streets teamed with a vibrant cross-section of life: itinerant traders and their customers, sailors, tourists, fortune seekers, soothsayers, musicians, thieves, prostitutes and many, many more. There were large glass, papyrus and linen factories, whose workers were formed into tradesmen's guilds, and smaller workshops owned by potters, carpenters, weavers, bakers and undertakers.

The concept of *tryphe* – boundless, ostentatious luxury as a manifestation of power – underpinned the Alexandrian court. Years of dedicated eating and drinking had rendered Ptolemies VIII, IX and X spectacularly obese. Proud of his appearance, and of the luxurious over-consumption that it represented, Ptolemy VIII 'Potbelly' celebrated his excesses, and scandalised Roman visitors, by dressing in the filmiest of robes that left nothing to the imagination. It cannot have been a pleasant sight, as 'his body had become corrupted by fat and a belly of such size that it would have been hard to measure it with one's arms'.[13] The *symposium*, or male after-dinner drinking club, was a flourishing Greek bonding ritual. Groups of wealthy men reclined on couches to drink wine, tell riddles, play childish games (a very popular game included flicking wine from a cup) and listen to music performed by slaves and prostitutes. Although the wine was mixed with water, the evening was quite likely to disintegrate into what today we might classify as an orgy of drinking. This did not matter overmuch. Immoderate drinking might be considered a tribute to Dionysos. It might even be beneficial to the system. Athenaeus, citing the respected Athenian physician Mnesitheus, advises us that:

> It happens that those who drink a great quantity of unmixed wine at banquets often receive great injury from so doing, both in their bodies and minds; but still occasional hard drinking for some days appears to me to produce a certain purging of the body and a certain relaxation of the mind ... Of all methods of purging, that which is caused by hard drinking is the most advantageous, for then the body is, as it were, washed out by the wine ... But when you are drinking hard you should guard against three things – against drinking bad wine, against drinking unmixed wine, and against eating sweetmeats when you are drinking. And when you have had enough do not go to sleep until you have had a vomit, moderate or copious as the case may be, and when you have vomited, then go to sleep after you have taken a slight bath.[14]

Excessive drinking naturally led to a great deal of casual sex: sex with fellow drinkers, sex with high-class prostitutes (*hetairai*), sex with flute girls and boys, sex with anyone, it seems, apart from wives. The Ptolemaic court allowed its men a great deal of sexual licence and even Ptolemy II, a twice-married man so devoted to his second wife that he deified her, was an inveterate womaniser:

> The second king of Egypt, Ptolemy Philadelphos by name ... had a great many mistresses – namely Didyma, who was a native of the country and very beautiful; and Bilistiche; and beside them,

Agathoclea; and Stratonice, who had a great monument on the sea-shore near Eleusis; and Myrtium; and a great many more; he was a man excessively addicted to amatory pleasures. And Polybius, in the fourteenth book of his History, says that there are a great many statues of a woman named Clino, who was his cupbearer, in Alexandria, clothed in a tunic only, and holding a cornucopia in her hand.[15]

The Romans, who (in theory at least) dined with their wives rather than their lovers, found this shocking. The air of dissoluteness was compounded for them by the presence of eunuchs, invariably ex-slaves, in positions of high authority at the Ptolemaic court. The Ptolemies respected their eunuchs as exceptionally loyal servants capable of running both the royal household (with no danger of an unsuitable alliance with a royal princess) and, by extension, the country. But Roman law forbade castration, even the castration of a slave, and the Romans would come to regard the Alexandrian eunuchs as typifying the emasculating strength of Egypt's women.

Outside the palace there were public festivals aplenty: the festivals of the Greek earth goddess Demeter, the female-based Adonia celebration in honour of Aphrodite and Adonis, which was hosted by the queen at the palace and, of course, the many exuberant festivals associated with the cult of Dionysos. Not all the celebrations were impressive, but most involved the consumption of alcohol:

When Ptolemy was instituting a festival and all kinds of sacrifices, and especially those which relate to Bacchus [Dionysos], Arsinoë asked the man who bore the branches what day he was celebrating now, and what festival it was. And when he replied 'It is called the Lagynophoria; and the guests lie down on beds and so eat all that they have brought with them, and everyone drinks out of his own flagon, which he has brought from home.' And when he had departed she, looking towards us, said, 'it seems a very dirty kind of party; for

*it is quite evident that it must be an assembly of mixed multitude,
all putting down stale food and such as is altogether unseasonable
and unbecoming.'*[16]

Religious processions had long been a regular feature of Egyptian life
and the principal cities were criss-crossed by ceremonial routes defined
by avenues of sphinxes. The days that the gods left the temple sanctuary to parade through the streets or sail on the Nile were eagerly anticipated public holidays, and crowds lined the processional ways to watch
and cheer as their gods sailed by in golden boats carried high on the
shoulder by priests. Eating and drinking were an important part of
festival days, and New Kingdom government records show that men
from the Theban tomb workers' village of Deir el-Medina absented
themselves from work to brew beer in advance of the festivities.

In wine-drinking Alexandria, the essentially Egyptian procession
was combined with Greek *tryphe* to make an unforgettable spectacle.
Athenaeus preserves some of the otherwise lost work of Callixeinos of
Rhodes, including a description of the celebration, in the winter of
275/4 (or 279/8 or 271/70), of the Ptolemaia, a four-yearly Dionysiac
festival with a grand parade and games commemorating the entry of
the deified Ptolemy I into Olympus, and hosted by his son Ptolemy
II.[17] Ptolemaiae were celebrated throughout Egypt, but the grandest
display was, of course, in Alexandria. Here celebrations started with
lavish sacrifices and with an opulent banquet held in a magnificently
decorated tent containing hundreds of ornate couches and golden
dining tripods. Callixeinos was struck by the fact that, even though it
was winter, the floor of the tent was so thickly strewn with flowers of
every description that it resembled a summer meadow. More flowers
were woven into garlands for the diners to wear.

The next day saw the processions: 'the procession of Lucifer (the
morning star)', the procession 'dedicated to the parents of the king'
and the procession 'of all the gods'. The wide city streets quite literally

flowed with wine (an estimated 25,000 gallons) and the people poured out of their houses to watch, wonder and drink. Towards the front of the procession came Dionysos himself: an enormous purple-clad statue pouring libations out of a golden goblet, and an even larger statue riding an elephant and supported by an army of satyrs (followers of Dionysos) crowned with golden ivy leaves and silenoi (elderly satyrs) dressed in purple and scarlet cloaks. Next came floats displaying gold and silver treasures (plate, tripods, armour, thrones and crowns, including the crown of Ptolemy I, made from 'ten thousand pieces of gold money'), floats presenting mythological tableaux, a vast array of exotic wild animals, including twenty-four lions and 2,000 bulls, costumed actors, musicians, divine and royal statues, priests and acolytes, and an automated statue of the personified Mount Nysa, birthplace of Dionysos, which entertained the crowds by repeatedly standing up, pouring a libation of milk out of a golden bottle and sitting down again. There were women dressed as maenads (female followers of Dionysos), with snakes and ivy wreaths in their dishevelled hair, an enormous wine press complete with sixty singing satyrs to trample the grapes, and a 180-foot-long phallus with a star at one end. A deep vine- and ivy-covered cave, constructed on the back of a float, released twin fountains of milk and wine. From deep within the cave flew doves, pigeons and turtledoves, their feet tied together with ribbons so that they might be caught (and later eaten) by the spectators. The military procession, with 57,600 foot soldiers and 23,200 cavalry, probably marched on the following day. This was *tryphe* at its extreme: a conspicuous display of public luxury and generosity designed to impress all – citizens, tourists and specially invited foreign dignitaries – who saw it. A *tryphe,* some might think, hovering dangerously close to hubris.

Alexandria could boast an eclectic religious profile and an embarrassment of temples dedicated to a diverse multitude of gods: there were temples dedicated to Greek deities, at least half a dozen temples dedicated to Isis, temples dedicated to other, lesser Egyptian gods, temples dedicated to the sole god worshipped by the monotheistic Jews, and many shrines and temples dedicated to Alexander and the growing number of deified Ptolemies.[18] The latter included the Arsinoeion, built by Ptolemy II in honour of his dead wife. Here, Pliny the Elder tells us, the priests planned to employ magnetism in their worship of the deified Arsinoë II:

> The architect Dionochares had begun to use loadstone for construct-ing the vaulting in the temple of Arsinoë at Alexandria, so that the iron statue contained in it might have the appearance of being sus-pended in mid-air; but the project was interrupted by his own death and that of King Ptolemy who had ordered the work to be done in honour of his sister.[19]

The magnetic floating statue would not have appeared out of place in a city filled with modern miracles: automated statues, steam-powered models, automatic doors and the word's first coin-operated machines.

Prominent among Alexandria's many deities stood Serapis, a god apparently designed by a committee. Legend tells how the canny Ptolemy I summoned the Egyptian priest Manetho of Sebennytos (modern Sammanud) and the Greek priest Timotheos of Athens, and invited them to submit designs for a new deity. Ptolemy wanted a modern god for the modern world, with no pre-existing allegiances to either cities or dynasties and no powerful, long-established priest-hood. Such a god could be used to support the new dynasty within Egypt, and could serve as an ambassador for Alexandria and the Ptol-emies outside Egypt's borders. If he proved acceptable to both Greeks and Egyptians, he might also go some way towards uniting Alexan-dria's religiously mixed population. The chosen god was Serapis, a combination of the Egyptian god Osiris and the Greek deities

Dionysos, Hades (god of the underworld), Asklepios (god of healing), Helios (the sun god) and Zeus. An anthropomorphic deity – animal and animal-human hybrid gods being unacceptable to non-Egyptians – Serapis personified divine kingship, healing, fertility and the after-life. The new god's name was derived from the name of the Memphite god Osor-Apis, himself a fusion of the deceased Apis bull, who was considered to be the living embodiment of the god Ptah and Osiris.

As we might expect, the story of Serapis's clinical conception is only partially true. Ptolemy I did deliberately set out to promote a new god, but it seems that a version of Serapis already existed as an obscure deity worshipped in the Greek colony of Sinope, on the Black Sea. Ptolemy's Serapis looked very much like the Greek Zeus. He was a mature gentleman with a mop of curly hair and a beard who dressed in Greek robes and carried a sceptre, but he was often shown with Egyptian features and he wore a *modius* crown in the form of a corn measure. Serapis was married to the universally popular goddess Isis, who, as the wife of Osiris, was already acceptable to both Greeks and Egyptians. As Ptolemy had planned, Serapis, Isis and their son Harpocrates quickly came to be associated with the ruling Ptolemaic dynasty.

While the native Egyptians were somewhat unconvinced by the new god, preferring to remain loyal to their traditional deities in their original forms, Serapis enjoyed a huge success throughout the Greek and Roman world. Soon every civilised city could boast a Serapeum, or temple of Serapis, each of which would include a subsidiary temple dedicated to the divine consort Isis, and also serve as a hospital for the sick. Egypt's doctors were respected throughout the ancient world, but their scientific understanding and practical skills were limited. In a land entirely controlled by capricious gods – gods who caused the sun to shine, the Nile to rise, the crops to grow and the dead to be reborn – it was entirely reasonable to assume that otherwise inexplicable illnesses were cause by malevolent powers. Invalids, faced with the choice of consulting a doctor or a priest, may well have viewed the latter as the more effective option. As both Serapis and Isis were blessed with the gift of healing, their temples attracted pilgrims from far and wide, with the Koptos Serapeum developing a particularly good reputation for curing the sick. Here, after a period of 'incubation', a night or two spent sleeping in the temple precincts and dreaming of Serapis, the faithful could expect to receive a divine cure. Restored to health – whether by the dream, the highly experienced temple staff or visiting doctors, who tended to use the Serapeum as a teaching hospital – they returned home to tell the world about the miracles wrought by Serapis and Isis.

The heart of the cult of Serapis lay in the raised south-western sector of Alexandria near the native Egyptian district. The temple complex was built by Ptolemy I and extensively remodelled by Ptolemy III. In its heyday it was one of the most famous and beautiful religious sites in the classical world. Today, however, it is a confusing ruin, topped by 'Pompey's Pillar', an ill-named granite column, possibly originally cut by an 18th Dynasty king and re-erected in Alexandria in AD 291 as a pedestal to support an image of the emperor Diocletian. Archaeologists have argued long and hard over the original architecture of the Serapeum: whether it was an essentially Greek-style building with some additional Egyptian touches, or whether it was an Egyptian building with Greek elements. Unfortunately, the few surviving written descriptions refer to the Roman Serapeum, built by Hadrian after the Jewish uprising of AD 116 destroyed the original Ptolemaic temple. Hadrian's Serapeum, and its archive of 700,000 papyrus scrolls, would itself be destroyed by Christians in AD 391.

Alexandria was a most un-Egyptian-looking city, filled with grand Greek buildings, Greek colonnades and Greek sculptures. The extent to which this most modern of cities was embellished with Egyptian artefacts acquired from other, more ancient sites is only just becoming clear. Today rival Franco-Egyptian teams are conducting extensive underwater excavations in the harbour. The team led by Jean-Yves Empereur is investigating the area around the Pharos lighthouse, while the team led by Franck Goddio concentrates on the area to the north of the Palaces and Antirrhodos. These are long-term projects, but the area around the vanished lighthouse has already yielded a series of pre-Ptolemaic monuments, including three broken obelisks inscribed with the name of Seti I, columns inscribed for Ramesses II and a series of sphinxes ranging in date from the Middle Kingdom to the Late Period. It seems that the cult centre of the sun god Re at Heliopolis, once the most splendid temple complex in Egypt, but sacked by the Persian Cambyses and in Ptolemaic times a ruin, was being quarried to provide Alexandria both with antiquities and with useful stone that could be recut and reused. Memphis, Bubastis and Sais, too, were being stripped of their antiquities to ornament Alexandria. It is not obvious when these artefacts were moved, and it is entirely possible that some at least were moved by the Romans. However, it seems that the Ptolemies did have the collecting habit: Pliny confirms that Ptolemy II had a dynastic obelisk raised in the Arsinoeion.[20] The obelisk was later transferred to Alexandria's forum, and then taken to Rome by the emperor Caligula. Eventually it was re-erected in St Peter's Square, Vatican City, where it still stands today.

Displayed alongside the genuine ancient Egyptian sculptures were modern pieces in the Egyptian style commissioned by the Ptolemies themselves. A series of statues, recovered from the Pharos lighthouse underwater site, includes a colossal Ptolemy II and a colossal queen, wearing a Hathoric headdress and a curly wig, who may be intended to represent the queen as the goddess Isis. Together, it seems, king and goddess guarded the entrance to the harbour. Today Ptolemy II, his face wiped blank by the water, stands tall and proud before the rebuilt Library of Alexandria.

London and New York each boasts a pink granite obelisk known as Cleopatra's Needle. Both obelisks come from Alexandria, but they have only the most tenuous connection with Cleopatra VII. The obelisk, a tall, tapering stone capped with a small pyramid, represented a solid ray of sunlight. To erect an obelisk in front of a temple was a splendid technical achievement, a sign of genuine devotion undertaken by only the richest and most powerful of kings. Cleopatra's Needles started life in the hot and dusty Aswan quarry, where they were cut on the orders of the 18th Dynasty king Tuthmosis III. Images preserved on the walls of the Karnak Red Chapel and the Deir el-Bahri mortuary temple of Hatshepsut (stepmother, aunt and co-ruler to Tuthmosis III) make it clear just how difficult it was to transport and raise such unwieldy artefacts. Twin obelisks, lashed to wooden sledges, are towed on a sycamore wood barge by a fleet of twenty-seven small boats crewed by over 850 oarsmen. Fortunately the flow of the river helps the barge on its way. The barge is escorted by three ships whose priests bless the proceedings. Upon their arrival at the temple there is a magnificent public celebration. A bull is killed and further offerings are made to the gods. Tuthmosis's obelisks were erected in the precincts of the temple of the sun god Re of Heliopolis. One and a half centuries later, still in place, they were reinscribed by the 19th Dynasty Ramesses II 'the Great', a pharaoh with an incorrigible tendency to usurp the monuments of his predecessor. In 13, with the temple of Re in ruins, Octavian had the obelisks brought to Alexandria. They were re-erected, supported by large bronze crabs, in front of the Caesareum, Cleopatra's unfinished monument to Julius Caesar, which now served as the focus for the imperial cult. Here they remained, one standing, one fallen, until the nineteenth-century ruler Mohamed Ali, an indefatigable moderniser, decided that Alexandria could manage without her needles. The fallen obelisk was given to Britain. It was transported to London and erected on the bank of the Thames in 1879. The sister obelisk, a gift to the USA, was erected in Central Park, New York, in 1880.

The obelisks, still in place in Alexandria in 1820, confirm the location of the Caesareum, which survives today as a series of massive foundation walls. The most complete description of this building dates to AD 40:

> For there is elsewhere no precinct like that which is called the Sebasteum, a temple to Caesar on the shipboard, situated on an eminence facing the harbours ... huge and conspicuous, fitted on a scale not found elsewhere with dedicated offerings, around it a girdle of pictures and statues in silver and gold, forming a precinct of vast breadth, embellished with porticoes, libraries, chambers, groves, gateways and wide open courts and everything which lavish expenditure could produce to beautify it ...[21]

A military text adds some welcome detail: there were at least two storeys, more than one staircase and a marble statue of Venus.

Cleopatra's palace has vanished, but is likely to have been situated in or close by the Palaces district, maybe on Antirrhodos.

CHAPTER FOUR

Cleopatra and Julius Caesar

… The young queen had little to fear so long as she had at her side the greatest Roman of the moment.

Grace Macurdy, *Hellenistic Queens*[1]

With Cleopatra and Ptolemy officially reunited there was perhaps a faint chance that the threatened civil war might be averted. The Roman poet Lucan, writing *c.* AD 65, tells us that Cleopatra threw a lavish banquet to celebrate this new beginning:

> *… The wanton's [Cleopatra's] prayers prevailed and, by spending a night of ineffable shame with her judge, she won his favour. When Caesar had made an expensive peace between the pair [brother and sister], they celebrated with a banquet. With pomp the Queen displayed her luxuries, as yet unknown to Roman fashions … There in her fatal beauty lay the Queen thickly daubed with unguents, content neither with her throne nor with her brother spouse. She lay laden with all the Red Sea spoils on her neck and hair, faint beneath the weight of gems and gold.*[2]

But Lucan is writing the equivalent of modern tabloid journalism, and his entertaining account needs to be taken with more than the usual pinch of salt. In reality no one, Caesar excepted, was happy with the new power-sharing arrangement and, as Pothinos secretly summoned Ptolemy's army from Pelusium, the Alexandrians started to arm their slaves. Caesar's meagre band of soldiers soon found themselves outnumbered by Ptolemy's far larger army of well-trained Gabinians. Securing the Palaces, Caesar hastily sent for reinforcements. He had just one card up his sleeve. Cleopatra and her siblings Ptolemy XIII, Arsinoë and Ptolemy XIV were all his guests – willing or unwilling – in the Palaces.

Suetonius summarises and sanitises the Alexandrian Wars:

> … *a most difficult campaign, awkward both in time and place, fought during winter within the city walls of a well-equipped and cunning enemy; but though caught off his guard, and without military supplies of any kind, Caesar was victorious.*[3]

In fact four months of vicious land and sea battles combined with a guerrilla-style urban war brought devastation to Alexandria. Caesar's own account of the struggles tells us that the city, built from stone and tile with very little wood, seemed virtually immune to fire.[4] 'Seemed' is the operative word here. When Caesar torched the Egyptian fleet in the harbour, the fire spread to the Palaces and part – maybe all – of the library was lost. Eventually Caesar was able to take control of Pharos, and to keep the harbour open. But things were not going well, and the Alexandrians managed to build a new fleet from scraps of wood recovered in the town. At one low point Caesar almost drowned in the Mediterranean. Forced to swim for his life, he kept his all-important military plans dry by holding them above his head, but lost his cloak to the sea. Retrieved by the enemy, it was displayed as a war trophy.

Just as Cleopatra had maintained a conspicuous silence during her elder sister's ill-fated reign and its bloody aftermath, so she remained silent and, as far as we can tell, inactive throughout the Alexandrian Wars. Younger and less experienced, the fourteen-year-old Arsinoë was not content to bide her time. Having escaped from the Palaces, and supported by her influential tutor Ganymede, she joined forces with Ptolemy's general Achillas. In November 48 the people of Alexandria proclaimed Arsinoë queen of Egypt: a rival to Cleopatra and a future wife for Ptolemy XIII, who was still the crowd's favourite. Soon after, Pothinos's treachery was discovered (Plutarch tells us that he was betrayed by Caesar's barber) and he was executed, while Achillas was killed by the ambitious Ganymede. This left Ptolemy XIII isolated, and Ganymede in command of the army. He was to prove an innovative commander, earning Caesar's grudging respect by polluting the subterranean water cisterns with saltwater. Caesar was only able to counter this by ordering his men to dig day and night until they struck ground water.

Next, the people of Alexandria, apparently tiring of life under Arsinoë and Ganymede, made a curious request:

The Alexandrians, perceiving that success confirmed the Romans, and that adverse fortune only animated them the more, as they knew of no medium between these on which to ground any further hopes, resolved, as far as we can conjecture, either by the advice of the friends of their king who were in Caesar's quarter, or of their own previous design, intimated to the king by secret emissaries, to send ambassadors to Caesar to request him, 'To dismiss their king and suffer him to rejoin his subjects; that the people, weary of subjection to a woman, of living under a precarious government, and submitting to the cruel laws of the tyrant Ganymede, were ready to execute the orders of the king: and if by his sanction they should embrace the alliance and protection of Caesar, the multitude would not be deterred from surrendering by the fear of danger.'[5]

It is hard to make sense of this development. Caesar's *Alexandrian Wars* tells us that Ptolemy, who had developed an intense loyalty to him, begged with tears in his eyes not to be sent from the Palaces. But Ptolemy was bluffing and Caesar, despite his belated recognition that the Alexandrians were 'false and perfidious, seldom speaking as they thought', was inexplicably naïve. Believing that Ptolemy's release might calm the situation, Caesar let him go. As soon as he got clear of the Palaces, Ptolemy wiped his eyes, took up his old command and, 'like a wild beast escaped out of confinement, carried on the war with much acrimony against Caesar, so that the tears he shed at parting seemed to have been tears of joy'.

Soon after Ptolemy's defection, troops commanded by Caesar's ally Mithridates of Pergamon and supplemented by Nabatean and Jewish forces, captured Pelusium and marched west to Alexandria. Caesar sailed to join them, surprising the Egyptians from the rear. There was a short, sharp battle outside the city. Caesar's allies won, Alexandria surrendered, Arsinoë was captured and Ptolemy XIII drowned trying to cross the Canopic branch of the Nile in a disastrously overcrowded boat. The heavy golden armour that had made it impossible for him to swim was recovered and displayed to the people of Alexandria as proof of their king's death, but his body was lost in the river. This was to cause Cleopatra problems years later, when a pseudo-Ptolemy appeared to claim the throne with a dramatic and plausible tale of a desperate swim to safety and many years spent in exile. The Egyptian army surrendered on 15 January 47. Caesar, a deeply unpopular victor, re-entered Alexandria in triumph, and joined the equally unpopular Cleopatra and her younger brother Ptolemy XIV in the Palaces. To thank them for their help in his campaign, Caesar later granted the freedom of the city to the Alexandrian Jews.

Caesar could have annexed Egypt, but did not. Instead, the widowed Cleopatra was reinstated on her throne alongside her thirteen-year-old brother, who, Dio tells us, now became her husband:

... Being afraid that the Egyptians might rebel again, because they were delivered over to a woman to rule, and that the Romans might be angry, both on this account and because he was living with the woman, he commanded her to 'marry' her other brother, and gave the kingdom to both of them, at least nominally. For in reality Cleopatra was to hold all the power alone, since her husband was still a boy, and in view of Caesar's favour there was nothing that she could not do. Hence her living with her brother and sharing the rule with him was a mere pretence which she accepted, whereas in truth she ruled alone and spent her time in Caesar's company.[6]

Together, brother and sister were to rule as the Theoi Philopatores Philadelphoi (the Father-Loving, Brother/Sister-Loving Gods), although Cleopatra, barely subscribing to the fiction of joint rule, would defy convention and always place her name first. Sister and brother were to be 'supported' in their rule by three, later four, Roman legions. Egypt was, in all but name, a Roman protectorate.

Caesar was now free to return to Rome, yet still he dallied in Alexandria. Contemporary observers, reluctant, perhaps, to suggest that the great Caesar was capable of the twin crimes of laziness and irresponsibility, made no mention of this delay. Modern historians are universally agreed that he dallied because of Cleopatra. The pragmatic view is that he wished to see her properly settled on her throne as a secure and useful Roman client-queen. The more romantic view is that he was simply worn out by many years of campaigning and wished to spend some time with his young mistress.

He often feasted with her to dawn; and they would have sailed together in her state barge nearly to Ethiopia had his soldiers consented to follow him.[7]

For many centuries Egypt's pharaohs had sailed up and down the Nile

– Egypt's highway – in order to confirm their presence to their people. Long, thin Egypt was an awkward country to administer. It could take two weeks for a message to pass from Memphis in the north to Aswan in the south, and there was an ever-present worry that officials living hundreds of miles from the administrative capital might be tempted to forget the king and assume their own quasi-royal prerogatives. A regular royal appearance was a simple and effective way of reinforcing the king's right to rule, and the Nile was dotted with minor palaces, 'mooring places of the pharaoh', where kings could hold temporary court while visiting local governors and making offerings in local temples. The link between large boats and earthly power remains an obvious one today. Only the wealthy can own a large boat; boat ownership brings access to greater wealth and the potential to build more boats. The link between boats and the divine is perhaps less clear to us. But Egypt's gods regularly processed on the Nile, travelling from temple to temple and crossing from the east bank to the west, while high above the river the sun god Re steered his solar boat across the clear blue sky each and every day.

Now, if Appian and Suetonius are to be believed, Cleopatra was preparing to sail down the Nile and Caesar had agreed to accompany her. Far from a romantic cruise, this was a triumphal public display; a calculated political move designed to make the new alliance crystal clear to everyone who mattered. The fleet of over 400 ships crewed by Roman soldiers which, Appian tells us, accompanied the royal barge simply reinforced the message.[8] We have no description of Cleopatra's barge. But we do have a description, penned by Callixeinos of Rhodes and preserved by Athenaeus, of the magnificent barge or *navis tha-lamegos* built by Ptolemy IV over one and a half centuries earlier.[9] This remarkable vessel was said to be half a stadium long, with a maximum width of thirty cubits and a maximum height of just under forty cubits. It was a multi-roomed, multi-storey floating pleasure palace with five separate restaurants and accommodation for king, queen, courtiers, servants and crew, and it may well have served as the model for Cleopatra's own barge.

It is reasonable to assume that Caesar wanted to inspect the land that was, in all but name, his. Lucan suggests that there may have been another motive behind the trip. For many years Caesar – and many others – had been intrigued by the unknown source of the Nile:

> *Despite my strong interest in science, said Caesar to Acoreus, Priest of Isis, nothing would satisfy my intellectual curiosity more fully than to be told what makes the Nile rise. If you can enable me to visit the source, which has been a mystery for so many years, I promise to abandon this civil war.*[10]

If this was the case, he was destined to be disappointed. The origin of the Nile would remain a mystery for another eighteen centuries, while Cleopatra's barge is unlikely to have passed further south than the notoriously rebellious city of Thebes. It might, indeed, have sailed no further than the ancient capital and traditional coronation city, Memphis.

At some time between 47 and 44 Cleopatra gave birth to a son whom she named Ptolemy Caesar. Her choice of name was highly suggestive, as was the fact that Caesar made no attempt to veto her use of his name. The people of Alexandria leapt to the obvious conclusion, and instantly renamed the baby Caesarion, or Little Caesar, after his 'father'. Of course, this is an assumption which is impossible to prove, although many have tried, focusing their attention on Caesarion's birth date and, by extension, the date of his conception. Plutarch is of little help here as he contradicts himself, telling us both that Caesarion was the son of Caesar, born in 47 – ' ... leaving Cleopatra on the throne of Egypt (a little later she had a son by him whom the Alexandrians called Caesarion)' (*Life of Caesar*) – and that 'Caesarion was believed to be a son of the former Caesar [Julius Caesar], by whom

Cleopatra was left pregnant' (*Life of Antony*), a loose statement which implies that Cleopatra was pregnant at the time of Caesar's death.[11]

Contemporaries and near-contemporaries are divided over the baby's paternity. Dio tells us that Cleopatra pretended that Caesarion was Caesar's child, while Suetonius tells us that Caius Oppius composed a careful text explaining that he was not. Suetonius himself sits on the fence. He says that Caesar, besotted with Cleopatra, 'even allowed her to call the son whom she had borne him by his own name. Some Greek historians say the boy closely resembled Caesar in features as well as in gait', and adds that Mark Antony, who is hardly an unbiased witness, nor one likely to support Octavian's claim to be Caesar's true heir, declared before the Senate that Caesar had acknowledged Caesarion as his son.[12]

For many years it was believed that a Ptolemaic or Roman stela recovered from the Memphite Serapeum and now housed in the Louvre, Paris, held the key to Caesarion's birth date. The demotic text on the stela is dated to 'Year 5, 23 Payni, day of the feast of Isis, birthday of King Caesar'. If we accept that the Year 5 in question is Cleopatra's Year 5, then, counting from Auletes's death in 51, this date would be 23 June 47.[13] Assuming that she carried her baby for the full nine months, this immediately suggests that Caesarion was conceived during the Alexandrian crisis, at a time when Cleopatra was separated from her brother-husband, Ptolemy XIII, and was living in close proximity to Caesar. But this is Egyptology, and nothing in Egyptology is ever simple. Cleopatra's co-regent in 47 was her brother Ptolemy XIV, not her son, so why would the stela give Caesarion an incorrect title? Was the stela carved later, when Caesarion had become king? Or does the Year 5 in question belong not to Cleopatra but to Caesarion himself? As his joint rule with Cleopatra started after the death of Ptolemy XIV in 44, this would effectively date the stela to 40. Could the stela refer to a later, Roman, ruler of Egypt who could also be called 'King Caesar'? Perhaps, as some Egyptologists believe, it is referring to the birthday of Octavian? The fact that Caesarion, as pharaoh, was never known as King Caesar – he was always 'Ptolemy named Caesar' – supports this last interpretation. Meanwhile, to add further to the confusion, a recent publication of the stela has suggested that the birth date should be revised to 25 Phaophi, or 28 October 48, and the name of celebrant to 'King Djoser', Djoser being the 3rd Dynasty builder of the Sakkara step pyramid who was revered as a god during Ptolemaic and Roman times. This revised reading would suggest that the piece has no relevance to either Cleopatra or Caesarion.[14]

Cleopatra refused to rise to the gossip and remained silent over the issue of her son's paternity. She, of course, had no need to explain herself and everything to gain from the assumption that she was the mother of Caesar's child. Caesarion offered the strongest of inducements for Caesar to ensure that Egypt remained an independent state for his son to inherit. The death of Ptolemy XIV would make Caesarion king of Egypt, ruling alongside his mother. With Caesarion and Cleopatra on the throne, and Caesar dictator of Rome, Egypt and the Ptolemies would receive Roman protection, Rome would benefit from Egypt's generosity, and Caesar's family would effectively rule the civilised world. Caesar, too, retained a dignified silence. Already married to a Roman wife, he was in any case unable to recognise any other woman's child as his son. His silence has been interpreted many ways. That the liaison was essentially unimportant to him; a fling on a par with his many earlier affairs. That there was no liaison; Caesarion was not his son. Or that Caesar, well aware of the dangers of being perceived as father of the heir to the Roman and Egyptian 'thrones', kept silent to protect his son.

With Caesar seemingly happy enough in his unacknowledged parentage, is there any reason to doubt Caesarion's paternity? Just a faint, lingering cloud of uncertainty hovers over Caesar's fertility. After a life of sexual excess, three marriages and countless affairs, he had produced just one acknowledged child. Julia, late wife of Pompey the Great, had been born to Caesar's first wife Cornelia thirty-six years before Caesarion's birth. Rumours that Caesar had fathered a string of natural children, including Brutus, son of Servilia, are of course unprovable. One surviving child was, however, by no means unusual: Cornelia, mother of Tiberius Gracchus, bore twelve children but only three survived infancy and childhood. While Egypt's women were famed for their fertility, something that can perhaps be attributed to their grain-rich diet, Rome was suffering an acute shortage of elite babies caused by a general wifely reluctance to reproduce and made worse by high rates of miscarriage, high rates of mother and baby mortality during pregnancy, labour and early infancy, and, perhaps, the use of lead water pipes.[15] Infant deaths and miscarriages frequently go unrecorded, making it difficult to obtain precise statistics, but an estimate that just over half of all babies born in Rome would reach five years of age does not seem unreasonable. Caesar's daughter Julia had herself died in childbirth, along with her baby.

In the summer of 47 Caesar left Cleopatra to resume his campaign against the followers of Pompey. He would not see her again for over a year, ill-documented in Egypt, which saw Cleopatra strengthen her hold on her throne through her astute manipulation of the cult of Isis. Caesar's year, in contrast, is well documented. A quick victory in Asia Minor saw the fall of Pharnaces II, son of Mithridates of Pontus (*'veni, vidi, vici'*). This was followed by the quashing of a potentially dangerous mutiny in Rome and a successful North African campaign that wiped out what he hoped would be the last remnants of Pompey's supporters. Caesar returned to Italy in June or July 46. In late September or early October he celebrated quadruple triumphs: four separate days of festivities honouring his victories in Gaul, Egypt, Pontus and Africa. There were games, plays, banquets, sacrifices and four extensive processions which started in the Field of Mars, entered Rome through the Triumphal Gate and wound their way through the Forum to the Capitol and the temple of Jupiter Optimus Maximus. Included in the processions were displays of war trophies and treasures, paintings and maps illustrating Caesar's many victories, and tableaux depicting, among other things, the River Nile and the Pharos lighthouse complete with imitation flames. The exhibition of prestigious prisoners included the great Gallic chieftain Vercingetorix, the four-year-old Juba II of Numidia, the Alexandrian eunuch Ganymede and his queen, the teenage Arsinoë IV. This was unusual – the Romans usually avoided displaying female captives in chains, although Pompey had exhibited the widow and daughters of Mithridates in 61 – and it proved very unpopular. Arsinoë gained the sympathy of the watching crowd, and Caesar deemed it wise to spare her life, banishing her to live in the temple of Artemis at Ephesus. Juba, too, was spared to be raised as a Roman gentleman. Vercingetorix, who had already suffered six years of solitary confinement, was garrotted immediately after his public appearance, while Ganymede simply disappeared, presumably to share Vercingetorix's fate.

Some time that same autumn Cleopatra, Ptolemy XIV and (probably) Caesarion arrived in Rome. They settled into Caesar's private estate, in Trastevere across the Tiber, and there, apparently, they stayed, even during Caesar's lengthy absence in Spain from December 46 to the summer of 45, until Caesar's assassination on the Ides of March (15 March) 44 prompted a return to Egypt. Whether Cleopatra followed Caesar to Rome of her own free will or was summoned, either as a lover or as a hostage, is unclear. There is certainly no evidence that she made the grand Roman entry beloved of film-makers; it is impossible to imagine Romans turning out to cheer a foreign queen unless they were cheering/jeering at her as a captive. Whatever its purpose, the visit played into the hands of Caesar's enemies, who were quick to spread malicious gossip: Caesar intended to divorce the barren Calpurnia and marry Cleopatra; Caesar had definitely decided to move his capital city to Alexandria; Caesar was planning to pass legislation that would allow him the right to as many foreign wives as he liked. Dio tells us that Caesar was unconcerned about the growing resentment:

> *... he incurred the greatest censure from all because of his passion for Cleopatra – not now the passion he had displayed in Egypt (for that was a matter of hearsay), but that which was displayed in Rome itself. For she had come to the city with her husband and settled in Caesar's own house, so that he too derived an ill repute on account of both of them. He was not at all concerned, however, about this, but actually enrolled them among the friends and allies of the Roman people.*[16]

Cicero, a dedicated republican, met Cleopatra at this time and despised her for her arrogance (*superbia*). In a letter written to his great friend Atticus on 13 June 44, he made his feelings clear:

> *I hate the queen! And the man who vouches for her promises, Ammonius, knows I have good reason to do so; although the gifts she promised me were of a literary nature and not beneath my dignity – the sort I should not have minded proclaiming in public .... The queen's insolence, when she was living in Caesar's house in the gardens beyond the Tiber, I cannot recall without indignation. So no dealings with that lot. They seem to think I have not only no spirit, but no feelings at all.*[17]

This extended Roman visit is yet another hazy period in Cleopatra's life. We can confirm from contemporary records that a visit did take place, but cannot be certain that an entire unbroken eighteen months were spent in Rome. Indeed, it seems unlikely that Caesar, having only just restored stability to Egypt, would wish to risk Cleopatra's precarious hold on her throne, while Cleopatra's own family history showed that neglecting Alexandria to holiday in Rome was a very bad idea indeed. It may therefore be that there were two entirely separate visits to Rome: an initial diplomatic mission with Ptolemy XIV to gain official recognition as a 'friend and ally', and a second visit a year later, with or without Ptolemy, to discuss the future of Egypt and Cyprus.[18]

The Egyptian royal party may well have been present to witness Caesar's dedication of a golden statue of Cleopatra in the Forum temple of Venus Genetrix (Venus the Mother). The story of this statue is recorded by Appian, who adds that it still stands in the temple as he writes in the second century AD. This superficially unlikely tale makes far more sense if we imagine Caesar dedicating a statue of the Egyptian goddess Isis to stand beside Venus. Within Egypt Cleopatra was strongly linked with Isis, who was in turn equated with the Greek Aphrodite and the Roman Venus, and she regularly dressed as the goddess. The dedication of a statue of Isis modelled on Cleopatra may not have been considered offensive to the people of Rome. The dedication of a statue of a living foreigner, on the other hand, would have caused huge public resentment. While it was acceptable, and even encouraged, for foreigners to recognise living Romans as divine beings, the Romans themselves did not worship living gods. Or did they? Caesar had always claimed descent from Venus, the divine mother of Aeneas. In 46 he had been publicly acknowledged as a demigod. In 45 his image was allowed to process with the images of the gods, and a temple statue was inscribed 'to the Invincible God'. There were sacrifices on his birthday, annual vows for his continuing good health, a new temple-style pediment fronting his house and a new title, 'Jupiter Julius'. It is quite clear that towards the end of his life Caesar, like Alexander the Great before him, was starting to investigate the intriguing question of his own divinity. At the same time, he was experimenting with the idea of kingship: his coy double refusal of a royal diadem tied with a laurel wreath, offered by Mark Antony during the February 44 Lupercalia (an ancient festival celebrated to purify the city of

Rome), had fooled no one. Diadems continued to appear on Caesar's statues, and Caesar himself continued to sit on a golden throne. Both aberrations were to be blamed fairly and squarely on the corrupting influence of the divine queen Cleopatra. Cicero's private letters suggest that Cleopatra was unpopular in Rome, although as he self-avowedly disliked the queen he cannot be considered a disinterested witness. Any unpopularity is unlikely to have arisen because Cleopatra tempted Caesar with sexual favours as, to a certain extent, it was expected that a great man would keep a suitably prestigious mistress. Cleopatra was unpopular because she was perceived as leading Caesar into dangerous Hellenistic ways. It was far easier to blame Cleopatra for Caesar's flirting with the trappings of royalty and divinity than it was to blame Caesar himself.

Caesar returned to Italy in the summer of 45, battle weary and suffering from worryingly frequent attacks of epilepsy. On 13 September, having bypassed Rome in favour of his private Lavicum estate (Monte Compatri, in Latium), he wrote a will which was to be lodged with the Vestal Virgins for safe-keeping. The will stipulated that a guardian was to be provided for any son and heir still to be born to him; an indication, perhaps, that Caesar and Calpurnia were still hoping to conceive a child together, or that Caesar was contemplating divorce and remarriage. Should he fail to father an heir, three-quarters of his estate was to pass to his great-nephew Gaius Octavius (Octavian), whom he adopted posthumously as his son. The remainder of his estate was to be shared between his nephew Quintus Pedius and his great-nephew Lucius Pinarius. His natural son Ptolemy Caesar was not mentioned. He could not have been. Roman law forbade bequests to foreigners.

A letter written by Cicero on 15 April 44 informs us that Cleopatra left Rome within a month of Caesar's assassination: 'I see nothing to object to in the flight of the queen.'[19] A letter written a few weeks later discusses the recent miscarriage suffered by Tertulla (Tertia), wife of

Cassius, before adding the cryptic comment, 'I am hoping that it is true about the queen and about that Caesar [Caesarion?] of hers.'[20] It seems that Cicero was hoping that Cleopatra, too, might miscarry. Freed from the constraints of a June 47 birth date for Caesarion, it is possible to use this letter to argue that Cleopatra's son was a posthumous child born soon after Caesar's death. But this interpretation would also suggest that Caesarion's conception occurred during Caesar's lengthy 46–5 Spanish campaign; Caesarion must therefore have been fathered by either Ptolemy XIV or someone else entirely.[21] The fact that contemporary Romans, who of course knew exactly when Caesarion was born, never mention a dating discrepancy when discussing Caesarion's paternity is a strong if indirect indication that Caesarion was not conceived in Caesar's absence. A far better interpretation of the letter is that Cicero is referring to a later pregnancy. If this is the case, we must assume that this second pregnancy ended in an early miscarriage as there is no record of a second child born to Cleopatra and Caesar.[22]

Cleopatra and her entourage returned to Alexandria. A papyrus dated to 26 July 44 confirms that Ptolemy XIV was still alive in July; he was, however, dead before the end of August. With no other heir to the throne, the three-year-old Caesarion became Ptolemy XV Theos Philopator Philometor (the Father-Loving, Mother-Loving God).

CHAPTER FIVE

The New Isis

*There existed at Armant till the year 1861 an extremely interest-
ing temple built by Cleopatra the Great in honour of the birth
of her son Caesarion. This was completely demolished between
the years 1861 and 1863 and the materials were taken and used
in the construction of a sugar factory; but prior to that date, it
had been visited and described by many travellers, and fortunately a number of drawings, plans and photographs of it were
taken by them. We are engaged upon a reconstruction of this
temple for publication and we should be very grateful for any
help which your readers may be able to give us, to make this as
complete as possible.*

Robert Mond and Oliver Myers, *Geographical Journal*[1]

Caesarion's birth was a triumph. It gave Cleopatra a new purpose
– the preservation of her throne for her child and his descendants – and, as both dynastic and Ptolemaic tradition allowed mothers
to rule on behalf of their infant sons, it freed her from the irksome
obligation to remain married to a male co-regent. It is perhaps no

coincidence that Ptolemy XIV died as soon as it became apparent that Caesarion's future lay in Egypt rather than in Rome, and Josephus, for one, has no doubt that the young king was murdered: 'She was also by nature very covetous, and stuck at no wickedness. She had already poisoned her brother, because she knew that he was to be king of Egypt, and this when he was but fifteen years old ...'[2]

Josephus, consistently anti-Cleopatra and prone to sweeping statements, offers no proof in support of his allegation. But, biased though they are, his remarks do carry a certain ring of truth. It is tempting to develop a dramatic reconstruction – the young and inexperienced Ptolemy left behind in Alexandria while his sister makes a second diplomatic trip to Rome; Ptolemy discovering that, with Caesar dead, the people were prepared to support his solo rule; Ptolemy considering marriage with the deposed and still-popular Arsinoë IV; Ptolemy succumbing to temptation and declaring himself king; Cleopatra returning sooner than expected and dealing swiftly with the crisis. However, it is important to remember that the estimated average life expectancy for men who survived infancy in Ptolemaic Egypt was only thirty-three. To die at just fifteen years of age was sad, but it was by no means unusual.

Ptolemy XV Caesar, king of Egypt, was to play a major part in his mother's propaganda. With a son by her side, Cleopatra VII could abandon any thought she might have had of adopting the role of a female king and could develop instead a powerful new identity as a semi-divine mother: an identity that had the huge advantage of being instantly recognisable to both her Egyptian and her Greek subjects. Divinity was nothing new. Cleopatra had become a goddess towards the end of her father's reign, when she had been united with her brothers and sister as the New Sibling-Loving Gods. But now she was to be specifically identified with Egypt's most famous single mother, the goddess Isis.

From the very dawn of the dynastic age, religion had been used to protect the position of the royal family. The belief in the king's ability to ward off *isfet* (chaos) by maintaining *maat* (an untranslatable concept which is best understood as a combination of 'rightness', justice, truth and the status quo) ensured that, although individual kings were occasionally removed from power, there was never any real attempt to abolish the monarchy. This overwhelming need to preserve *maat* encouraged a slow, conservative approach to life. Experimentation was seen as dangerous and unnecessary – it might upset the gods and bring chaos – and it was both safer and more comforting to stick to the tried and tested ways. This conservatism is particularly obvious in official art, which, to the non-specialist, shows surprisingly little development from the beginning of the Old Kingdom until the end of the Ptolemaic age.

Maat the concept was personified in the form of Maat the goddess, the beautiful, truthful daughter of the sun god Re. Many dynastic scenes show kings standing with Maat, or offering a miniature squatting image of Maat to much larger gods. As both Maat and the queen consort were companions of the king, it was perhaps inevitable that their roles and appearances would become confused. Only the single feather of truth worn on her head distinguished Maat from the living queen. Official Egyptian art was never spontaneous, and this confusion was far from accidental. As the dynastic age progressed, Egypt's queens developed a high public profile, an array of secular and religious titles, and a wide range of headdresses incorporating divine symbols such as the vulture crown, the double or multiple uraeus, the cow horns of Hathor, the solar disc associated with the sun gods and the tall, twin plumes associated with the gods Amen, Montu and Min. With both Hathor and Isis sporting near-identical headdresses, the blurring of the boundary between the mortal and the immortal intensified.

While the Egyptians compared their queens to goddesses, many early Egyptologists saw them as breeding machines and little else. An increasing awareness of the complexities of Egyptian thought over the past century has confirmed that the consort was in fact an essential feminine part of the complex theology of kingship.[3] Yes, the consort was expected to produce a son and heir, but this was by no means essential. If necessary, an heir could be found in the harem, or could be adopted from an elite family. It was far more important that the consort be politically astute and theologically acceptable. She was expected to rule the country in her husband's absence, and to participate in religious rituals that demanded a female celebrant. She might even, in the absence of an heir, be expected to rule Egypt as a female king. As the spouse of a semi-divine being, and the potential mother of a demigod, the dynastic consort was herself considered a source of religious and political power.

Egypt's first 'goddesses' appear before her first kings and queens. Prehistoric cemeteries have yielded bone and ivory female figurines whose obvious pubic regions and breasts indicate that they are to be associated with sexuality, fertility and, perhaps, rebirth. Near-contemporary pottery is decorated with scenes of daily life and life beyond death. Water and boats feature prominently: there are animals, birds, men and boats sailing on rivers of wavy lines. Occasionally in these scenes we see a plump, obviously female figure accompanied by smaller-scale men. This woman is paralleled by small terracotta female figurines that, with simple, bird-like faces but well-defined breasts and hips, perform a strange dance with their arms curved above their heads. The faceless females belong to an age before writing. We cannot name them, but it seems that we are looking at Egypt's original mother goddesses.

By 3100 we have both a royal name and a recognisable goddess. The Narmer Palette is a large slate votive palette recording the victories of a king whose two-symbol name is represented by the hieroglyphic signs of the catfish and the chisel: *N'r Mr*.[4] The palette displays scenes of royal dominance and celebrates the triumph of order over chaos. On one face Narmer, wearing the white crown of southern Egypt, raises a club to smite an enemy who cringes at his feet. On the reverse Narmer, now wearing the red crown, marches with a troop of soldiers. Before him lie five decapitated victims of war, their heads placed neatly between their legs. Below, in a separate scene, Narmer takes the form of a bull to gore an enemy. Gazing down on both sides of the palette is the face of the cow goddess Bat, an ancient version of the mother goddess Hathor.

Egypt's gods started life as independent totemic local deities. Soon they were linked by an intricate mythology designed to explain the otherwise inexplicable: matters that today we explain by science. To address the fundamental need for understanding, to explain creation and death, each priesthood devised a mythology featuring their own particular god. Hathor, Lady of Perfume, was celebrated as the daughter of the sun god Re; an uninhibited goddess of motherhood, music, love and drunkenness. In some tales she assumed the role of the Golden One to accompany Re on his daily journey across the sky. In others she was the gentle cow who suckled the king of Egypt. At Memphis she was the Mistress of the Sycamore, who sustained the dead with food and drink; at Thebes she became the compassionate Mistress of the West, who cared for the dying sun. But when she was roused, mild-mannered Hathor transformed into Sekhmet, the Powerful One. Sekhmet, an uncompromising lion-headed goddess who breathed fire and was armed with plagues and pestilence, was the protector of Egypt's kings. From the reign of Narmer onwards, the cult of Hathor grew in importance until it became Egypt's dominant female-based cult.

Isis, several centuries younger than Hathor, is first named as a protective goddess, 'the Great Isis', in the 5th Dynasty Pyramid texts, where she appears as one of the nine original gods (the Ennead) of Heliopolis. Her name, Aset in the original Egyptian, is represented by the sign of a throne, and Isis herself often appears with a small throne sign topping her crown. Alternatively Isis could be identified with the cobra or uraeus worn on the royal brow. This obvious connection between the goddess and kingship, both living and dead, would persist as long as the cult of Isis survived. As the dynastic age progressed, Isis grew in status and power, absorbing the roles, traditions and accessories of other Egyptian goddesses, including the once-dominant Hathor, so that by the start of the Ptolemaic age Hathor and Isis were virtually indistinguishable in appearance. Both were beautiful women who wore the tall cow horn and solar disc headdress, and both carried the sistrum or sacred rattle whose rhythms could stimulate the gods.

Outside Egypt the cult of Isis was spread by the sailors, merchants and travellers who regularly sailed around the eastern Mediterranean, using the Greek island of Delos, home to a flourishing cult of Isis, as a trading post. Herodotus, writing in c. 450, was tolerably familiar with the goddess:

> *All Egyptians use bulls and bull-calves for sacrifice, if they have passed the test for 'cleanness'; but they are forbidden to sacrifice heifers, on the ground that they are sacred to Isis. The statue of Isis shows a female figure with cow's horns, like the Greek representations of Io ...*[5]

Just as she had absorbed Hathor, Isis gradually assimilated the attributes and appearance of several Greek goddesses. The earth mother Demeter, the wise Athene, the sister-consort Hera, the virgin huntress Artemis and, most particularly, the beautiful and loving Aphrodite all donated aspects of their mythology, allowing Isis to develop into a versatile, powerful, universal goddess with an appeal strong enough to make her, in the first century AD, a serious rival to the growing cult of Christianity.[6] The first apparent reference to a cult of Isis in mainland Greece comes from Piraeus, the port of Athens, and pre-dates Alexander's arrival in Egypt. The next, more firmly established reference dates to the second century BC. In Rome, the first temple to Isis was raised on the Capitoline Hill in *c.* 80. It was destroyed almost immediately, then quickly replaced. Successive temples were destroyed (and subsequently rebuilt) in 58, 53, 50 and 48 and in AD 19. Meanwhile, the official Roman attitude to Isis was both cautious and inconsistent. Julius Caesar refused the priesthood of Isis permission to enter Rome, yet the triumvirate permitted a sanctuary dedicated to the gods of Egypt, Isis included, in 43.

This Graeco-Roman Isis was a healer, a wise woman and a powerful magician. She could cause the River Nile to flood and, undying herself, could bring the dead back to life. She was both the queen of heaven and the fertile soil of Egypt. In the dark night sky she twinkled as the bright star Sothis (Sirius or Sepedet). In Alexandria Isis Pelagia (Isis of the Sea) protected the sailors entering and leaving the safety of the harbour; outside the city, Isis Medica cured the sick in her temple-hospitals. But Isis's most celebrated role was that of the faithful wife and compassionate mother. The elaborate story of Isis, her husband-brother Osiris and their son Horus is one of Egypt's most ancient and intricate myths, but no original version survives. To read the story – and we always have to remember that this is just one, late, version of an often repeated tale – we have to turn to Plutarch's masterpiece, *Of Isis and Osiris*. Plutarch based his interpretation on stories preserved in the oral tradition, and on fragments of original Egyptian myths preserved in the writings of earlier classical writers. He dedicated it to Clea, a priestess in the cult of Isis at Delphi:

> *Many years ago the sky goddess Nut bore two sons, Osiris and Seth, and two daughters, Isis and Nephthys. Osiris was good and true but Seth was troubled and angry, and his birth caused Nut great pain as he forced his way into the world through her side. Osiris ruled Egypt as king with his sister-wife Isis. Osiris taught men how to plant crops, obey laws and worship the gods, while Isis taught women the secrets*

of weaving, baking and brewing. With Egypt at peace, Isis ruled Egypt alone as Osiris travelled the world, beguiling the people with his songs and his poetry.

Seth was unhappy. His heart was consumed with jealousy and he had determined that his brother must die so that he might take his place. He planned a magnificent banquet. The food stands were piled high with meat. There was every kind of fowl and fish, pyramids of bread and sweet cakes, heaps of fresh vegetables and succulent fruit, and jars of fine wine and strong beer. Seth had invited seventy-two friends to his banquet, but the guest of honour was his brother Osiris. The guests drank and ate and drank again. Finally, Seth signalled to his servants and a long, narrow chest was carried into the banqueting chamber. Carved from the finest wood, the chest was inlayed with bands of gold and silver and decorated inside and out with ebony, ivory and precious stone. Here was a new game. Whoever could fit inside the chest could keep it. The guests rushed forward and attempted to squeeze into the narrow space. But none fitted. Then the slender Osiris stepped forward to take his turn. He lay down in the chest: it was a perfect fit. Instantly, Seth slammed the lid shut and shot the bolt home. The chest had become Osiris's coffin. Seth dragged the chest to the mouth of the Nile and threw it in.

News of the tragedy reached Isis in her palace at Koptos. Refusing to forget Osiris, Isis spent many years wandering the length and breadth of Egypt hoping to find news of her vanished husband. Eventually she heard a rumour that the chest had washed ashore in the faraway land of Byblos. Here it had lain against a young cypress tree, which had grown to envelop the chest so that Osiris became completely hidden within its trunk. The tree had been felled and had been used to hold up the roof in the great pillared hall of the palace of the king of Byblos.

Isis left Egypt to become nursemaid to the younger son of the queen of Byblos. At night, when no one could see, she set the baby at the centre of a ring of immortal fire so that he might gain eternal life. She turned herself into a bird to fly round the pillar that still held

Osiris. And as she flew, she gave great cries of grief. Her cries woke the queen, who rushed to the hall. Seeing her child in the flames, the queen gave a scream of horror. This broke the spell. Isis regained human form and, taking the pillar from beneath the roof, cut into its wood to reveal the coffin. The discarded remains of the pillar would be venerated for ever in the temple of Isis at Byblos.

Isis took the coffin and set sail for Egypt so that she might bury Osiris in his own land. But Seth, hunting in the moonlight, stumbled across Osiris lying in his coffin in the Egyptian desert. Furious, he hacked his brother into pieces, which he flung far and wide. Isis and the jackal-headed god Anubis searched high and low, recovering the scattered parts until only the penis was missing. This would never be found, for the greedy Nile fish had eaten it.

Isis, the divine healer, equipped her husband with a replica penis, bandaged him, then sang the spell that would bring him back to a semblance of life. Transforming herself into a bird, she hovered over her husband's restored body, flapped her wings and breathed air into his nose. Her magic was very powerful; nine months later she bore Osiris a son. As Osiris retreated to the afterlife to become king of the dead, Isis fled with the baby Horus to the papyrus marshes. Here she protected her son with her potent magic until he was old enough to challenge his uncle and claim his inheritance.[7]

The Isis of this tale is the ideal wife for any man, be he king or commoner, and she is the ideal role model for any queen. She is beautiful, wise, faithful and fertile. While things go according to plan, she remains modestly in the background, supporting her husband and attending to the domestic tasks that are traditionally the wife's lot. When her husband dies, she grieves for him. But we should not underestimate her. Isis is cunning and well versed in magic, and she is quite capable of independent action should the need arise. It is she who poses the greatest threat to Seth's ambition. Her healing powers, in particular, are unsurpassed, magic being an important aspect of the

Egyptian healer's training. While Osiris takes a sabbatical to travel the world it is Isis, and not Seth, who is left to rule in his absence; the tradition of the wife deputising for the husband is a well-documented one, and we have examples of women from all walks of life directing their absent husbands' affairs. When Osiris departs to the land of the dead, it is Isis who rules on her infant son's behalf.

Osiris quickly came to symbolise all of Egypt's dead pharaohs. They, mummified like their new sovereign, became eternal kings in the shadowy afterlife, while their successors, the Horus kings, ruled the living Egypt. And, as Isis was the mother and protector of Horus the living king, she naturally became the mother of all of Egypt's living kings. Two- and three-dimensional images of Horus sitting on his mother's knee may therefore be 'read' as images of the living king sitting on his throne, while images of Isis suckling Horus (or his late variant Harpocrates) may be read as images of any and all Egyptian queens suckling their sons. Conversely, any image of an Egyptian queen with her son may be interpreted as an image of Isis with Horus. Soon after Caesarion's birth, mother and son were featured on the bronze Cypriot coin already mentioned (page 61). The obverse of this coin shows Cleopatra carrying a sceptre and wearing the raised diadem known as a *stephane*, a Hellenistic symbol of divinity. Caesarion is an indistinct, featureless blob at his mother's breast. This is not Cleopatra the queen, but Cleopatra the mother goddess Isis/Aphrodite, suckling the infant Horus/Eros. The reverse of the coin features the double cornucopia, symbol of never-ending fertility, and the legend 'of Cleopatra the Queen' (*Kleopatras Basilisses*).

No equivalent Egyptian coin was issued, but reliefs carved in the Armant birth house associate Cleopatra with Rat-tawi (Female Sun of the Two Lands; a late form of Hathor) and Caesarion with the infant Harpre-pekhrat (Horus the Sun, the Child; a late version of Horus/ Harpocrates). We have already noted Cleopatra's presence, either in body or in spirit, at the installation of the Buchis bull of Armant. Now we find her building a birth house (*mammisi*) within the precincts of the Armant Montu temple. Cleopatra's birth house was a temple dedicated to the celebration of Harpre's nativity, a birth which native theology linked both to the daily rebirth of the sun and to the cyclical renewal of kingship. During Ptolemaic times birth houses took the form of a small chapel with an antechamber and a flat roof that could be used for ritual purposes, surrounded by a columned walkway. At Armant the central chapel included an outer hall, an inner hall and a birth room.

An inscription on the Armant birth-house wall provided Cleopatra with an Egyptian-style titulary, including a cartouche (the oval loop enclosing royal names) and a female Horus name (the first part of the traditional king's titulary) which classifies her as a female king: 'the female Horus, the great one, mistress of perfection, brilliant in counsel, Mistress of the Two Lands, Cleopatra Philopator'. Ptolemaic kings bore five formal names or titularies, based on the traditional New Kingdom model (Horus name; Two Ladies name; Golden Horus name; prenomen; nomen) plus a sixth name, a translation of the king's Greek epithet. The last traditional name, the nomen, was the king's personal name, introduced by the phrase 'Son of Re'. The penultimate name, the prenomen, was the name by which his subjects knew him. Both the nomen and the prenomen were written within a cartouche. All five names were used on formal occasions, but when a shorter name was required it was acceptable to use just the nomen and prenomen. By the Ptolemaic period this custom had undergone a slight change and the nomen alone sufficed. This was preceded, not by 'Son of Re' but by 'pharaoh', literally 'Great House'.[8]

A cartoon-like series of drawings decorating the inner walls of the Armant birth house showed the birth of Harpre in the presence of divine midwives, the goddess Nekhbet, the god Amen-Re and Cleopatra. The mother of the child is clearly identified as Rat-tawi, but his father is not obvious. Given the situation of the birth house, he should

Scenes from the sanctuary of the now-demolished Armant temple, recorded by Lepsius (Denkmäler IV, 60a and 59b). Above: the divine mother gives birth to 'Horus the sun, the child' in the presence of Amen-Re, Nekhbet and Cleopatra VII. Below: multiple versions of the goddess Hathor suckle a newborn king: the young god of the temple, or the infant Caesarion? The confusion is deliberate.

be Montu, but the preserved hieroglyph appears to be that of Amen (divine father of, among others, the earthly kings Hatshepsut, Amenhotep III, Ramesses II the Great and Alexander the Great). Nearby, seated on a couch, two identical cow-headed goddesses each suckle a baby. These identical infants have been identified as Harpre and Caesarion, whose cartouche appears throughout the birth house. In an age eagerly anticipating the arrival of a saviour on earth, Caesarion has clearly been born a god. An educated Egyptian 'reading' the scene might also understand that Caesarion, like Horus before him, is a god destined to avenge his assassinated father. Unfortunately the Armant temple was substantially dismantled during the reign of the emperor Antoninus Pius, when its stone was reused in a monumental arch. Later, blocks from the temple would be incorporated into a church and a sugar-cane factory. Cleopatra's images are fortunately preserved in the form of line drawings made by Napoleon's scholars following his invasion of Egypt, and by the pioneering nineteenth-century Egyptologist Karl Richard Lepsius.

The 30th Dynasty temple of Hathor at Dendera had been substantially redesigned by Auletes, who started building works on 16 July 54 and died just four years into the programme. Work at the temple continued throughout Cleopatra's reign and was eventually finished a decade after her death. Here, on the outer rear wall of the temple, we find the above life-size double scene of Cleopatra and Caesarion mentioned in Chapter 2 (page 65). Mother and son are offering to a line of gods. In the left-hand scene they offer to Osiris, his sister-wife Isis and their son Harsiesis; in the right-hand scene they offer to Hathor, her son Ihy/Harsomtus and the Osirian triad (Osiris, Isis and Horus). Hathor, in this context, may be read as a representative of female royal power and solar authority, while Isis represents the universal mother. Between the two lines of gods, in the middle of the wall, is the head of Hathor, the main goddess of the temple complex.

Ptolemy Caesar, as king, takes the dominant role in the offering scene, a role which Cleopatra has previously denied both Ptolemy XIII and Ptolemy XIV and which she reverses in the accompanying text, where she is mentioned before Caesarion. The texts, we may assume, follow actual practice, while the illustration follows the time-honoured Egyptian tradition that will always place a ruling king ahead of his supportive mother. Nevertheless, tradition or not, it seems reasonable to assume that Cleopatra approved the temple artwork. Dressed in a long kilt and double crown plus ram's horns, Caesarion stands in front of his mother to make an offering of incense to the gods. Above Caesarion hover the protective deities Horus (left-hand scene) and the vulture goddess Nekhbet (right); immediately behind him stands a tiny male figure, his *ka* or spirit. Standing behind her son's *ka*, Cleopatra wears a tight sheath dress, tripartite wig and a *modius* with multiple uraei, solar disc, cow horns and double plumes. She carries a sistrum and the stylised necklace known as the *menyt* which is associated with Hathor, and she does not have a *ka* figure. Work on this entirely Egyptian scene started in 30, the year that both Cleopatra and Caesarion died, and was continued under Octavian. The message is not a subtle one. Hathor the mother goddess of the Dendera temple is a single parent: the partner of Horus, who lives in his own temple many miles away at Edfu (Greek Apollinopolis Magna). Each year, at the Festival of the Beautiful Union, the cult statue of Hathor would process to the river and sail to Edfu. Here she would reside in the temple with the father of her child for fourteen days, before returning by river to Dendera. Parallels between the earthly triad of Cleopatra, Caesarion and the absent Caesar, and the divine triad of Horus, Hathor and Ihy/Harsomtus are clear. Meanwhile, at Edfu, scenes carved into the temple walls, and the annual celebration of the victory of Horus over his father's killer Seth, served to hammer home the message of the avenging royal son.

The Dendera Cleopatra is a deliberate mixture of queen, mother and goddess. In 1873 the novelist and journalist Amelia B. Edwards hired the *Philae* – a large flat-bottomed *dahabeeya* boat – and embarked upon a lengthy, leisurely cruise along the River Nile. Four years later she published an eminently readable account of her travels.[9] Visiting Dendera, she despaired at the damage wrought by the early Christians, who had hacked away at the stonework in an attempt to erase all trace of the temple's pagan gods:

> *…one can easily imagine how these spoilers sacked and ravaged all before them; how they desecrated the sacred places, and cast down the statues of the goddess … Among those which escaped, however, is the*

> *famous external bas-relief of Cleopatra on the back of the Temple. This curious sculpture is now banked up with rubbish for its better preservation, and can no longer be seen by travellers. It was however, admirably photographed some years ago by Signor Beati; which photograph is faithfully reproduced in the annexed engraving. Cleopatra is here represented with a headdress comprising the attributes of three goddesses; namely the vulture of Maut [Mut] (the head of which is modelled in a masterly way), the horned disk of Hathor, and the throne of Isis … It is difficult to know where the decorative sculpture ends and portraiture begins in a work of this epoch. We cannot even be certain that a portrait was intended; though the introduction of the royal oval in which the name of Cleopatra (Klaupatra) is spelt with its vowel sounds in full, would seem to point that way …*

There was a good reason why Miss Edwards could not see the famous

Cleopatra portrait *in situ*. It did not exist. The 'queen' beneath the complicated crown (a vulture headdress topped by a *modius* crown with multiple uraei, a solar disc, cow horns and the 'throne' symbol of Isis) was actually the goddess Isis herself. The Cleopatra cartouche was a modern enhancement, added to a plaster cast of the original scene by an enterprising curator at Cairo Museum.[10] Unfortunately, Miss Edwards had allowed her assumed knowledge to influence her perceptions:

> *Mannerisms apart, however, the face wants for neither individuality nor beauty. Cover the mouth and you have an almost faultless profile. The chin and the throat are also quite lovely; while the whole face, suggestive of cruelty, subtlety and voluptuousness, carries with it an indefinable impression not only of portraiture, but of likeness.*

A good description of Cleopatra perhaps, but less appropriate for the healing mother goddess Isis.

The classical authors are agreed that Cleopatra occasionally dressed in the ceremonial robes of Isis. Quite what these robes might have been is not made clear. The traditional Egyptian Isis, as seen at Dendera, wore a simple white linen sheath dress, an assortment of jewellery, a heavy tripartite wig and either her 'throne' sign or the vulture headdress, *modius*, double plumes, cow horns and solar disc borrowed from Hathor. This image may be compared with a marble statue recovered from Alexandria and dated to the mid-second century AD (and now in the Graeco-Roman Museum, Alexandria) which shows a Hellenic Isis wearing a wig of corkscrew curls, a crown composed of a solar disc, cow horns and double plumes, and a flowing woollen chiton or robe covered with a rectangular mantle or shawl tied with a distinctive knot which, as a symbol of magical power, had come to symbolise the goddess. A colourful Graeco-Roman Isis is described in *The Golden Ass*, written by Lucius Apuleius in *c.* AD 155.

Here, in Adlington's 1566 translation, Isis, Queen of Heaven, appears to Lucius in a dream:

> *I purpose to describe her divine semblance, if the poverty of my humane speech will suffer me, or her divine power give me eloquence thereto. First shee had a great abundance of haire, dispersed and scattered about her neck, on the crowne of her head she bare many garlands enterlaced with floures, in the middle of her forehead was a compasse in fashion of a glasse, or resembling the light of the Moone, in one of her hands she bare serpents, in the other, blades of corne, her vestiment was of fine silke yeelding divers colours, sometime yellow, sometime rosie, sometime flamy, and sometime (which troubled my spirit sore) darke and obscure, covered with a blacke robe in manner of a shield, and pleated in most subtill fashion at the skirts of her garments, the welts appeared comely, whereas here and there the starres glimpsed, and in the middle of them was placed the Moone, which shone like a flame of fire, round about the robe was a coronet or garland made with flowers and fruits. In her right hand shee had a timbrell of brasse, which gave a pleasant sound, in her left hand shee bare a cup of gold, out of the mouth whereof the serpent Aspis lifted up his head, with a swelling throat, her odoriferous feete were covered with shoes interlaced and wrought with victorious palme.*[11]

Robert Graves's 1950 more down-to-earth translation of this same text clarifies the description to a moon-disc crown held in place by twin snakes (evolved cow horns?), and a multicoloured robe with an embroidered hem of fruit and flowers covered with a pleated black mantle tied in an Isis knot. Plutarch confirms this: 'the robes of Isis are variegated in their colours, for her power is concerned with matter which becomes everything and receives everything, light and darkness, day and night, fire and water, life and death.'[12] Faced with a choice of two very different costumes, it seems likely, then, that

Cleopatra would choose the dress, either Greek or Hellenistic, which would best suit her intended audience.

The Ptolemies never neglected Egypt's traditional temples. Their support for the native priesthood ensured that the elite Egyptians were in turn able to support the artists and craftsmen who preserved Egypt's cultural heritage. Kings continued to maintain and restore the cult temples of the state gods, while the elite used their wealth to build stone tombs and commission statues and stelae just as their predecessors had always done, but everything now had a distinct Hellenistic twist. The walls of the elite tombs show Greek-inspired figures participating in traditional Egyptian scenes and accompanied by hieroglyphic texts. The temples which the Ptolemies raised, rebuilt or substantially enhanced at Philae (Ptolemies II and VIII), Edfu (Ptolemies III, VIII and XII) and Dendera (Ptolemy XII) were based on ancient beliefs and designs, yet are instantly recognisable today, even to the non-expert, as Ptolemaic. Their walls are decorated with an increasing amount of hieroglyphic text, almost as if the priests realised the need to preserve their heritage in stone. It is ironic that these, Egypt's atypical but best-surviving temples, heavily influenced by contemporary Hellenistic architectural thought, have to be used to reconstruct the rituals con-ducted in Egypt's 'purer' and now vanished dynastic temples.

Their obvious interest in the native gods earned the Ptolemies valuable propaganda points and encouraged national stability. Thebes was far less likely to rebel if the influential priests were happy with their lot. But this was not necessarily their primary consideration. The Ptolemies ran Egypt outside Alexandria as a profitable business and their decision to invest in the temples was a part of their wider decision to keep the traditional bureaucracy functioning. For many centuries the cult temples of the state gods had played an important role in Egypt's redistributive economy. The system was a simple but effective one. The crown both generated its own income (farming its own lands, operating mines, quarries and workshops, etc.) and collected taxes and rents in both coin and kind. This income was used to pay the crown's expenses, and any surpluses were stored in the large warehouses within the local palace complexes, where they offered a shield against future bad harvests. Part of the royal income was used to provide offerings to the local temples. Here the god, in the form of a statue, lived in the sanctuary. He was served by priests who cared for him as they might care for a child: he was roused in the mornings, washed, dressed, fed, entertained, fed again and put to bed at night.

The temple, the house of the god, was the one place where the mortal could communicate with the divine, but this communication could be achieved only via the king and his deputies. It was, in theory, the king and the king alone who supplied the god with regular offerings of food, drink, clothing, incense and recitations. The god was capable of accepting or rejecting these offerings, but he could not physically consume anything. His leavings were therefore redistributed among the temple staff (essentially, they paid the temple staff), with any surpluses being stored in the temple warehouses, which also housed the revenue from the temple's assets. These assets, for a prosperous temple, might include land, peasants, mines, workshops and ships which, distributed throughout Egypt, were either owned outright or leased from the crown. The temple priests administered and accounted for these assets and the gods paid tax on their income and duty on the goods that they manufactured in their workshops. An investment in Egypt's temples was therefore a thinly disguised investment in the Egyptian economy and it comes as little surprise to find Ptolemies VIII and XII, kings whose reigns were characterised by uncertainty and civil unrest, donating generously to the traditional gods. Cleopatra lacked the time and resources to be the great temple builder that her father had been. However, as well as completing her father's work at Edfu and Dendera, she built the now-demolished birth house in the Armant temple of Montu, and the barque or boat shrine of Geb at Koptos. She also, as we noted in Chapter 2 (pages 42–3), showed an interest in Egypt's bull cults.

The dynastic Egyptians had embalmed a wide range of animals (including fish, mice, snakes, crocodiles and bulls) prior to burial in dedicated animal cemeteries. However, during the Late and Graeco-Roman periods, at a time when the traditional Egyptian culture was threatened by foreign influences, interest in the animal cults blossomed. Diodorus Siculus tells the story of one Roman unfortunate, lynched for inadvertently offending against Graeco-Egyptian superstition:

> ... Once, at the time when Ptolemy [XII] their king had not yet been given by the Romans the appellation of 'friend' and the people were exercising all zeal in courting the favour of the embassy from Italy which was then visiting Egypt and, in their fear, were intent on giving no cause for complaint or war, when one of the Romans killed a cat and the multitude rushed in a crowd to his house, neither the officials sent by the king to beg the men off nor the fear of Rome which all the people felt were enough to save the man from punishment, even though his act had been an accident. And this incident we relate, not from hearsay, but we saw it with our own eyes on the occasion of the visit we made to Egypt.[13]

Greeks and the Romans, misreading the situation, dismissed the animal cults as a primitive form of animal worship. The theology was, as we might expect, far more complicated. The 'animal' aspect of a god represented his or her essential nature expressed in easily recognisable terms. To show Hathor as a cow stressed her placid, nurturing nature; it did not mean that Hathor was to be imagined looking or behaving exactly like a cow, and nor did it mean that each and every cow was to be equated with Hathor. Most of Egypt's deities could be depicted in several equally valid ways, and in many cases a god's appearance was dependent upon context. Thoth, the scribe of the gods, for example, could appear as either a baboon or an ibis, while Amen of Thebes, who normally appeared in human form, could also be represented by the goose or the ram. Hathor could appear either as a beautiful woman or as a cow. If she was required to participate in a set-piece scene, to sit on a throne to receive an offering, or to rattle a *sistrum*, she had to have the conventional female body that would allow her to perform these actions – but there was no reason why that human body could not be topped by a cow's head complete with horns and a crown. Realism was never an issue: in all their work, Egypt's artists set out to convey the essence of their subjects and, in a land where words were pictures and pictures were words, the image of a cow-headed woman told its own story.

It was perhaps inevitable that animals specifically linked to gods would become imbued with an aura of divinity. Initially only a few animals from each species were singled out. While some temple geese may have symbolised Amen within the precincts of the Karnak temple, for example, most dynastic geese were bred as food. Gradually, however, the idea developed that any animal from a 'sacred' class might have its own divine attributes, and Egypt's temples came to resemble informal zoos. The temple of Thoth at Hermopolis Magna became a sacred safari park, with hundreds of baboons and thousands of ibises wandering around, while the Bubastis temple of Bast was soon overrun with cats. At death these temple animals were mummified, packed into miniature coffins or purpose-made pots, and interred in their thousands in galleries in the nearby desert cemeteries.

The Apis bull, the living embodiment of the Memphite creator god Ptah, had been revered from the beginning of the dynastic age, but little is known of his cult before the New Kingdom, when the 19th Dynasty Khaemwaset, priestly son of Ramesses II, constructed the 'lesser vaults', an underground gallery to house the Apis burials in the Sakkara cemetery. The cult grew in popularity until, by the Ptolemaic period, it had assumed a huge significance. By now the bulls were being buried in enormous stone sarcophagi in the 'greater vaults', the focus of modern tourist visits to the Memphite Serapeum. At a time when standards of human mummification were declining, increasing attention was being paid to the mummification of sacred animals, and the dead Apis underwent a sixty-eight-day stay in an embalming house in the precincts of the Ptah temple, followed by a series of elaborate rituals (including a journey to the sacred temple lake and a visit to the tent of purification, where the opening of the mouth ceremony was performed) leading to the funeral on the seventieth day. The Ptolemies made a financial contribution to these expensive ceremonies, with Cleopatra donating 412 silver coins plus food and oil at the death of the Apis, son of the cow Ta-nt Bastet.

The Memphite Serapeum lies in the sacred animal cemetery in the Sakkara necropolis, to the north-west of the step pyramid built by the 3rd Dynasty king Djoser. This is a complicated site incorporating a ruined Ptolemaic temple complex, a sphinx-lined processional avenue, a temple built by the Late Period king Nectanebo, and a series of sacred-animal catacombs and cemeteries including the galleries dedicated to the Apis bulls. The Isis cows, the mothers of the Apis bulls, had their own cemetery nearby, with the last cow being interred during Cleopatra's Year 11. Further catacombs were dedicated to ibis, baboon and falcon burials, while the neighbouring Anubeion (dedicated to the jackal-headed god of mummification, Anubis) and Bubasteion (dedicated to the cat goddess Bast) housed dog and cat burials. The scale of these animal interments is extraordinary: excavations at Sakkara have so far yielded an estimated four million ibis mummies and 500,000 hawks, plus many domestic artefacts and papyri which make it clear that the Ptolemaic Serapeum was a living community with accommodation for priests and lay workers, a palace for the frequent royal visits, and a library and archive second only to the Great Library of Alexandria.

A curious Ptolemaic construction, the *exedra,* built along the processional avenue of the sphinxes close by the Serapeum entrance, has yielded a semicircular podium displaying seated statues of the more important Greek philosophers and poets. The statues are unlabelled and in a poor state of preservation, but various experts have identified Homer, Hesiod, Plato, Xenophon and Aristotle among the figures. Nearby, lining the avenue, is a collection of statues and reliefs connected with the cult of Dionysos: the young Dionysos riding various wild animals; peacocks bearing grapes; mythological creatures including female sphinxes and sirens. The age of the *exedra* is uncertain, with some scholars dating it as early as the reign of Ptolemy I, others as late as the reign of Ptolemy XII. Its purpose is equally obscure, although there has been some speculation that the Greek sages and Dionysiac beasts may have been charged with guarding the entrance to the original Egyptian burial place of Alexander the Great.

Parallel to the native temples and the animal cults were the Hellenistic temples and the new royal cults, which were primarily designed to appeal to Egypt's Greeks. The Ptolemaic interest in royal divinity was by no means a new phenomenon. Egypt's living kings had long been recognised as mortals transformed by the powerful coronation rituals into demigods. At death, mummification made them fully divine. Rising into the heavens, they would twinkle as undying stars in the velvet night sky, sail across the heavens in the flaming sun-boat of Re, or descend to the underworld to rule at one with the king of the afterlife, Osiris. Egypt's last native king, Nectanebo II, had been profoundly interested in his own divinity. But he lived in difficult times, his throne constantly under threat from the Persians. He set out to prove his piety by building and restoring the cult temples of the state gods; this was a traditional and very obvious means of bringing *maat* to chaos, establishing links with Egypt's glorious past, raising finances and boosting national morale.[14] Within the temples Nectanebo placed royal statues which had their own priesthoods and were financed by their own endowments. For the first time, it seems, Egypt's kings were considered worthy of sharing the houses of the gods. Nectanebo simultaneously emphasised his own role as the one true pharaoh by promoting the image of Nectanebo the Falcon: a direct reference to the falcon god Horus, who represented all of Egypt's living kings. Following the 343 Persian invasion led by Artaxerxes III, Nectanebo fled Egypt, probably heading south, to Nubia. He left behind the impression of a mysterious, semi-legendary figure whose mythology grew with time. Nectanebo appears in *The Alexander Romance* as a wily magician who befriends Olympias of Macedonia. Aware of the queen's penchant for snakes, Nectanebo turns himself into a serpent, sleeps with the queen and fathers Alexander the Great. Thus Alexander, son of Nectanebo, was justified in claiming the throne of Egypt.

Alexander appreciated the importance of Egypt's gods and the priests who served them. *The Alexander Romance* tells us that Alexander chose to be crowned King of Upper and Lower Egypt by Egyptian priests in the temple of the creator god Ptah of Memphis. This – if true – was a wise move. His conspicuous coronation, an abbreviated version of the traditional Egyptian ceremony, made clear Alexander's acceptance of the time-honoured rituals and responsibilities of Egyptian kingship while demonstrating the priesthood's acceptance of Alexander as king. Lest there be any doubt over his sincerity, the new king selected a throne name, Meryamen Setepenre (Beloved of Amen, Chosen of Re), that confirmed his commitment to the Egyptian pantheon. Impressive, and very public, sacrifices in the temples of Memphis and nearby Heliopolis followed. Traditional Greek-style games were held at Memphis, while, 400 miles upriver, the walls of the splendid new barque shrine in the Luxor temple were carved with images of Alexander offering to the gods of his new land. Shown in profile, shaven-headed, bare-chested and dressed in a kilt and crown, the Greek Alexander was indistinguishable from all the pharaohs who had gone before.

Alexander counted Zeus among his remote ancestors, and his

mother had for many years dropped strong hints that her son was no ordinary boy. Traditional Greek theology, however, did not accept that a living person could be divine. Now, following his Egyptian coronation, Alexander was officially semi-divine in Egypt, where he was recognised as the son of Amen-Re, father of all of Egypt's kings. But to be half divine was not enough. Soon after his coronation ceremony Alexander made a 300-mile trek across the Libyan Desert to consult the oracle of Zeus-Ammon in the remote Siwa Oasis. Zeus-Ammon was a ram-headed hybrid of the Greek Zeus and the Egyptian Amen, tinged with more than a hint of the native Libyan god who had originally been celebrated at Siwa. Worshipped in the Egyptian style, Zeus-Ammon was essentially a Greek oracle famed for his accurate pronouncements. After eight days wandering in the desert – contemporary histories tells us that he was guided on his way by friendly crows and a succession of talking snakes, and sustained by unexpected rains – the weary Alexander arrived at the temple and entered the sanctuary with the chief priest, leaving his entourage outside. No one knows what questions Alexander asked; indeed, no one knows how he asked them or how the god responded. But the whole world soon knew how the chief priest had greeted Alexander as the son of Zeus-Ammon himself. The living Alexander was definitely, undeniably, divine.

Ptolemy I developed the link between the royal family and the gods by promoting the cults of Serapis and Alexander, and by instigating a Ptolemaic programme of temple building and restoration which, initially confined to northern Egypt, soon spread southwards. Ptolemy II took things further. His incestuous marriage with his sister mirrored the unions of Osiris and Isis and Zeus and Hera, and led directly to the deification of his late parents. Ptolemy I and Berenice I, descendants of both Dionysos and Heracles, were to be worshipped together as the Theoi Soteres ('Saviour Gods'). The royal ancestor cults, a new and entirely Graeco-Egyptian focus for worship, were to prove an effective means of channelling the loyalty of the elite of Alexandria and the southern city of Ptolemais Hormou, whose sons were happy to serve as eponymous priests for a year and whose daughters were eager to become priestesses in the cults of the deified queens. Outside the Greek cities the royal cults were quietly absorbed into the traditional theology, as many other gods had been before.

In 272/1 the Ptolemies acquired an enhanced divinity, as Ptolemy II and Arsinoë II were officially designated living gods. Together they became the Theoi Adelphoi ('Brother-Sister Gods'). Arsinoë II, sister-wife of Ptolemy II, was queen consort of Egypt for less than seven years. Within the royal family she entirely supplanted her husband's divorced first wife, Arsinoë I, and at Karnak we can see her stepson Ptolemy III making offerings to the dead Arsinoë II as if she had been his birth mother. A gold coin issued between 285 and 246 made Arsinoë the first Egyptian queen to be featured on her husband's coinage. She was also the first Ptolemaic queen to be shown accompanying her husband as he offered to the gods, the first to wear the double uraeus which distinguished her from her predecessor, Arsinoë I, and the first to design her own Egyptian-style crown: an elaborate combination of the king's red crown (the crown of Lower or northern Egypt), a solar disc, two tall feathers, the cow horns associated with Hathor and Isis, and the ram horns associated with Amen. The crown, which somewhat resembles the one worn by the earth god Geb, suggests an interest in Egypt's dynastic history and, maybe, some understanding of traditional Egyptian solar theology, which is reinforced by references to Arsinoë as a 'daughter of Amen' and 'daughter of Shu'. A colossal granite statue of Arsinoë recovered from the Gardens of Sallust, Rome, shows her as an entirely Egyptian queen with a now-vanished crown and a double uraeus still on her brow. The statue inscription confirms that she is:

The princess, inherent; daughter of Geb, the first, the daughter of the bull, the great generosity, the daughter of the king, sister and spouse, woman of Upper and Lower Egypt, image of Isis, beloved of Hathor, Mistress of the Two Lands, Arsinoë, who is beloved to her brother, beloved of Atum, Mistress of the Two Lands.[15]

Arsinoë's image, both Greek- and Egyptian-style, living and posthumous, spread throughout the Ptolemaic empire on coins, cult vases, statues and reliefs, while back home her name was celebrated in the growing number of towns named, or renamed, Arsinoë. By 256 the reclaimed land of the Faiyum had been renamed the Arsinoite nome, and Arsinoë, assisted by the crocodile god Souchos, had become its patron deity. An early death, in *c.* 270, had merely enhanced Arsinoë's status. She was posthumously deified as an individual in her own right, with her personal cult based at Alexandria, where she was served by a priestess known as the basket-bearer (*kanephoros*). As temples were raised with shrines to both the deified Arsinoë and Arsinoë as half of the Theoi Adelphoi, the canny Ptolemy taxed Egypt's vineyards to pay for his sister's new cult. Arsinoë was now one of the Sunnaoi Theoi ('Temple-Sharing Gods'), and her statue was officially placed beside that of the main deity in all of Egypt's Greek and Egyptian temples. The Mendes Stela, recovered near Cairo in 1871, shows a scene of Ptolemy II, accompanied by his second wife and son, offering to a ram, to the gods of Mendes and to the deified Arsinoë. The text beneath details the dead queen's metamorphosis into a goddess:

His Majesty [Ptolemy II] decreed that her image be erected in all the temples. This pleased the priests, for they were aware of her noble attitude towards the gods, and of her excellent deeds to the benefit of all the people ... Her name was proclaimed as the beloved of the Ram, the goddess Philadelphos, Arsinoë.[16]

Arsinoë's association with sacred rams (an association with the god

Amen and the divine Alexander the Great rather than a specific ram cult) is confirmed by coins which show her with a ram's horn discreetly curling around her ear. Our best preserved images of the deified queen come from the Philae temple. Here just one scene, in Room V, shows Arsinoë standing alone to receive an offering from her husband. In other scenes she appears as the companion of Isis. Arsinoë wears a sheath dress, a full wig, a vulture headdress and her own red crown. She carries a sceptre and the *ankh* sign of life. She is entirely Egyptian in appearance and virtually identical to Isis. Two and a half centuries after Arsinoë's death, Cleopatra VII would occasionally don Arsinoë's personal crown and display the double cornucopia, the Greek horn of plenty, on the reverse of her coins and on at least one of her (assumed) statues. As the double cornucopia was already strongly identified with Arsinoë II, being found on her coins, statues and vase images, Cleopatra's choice of symbols suggests that she was deliberately identifying herself not only with Isis, but also with the politically powerful and still-popular Arsinoë II, who was herself identified with Isis.

Arsinoë II clearly had an enormous influence on the developing political and religious role of the Ptolemaic queen. Cleopatra I expanded the role further, drawing on the traditional Egyptian theology which allowed a mother to serve as regent for her infant son by establishing the tradition of the queen regent. Born a Syrian princess, Cleopatra outlived her husband Ptolemy V (died 180), and ruled alongside her son Ptolemy VI. She became a goddess in her own lifetime, taking the title Thea, and was the first queen to mint her own coins. Her reign marks another substantial increase in the power of the Ptolemaic women, and a corresponding decrease in the power of the Ptolemaic men.

In 168 the goddess Isis spoke in a dream to Hor of Sebennytos, who recorded his dream on an ostracon. This was discovered in modern times in the ruins of the Sakkara Serapeum, where Hor had lived and worked in the ibis shrine of Thoth:

I was told in a dream: Isis, the great goddess of Egypt and the land of Syria, walks upon the face of the waters of the Syrian sea. Thoth stands before her and takes her hand. She has reached the harbour at Alexandria. She says 'Alexandria is safe against the enemy. Pharaoh resides within it with his brethren. His eldest son wears the crown. This son's son wears the crown after him. The son of the son of the son of this son wears the crown after him, for a great length of days. The proof of this is that the queen bears a male child.'[17]

The Egyptians were famed throughout the ancient world for their oracles and their dream interpretations. Hor's dream, however, needs little in-depth analysis. It illustrates the general acceptance of a strong link between the goddess Isis and the mortal queen who is destined to become the mother of the next Horus king. In this case the queen in question is Cleopatra II, daughter of Cleopatra I and, at the time of the dream, sister-wife of Ptolemy VI. Isis was only half correct in her prophecy. The Ptolemaic dynasty would indeed continue, but the sons born to Cleopatra II would all die untimely deaths and it would be Cleopatra's daughter, Cleopatra III, who maintained her line.

The late second century BC saw the royal house plagued by near-disastrous inter-family strife as brother kings Ptolemy VI and Ptolemy VIII competed for the throne. This dynastic uncertainty had the effect of strengthening rather than weakening the role of their queens, with Ptolemy VIII in particular realising that an association with a powerful divine consort could only enhance his own position. As consort to Ptolemy VI, Cleopatra II earned the respect of the Alexandrians and achieved a status approaching political equality with her brother. As consort to Ptolemy VIII she was challenged by her daughter Cleopatra III, who was also married to Ptolemy VIII. Ptolemy favoured the younger Cleopatra, yet was unable to strip his sister of her power, and his simultaneous queens became known as Cleopatra the Sister and

Cleopatra the Wife. As an abandoned wife, Cleopatra II claimed sole rulership of Egypt as Clepatra Thea Philometor Soteira (Cleopatra the Mother-Loving Goddess, the Saviour).

Cleopatra III was, even by Ptolemaic standards, a particularly ruthless woman. On 18 February 142 she gave birth to her stepfather's son, a rival to her half-brother born to Cleopatra II. The day was considered a particularly auspicious one, as it was also the birth date of the new Apis bull. Cleopatra was rewarded with a string of religious promotions and, in 140, marriage. Even before she became queen, Cleopatra was given a personal divinity. Following her marriage she became the living embodiment of Isis. The earlier Ptolemaic queens Arsinoë II, Berenice II, Arsinoë III and Cleopatra I had each, to a greater or lesser extent, been associated with Isis as the mother of Horus. This, however, was very different. Cleopatra III was totally identified with the goddess in all her aspects: queen and goddess essentially became one. The new cult was served by a male priest known as the 'Holy Colt of Isis Great Mother of the Gods'; this was a significant development, as earlier queens' cults had been served by priestesses. Cleopatra was by now the most divine of the Ptolemaic queens. Yet her role as Isis incarnate was apparently not enough. Following the death of Ptolemy VIII she awarded herself three further cults intended to reflect specific aspects of her divine persona. Records now make reference to priestesses known as the 'crown-bearer' (*stephanophoros*), the 'torch-bearer' (*phosphoros*) and the priestess of 'Queen Cleopatra, the Mother-Loving Goddess, the Saviour, Mistress of Justice, Bringer of Victory'. To modern eyes this is incomprehensible: why would the all-powerful Isis wish to add to her already boundless divinity? No explanation is offered, but it seems that Cleopatra may simply have wished to ensure that her priestesses outranked the individual Alexandrian cult priestesses of her predecessors: the 'basket-bearer' of Arsinoë II, the 'victory-bearer' (*athlophoros*) of Berenice II and the priestess of Arsinoë III.

A century after the death of Cleopatra III, Cleopatra VII used a combination of ancient Egyptian and recent Ptolemaic tradition to develop her own powerful divinity. Slowly but steadily, she rewarded herself with religious titles. In 36 she became the Thea Neotera (Younger Goddess, a title which suggested an association with Cleopatra Thea, daughter of Ptolemy VI and highly successful queen of Syria. Two years later she was formally proclaimed the Nea Isis (New Isis), a title that distinguished her from the earlier Ptolemaic incarnation of Isis, Cleopatra III, while linking her to her father, the New Dionysos. The cult of Cleopatra-Isis was to prove popular throughout Egypt, and long after the introduction of Christianity a statue of the goddess queen was still being maintained on Philae Island. A graffito scribbled by Petesenufe, Scribe of the Book of Isis, in AD 373 tells us, 'I overlaid the [wooden] figure of Cleopatra with gold.'

CHAPTER SIX

Cleopatra and Mark Antony

… The princesses of the house of the Ptolemies had always apparently been very much averse to taking casual lovers, especially from outside the royal house. They were not, like later Roman imperial ladies, both murderous and adulterous. They were murderous and chaste.

Michael Grant, *Cleopatra*[1]

Cleopatra now ruled Egypt for three difficult but essentially peaceful years. Seneca tells how, for 'two years in succession, under Cleopatra's administration, during her tenth and eleventh years [42 and 41] the Nile did not flood'.[2] These worryingly low inundations resulted in failing crops, high inflation and, despite an extensive relief programme, hunger, plague and civil unrest. Persistent inflation would force Cleopatra to lower the silver content of her coins, making them compatible, in terms of silver content, with the Roman denarius. At the same time she increased the production of bronze coins at the Alexandria mint, while cutting their weight by as much as 75 per cent. To prevent traders simply weighing out the reduced-value coins, she had them inscribed with their official denominations (40 and 80 drachmas), a simple but highly effective move which forced acceptance of the coin's nominal value.

On 12 April 41 a decree was issued to protect city-dwelling landowners from harassment by over-zealous tax collectors. Josephus tells us that Cleopatra was able to feed the people of Alexandria but 'refused to distribute the necessary grain to the Jews', presumably because they were not full citizens.[3] This allegation is unconfirmed and, given the strong Jewish support for Cleopatra and Caesar during the Alexandrian Wars, seems unlikely, particularly as we find Cleopatra now renewing a grant of asylum originally made for a Jewish temple (possibly the temple in the Delta town of Leontopolis) by either Ptolemy III or Ptolemy VIII. Southern Egypt coped well under these trying conditions: a stela set up at Karnak some time between 44 and 39 mentions the heroic efforts of the *epistratagos* Callimachos, who apparently saved the city during the years of famine. His achievements were to be celebrated by public festivals held on his birthday.

On 14 July 41, in Cleopatra's Year 11, the high priest of Ptah, Pasherenptah III, died. His funerary stela (known as the Harris Stela), recovered from his Sakkara tomb and now in the British Museum, tells a story of elite Egyptian life outside Alexandria. Pasherenptah came from a long line of hereditary priests who formed a parallel, supportive religious dynasty to the Ptolemies. Pasherenptah himself appears at the top of his stela, wearing the panther skin and the side-lock hairstyle (a ponytail worn on the side of an otherwise shaven head) that identify him as a priest of Ptah of Memphis. Below, in a beautifully carved hieroglyphic text, we read a series of offering formulae for the deceased, then an autobiography.[4] This tells how, as a newly appointed priest just fourteen years old, Pasherenptah officiated at the coronation of Auletes, whom he, in his Egyptian text, describes as the 'Young Osiris' rather than the 'New Dionysos'. Relationships between the king and his priest were cordial. Pasherenptah travelled to Alexandria, where he was crowned with a golden chaplet and made a priest of Auletes's own cult, and Auletes paid frequent visits to Memphis, where he stayed at the Serapeum palace with 'his chiefs, his women and royal children'.[5] The king was happy to play his part in the regular religious festivals, maintaining an obvious royal presence in the traditional cults. There was just one sadness. Pasherenptah had several daughters, but no son to follow him as high priest of Ptah. Finally, when he was forty-three years old, the god Imhotep heard his prayers. A much-wanted son was born and named Imhotep in honour of the god; later Imhotep would be known as the high priest of Ptah Pedibastet III. The limestone stela (also in the British Museum) of Tayimhotep, wife of Pasherenptah III, tells us that she died at thirty years of age, a year before her husband. Her autobiography confirms the story of her son's miraculous birth and ends with a poignant plea:

> The west, it is a land of sleep,
> Darkness weighs on the dwelling-place,
> Those who are there sleep in their mummy-forms.
> They wake not to see their brothers,
> They see not their fathers, their mothers,
> Their hearts forget their wives, their children ...
> Say to me 'You are not far from water'.
> Turn my face to the north wind at the edge of the water,
> Perhaps my heart will then be cooled in its grief.[6]

In spite of her economic problems, Cleopatra found herself in a more secure position than ever before. With both her brothers dead, her sister in exile and their supporters removed, she had absolute power and no obvious rival to form a rallying point for dissidents. Her co-ruler was an infant who, although invaluable for propaganda purposes, posed no threat to her authority. Caesarion, Ptolemy Caesar

Theos Philopator Philometor ('the Father-Loving, Mother-Loving God'), was proclaimed king of Egypt in Alexandria in the summer of 44.

In the wider Mediterranean world things were far from peaceful. The second triumvirate of Caesar's friend Mark Antony, his great-nephew and heir Octavian and his supporter Marcus Aemilius Lepidus had united in their determination to capture Caesar's principal assassins, Brutus and Cassius. They were intent on public revenge and Egypt – still, in spite of her suffering, the richest land in the eastern Mediterranean – was expected to provide practical help. Meanwhile, Brutus and Cassius, having realised that they had few friends in Rome, were looking to the eastern provinces for support and they, too, expected Egypt to help. When Cassius occupied Syria and formed an alliance with the powerful king of Parthia (whose extensive territories covered much of modern Iran and Iraq), Cleopatra was forced to take sides. She hesitated as long as she could, then committed herself by returning the four Roman legions, stationed in Egypt by Caesar in 48, to the triumvirs' general, Publius Cornelius Dolabella, who was now in Syria. As an acknowledgement of her support, or as payment for services rendered, the triumvirs officially recognised Caesarion as co-ruler of Egypt. This decision would, it was hoped, persuade Cleopatra, mother of Caesar's natural son, to continue to support Octavian, Caesar's legal heir.

Cassius had been able to intercept and subvert Cleopatra's Roman troops. They had changed sides without putting up a fight and were now stationed with his own legions along Egypt's north-eastern border. When Cassius appealed directly to Cleopatra for aid – surely a prelude to invasion – she pleaded famine, plague and a manpower shortage that would prevent her from taking any direct part in the war. Meanwhile, Serapion, *strategos* or governor of Cyprus, had unilaterally declared his support for Cassius and had supplied him with ships. It seems that Serapion was planning to depose Cleopatra in favour of Arsinoë IV, who, currently living in the temple of Artemis at Ephesus, had maintained close contact with Cyprus. When, in 42, Brutus summoned Cassius and his troops to Smyrna, the threat of invasion lifted and Cleopatra breathed a huge sigh of relief.

Now openly on the side of the triumvirs, Cleopatra raised a fleet and set sail to join Octavian and Antony in Greece. Unfortunately (or perhaps fortunately), a mighty Mediterranean storm blew up, her ships sustained serious damage and Cleopatra herself fell ill, possibly with seasickness. As Egyptian wreckage washed up on the Greek shore, the badly battered fleet limped home to Alexandria. It is impossible not to suspect that this may have been another delaying tactic. If so, it was successful. While Cleopatra waited for a second fleet to be made ready, news came that Brutus and Cassius had committed suicide following a heavy defeat at the two battles of Philippi in Macedon in October 42. Two men now effectively held power in Rome: Octavian, Caesar's twenty-one-year-old great-nephew and legal heir, controlled the bulk of Rome's western empire; while Antony, Caesar's forty-year-old friend and general, controlled Gaul and the eastern provinces of Achaea (Greece), Asia, Bithynia-Pontus and Cilicia. Lepidus, who was eventually to be given control of Africa, remained a triumvir but was a political nonentity. There remained just one problematic region. Sextus Pompey, the younger son of Pompey the Great, had occupied part of Sicily and could not be dislodged. His ships – pirate ships – were threatening the vital Mediterranean trade networks.

Octavian left the battlefield of Philippi ill – it was widely believed that he was dying – and returned to Rome, leaving Antony to establish control over his eastern territories. Cleopatra and Caesarion were extremely vulnerable in Egypt. They needed a protector and Antony was their natural ally. Not only was he the controller of the east, he was the dominant triumvir: older, more popular and demonstrably healthier than the sickly Octavian. Antony, in turn, needed money. He had promised each of his veterans a reward of 500 drachmas, which he had no means of paying, and he had vowed to resurrect the campaign against the Parthian empire that Julius Caesar had been planning at the time of his death. Success against Parthia would finally avenge Crassus, and would demonstrate to the whole world that Antony was Caesar's natural, if not his legal, heir. Antony spent the winter of 42/1 raising funds in Greece, then moved on to Ephesus. Here the priestesses of the Artemis temple were persuaded to greet him as the living incarnation of Dionysos the Gracious, 'Giver of Joy'. He was welcomed into a celebrating city filled with ivy, *thyrsos* wands, harps, pipes and flutes, dishevelled women dressed as maenads and men and boys dressed like satyrs and Pans. The political implications of this religious honour would not have been lost on Octavian. While he was confined to Rome, the eastern territories were starting to identify Antony as the successor of all the former earthly Dionysoi, including Alexander the Great, the Ptolemies of Egypt and Pompey the Great. As Caesar had been granted posthumous divine honours in 42, his adopted heir Octavian could legitimately claim to be the 'Son of the Divine Julius', but this must have seemed poor compensation. Octavian fought back the only way he could: by circulating rumours of his own familial relationship with the Olympian Apollo, who, as an Italian god of light, might reasonably be considered the theological opposite of the dark, eastern Dionysos. Soon everyone knew the story of his mother, Atia, who had fallen asleep in the temple of Apollo and been ravished by a snake. Nine months later, Octavian was born, and Atia was left with an indelible snake mark on her stomach.

Ephesus was not Antony's first brush with divinity. He came from an impoverished junior branch of the Antonius family, and Plutarch tells us that his father, Antonius Creticus, was 'a man of no great repute in public life, nor illustrious, but kindly and honest and generous'. Both his father and his stepfather were careless with money and when Creticus died he left such steep debts that his son refused to inherit his estate. Perhaps to compensate for this undistinguished background, Antony claimed descent from Anton, one of the sons of Heracles. This gave him a distant kinship with the Ptolemies, who also claimed Heracles as an ancestor through Arsinoë, mother of Ptolemy I, and who were occasionally depicted wearing his trademark lion-skin headdress. Antony did not don a skin, but he did, or so Plutarch claims, emulate his hero in public by wearing a tunic hitched up to his thigh, a heavy cloak and a large sword: 'a shapely beard, a broad forehead, and an aquiline nose were thought to show the virile qualities peculiar to the portraits and statues of Heracles'. In citing Heracles as an ancestor, Antony was clearly thinking of his hero's bravery and exceptional strength, and maybe even of his multiple fruitful relationships with women. Later, under the influence of Octavian's propaganda, others would draw a crueller comparison. At one stage in his colourful career Heracles had been sold into slavery. He became the property of Omphale, the forceful queen of Lydia, who dressed him in women's clothing and forced him to spin and weave at her command. When Omphale donned his discarded lion-skin garment, Heracles's humiliation was complete. Yet Heracles the slave and Omphale the mistress were known to be lovers, and Omphale bore Heracles's children. The parallels between the weak Antony and the unnaturally forceful Cleopatra were obvious.

The *tryphe* of the Hellenistic courts was far more to Antony's taste than the puritanism of Rome, and he found much to appreciate in the cult of Dionysos, with its ecstatic rituals, and its heavy consumption of wine. Antony had enjoyed a well-documented dissolute youth when, heavily influenced by his friends, he indulged in binge drinking, promiscuous sex and immoderate expenditure that left him heavily in debt. A distinguished military career and a growing reputation as a politician and orator followed, but the tendency to overindulge was never quite suppressed. Military life brought out the best in him: Antony was a brave and able soldier, a generous man well regarded by his troops. But the dull routine of civilian life brought out the worst. Plutarch gives a report of his behaviour when, with Julius Caesar busy in Egypt, he was left unsupervised to maintain order and promote Caesar's cause in Rome:

> *[Men of worth and uprightness] loathed his ill-timed drunkenness, his heavy expenditures, his debauches with women, his spending the days in sleep or in wandering about with crazed and aching head, the nights in revelry or at shows, or in attendance at the nuptial feasts of mimes and jesters. We are told, at any rate, that he once feasted at the nuptials of Hippias the mime, drank all night, and then, early in the morning, when the people summoned him to the forum, came before them still surfeited with food and vomited into his toga, which one of his friends held at his service. Sergius the mime also was one of those who had the greatest influence with him, and Cytheris, a woman from the same school of acting, a great favourite, whom he took about with him in a litter on his visits to the cities, and her litter was followed by as many attendants as that of his mother.*[7]

Plutarch is, of course, deliberately painting a portrait of a weak man made weaker by over-indulgence; he is preparing us for Antony's first encounter with Cleopatra. The consistent emphasis on Antony's drinking links him firmly in the Roman reader's mind with disreputable Dionysiac rituals, while repeated references to his sex life invite the manly reader to imagine not a stud, but a man who is somehow softened by his constant association with women. Plutarch was by no means the only classical writer to consider *eros*, or sexual desire, a form of madness. Heterosexual sex was, in theory at least, an unclean act forced on men by women and nature: an activity to be endured in the dark rather than enjoyed in the daylight.[8]

Antony was a much-married man. His first wife, Fadia, was the daughter of a freedman. We know little about this most unsuitable union, but it seems that Fadia's father, Quintus Fadius Gallus, had been able to provide a dowry large enough to tempt a chronically impoverished young aristocrat. Fadia soon disappeared, and it is assumed that she and her children, with their embarrassing origins, died young. Antony's next and far more suitable wife was his first cousin Antonia. She bore him a daughter, also named Antonia, and then was divorced in 47 on the grounds of adultery with the notorious rake Dolabella. Antony undoubtedly allowed himself a great deal of sexual licence while expecting his long-suffering wife to remain chaste, but the speed with which he subsequently remarried suggests that Antonia, like Fadia before her, was simply discarded when the chance of a better wife came along. In 47/6 Antony married Fulvia, widow of the murdered popular hero Publius Clodius. This was an extremely advantageous match. Fulvia was beautiful, intelligent and capable, and her role as the mother of Clodius's young children gave her great political standing.[9] Furthermore, she was immensely wealthy and Antony was in desperate need of funds, as Caesar was now forcing him to pay for Pompey's estate, which he had 'bought' and squandered. Fulvia bore Antony two sons, Marcus Antonius (Antyllus) and Julius Antonius, and did much to protect his interests while he was campaigning away from Rome:

> She was a woman who took no thought for spinning wool or housekeeping, nor would she deign to bear sway over a man of private station, but she wished to rule a ruler and command a commander. Therefore Cleopatra was indebted to Fulvia for teaching Antony to endure a woman's sway, since she took him over quite tamed, and schooled at the outset to obey women.[10]

Now, with Fulvia fully occupied in Rome, Antony was travelling with the well-known courtesan Volumnia Cytheris. This did not prevent him from casting his eye over other women. In the summer of 41 he was rumoured to have had an affair with the beautiful Glaphyra, the daughter-in-law of Archelaos, the twice-married husband of Berenice IV, and to have fathered her son Archelaos.

Antony, now stationed in the Cilician city of Tarsus (in the south of modern Turkey), was busy raising funds, rewarding those who had been loyal to the triumvirate and punishing those who had not by demanding ten years' back-tax to be paid within two years. Cleopatra can hardly have been surprised when first a series of letters, then an emissary, Quintus Dellius, arrived in Alexandria to summon her to Tarsus. She was to answer the charge that she and her *strategos* Serapion had aided the traitor Cassius. Whatever the truth of the matter, this would be a hard charge to disprove and Antony, his eyes firmly fixed on Egypt's wealth, would need to be persuaded of her innocence. As always, Cleopatra hesitated, considering her options. It would be surprising if she had not already met Antony during her visit(s) to Rome. She may even have met him much earlier: Appian, for one, believed that Antony had fallen in love with the teenage Cleopatra while campaigning in Egypt with Gabinius.[11] Her personal knowledge of Antony the man allowed Cleopatra to settle on a tactic that would give her genius for showmanship full rein. If Antony was Dionysos, she would greet him as Isis, consort of Dionysos-Osiris. Cleopatra sailed along the Cydnus River to enter Tarsus in a gilded ship fitted with silver oars and a splendid purple silk sail. Flutes, pipes and lutes played on deck, and powerful incense perfumed the air. Cleopatra herself reclined beneath a gold-spangled canopy dressed in the robes of Isis (a colourful dress covered by a black mantle, we must assume), attended by beautiful small boys dressed as Cupids. The people of Tarsus flocked to the harbour to watch this spectacular arrival, leaving Antony alone and disconcerted in the marketplace. When he sent the queen an invitation to dine that night she declined, declaring that she would rather he ate as her guest. She entertained him with a banquet so splendid that the usually verbose Plutarch simply refuses to attempt a description, and they sat together that evening on the deck of her boat amidst a multitude of twinkling artificial lights.

Plutarch is quite clear that Cleopatra deliberately set out to seduce Antony and that he, more naïve than Caesar, almost immediately succumbed to her practised charms:

> … *Caesar and Pompey [Gnaius Pompeius] had known her when she was still a girl and inexperienced in affairs, but she was going to visit Antony at the very time when women have the most brilliant beauty and are at the acme of intellectual power. Therefore she provided herself with many gifts, much money, and such ornaments as high position and prosperous kingdom made it natural for her to take; but she went putting her greatest confidence in herself, and in the charms and sorceries of her own person.*[12]

Again, he sets the scene for what is to come by telling us that, while Cleopatra deliberately schemed to captivate the simple Antony, Antony's decision to ally himself with Cleopatra was a decision taken with the heart, not the head. Dio agrees that the weak Antony is easily corrupted by power, by Cleopatra and by the luxury with which she surrounds herself:

> *It is indeed true that he had earnestly devoted himself to his duties so long as he had been in a subordinate station and had been aiming at the highest prizes, but now that he had got into power, he no longer paid strict attention to any of these things, but joined Cleopatra and the Egyptians in general in their life of luxurious ease until he was entirely demoralized.*[13]

It is important to see through this propaganda and to remember that Antony was not only a bluff, naïve, simple fellow; he was also an extremely ambitious and capable man.

Athenaeus tells the story of that first evening together.[14] In a room decorated with purple and gold wall hangings Cleopatra served delicious food on golden plates inlaid with precious stones; she ended the banquet by presenting all her golden plates to Antony. The next night's banquet was even more splendid and Antony went home with yet more golden tableware, while his invited guests were allowed to keep their couches and their goblets. Banquets were times when luxury could come dangerously close to debauchery. The connection between eating, drinking and sex was an obvious one, and the dynastic Egyptians had chosen to decorate their tombs, places of rebirth, with images of perpetual banquets where men and women sat before tables groaning with produce. Cleopatra, it is suggested, habitually used the banquet as a means of seduction. She feasted with Caesar, a man so remarkably abstemious that he legislated against personal luxury, lavish food, extravagant clothing and pearls. And now she feasted with Antony, a notoriously weak and lazy man. Indeed, if we take the accounts of the classical writers at face value, it seems that Cleopatra and Antony did nothing other than eat, drink and fornicate. The sheer amount of food consumed, and wasted, at Cleopatra's court is enough to make a restrained man, in this case Plutarch, shudder:

> *Philotas, the physician of Amphissa, used to tell my grandfather, Lamprias, that he was in Alexandria at the time, studying his profession, and that having got well acquainted with one of the royal cooks, he was easily persuaded by him (young man that he was) to take a view of the extravagant preparations for a royal supper. Accordingly, he was introduced into the kitchen, and when he saw all the other provisions in great abundance, and eight wild boars a-roasting, he expressed his amazement at what must be the number of guests. But the cook burst out laughing and said: 'The guests are not many, only about twelve; but everything that is set before them must be at perfection, and this an instant of time reduces. For it might happen that*

Antony would ask for supper immediately, and after a little while, perhaps, would postpone it and call for a cup of wine, or engage in conversation with someone. Wherefore, he said, 'not one, but many suppers are arranged; for the precise time is hard to hit.'[15]

Octavian, a moral, upright man who famously wore homespun clothes made (or so he fondly imagined) by his wife and daughter, could not be seduced either by Cleopatra or by her food. In his one interview with her he refused to meet the queen's eye and, after her death, he melted down all the gold plates in the Alexandria palace.

Pliny the Elder tells the story of Cleopatra's earrings, inherited from 'oriental kings' and made from the largest pearls ever discovered.[16] One day, bored and irritated by the quality of the food served at Antony's table, Cleopatra wagered that she could serve him a banquet worth ten million sesterces (this at a time when the annual pay for a legionary soldier was a mere 900 sesterces). The next evening she offered Antony the choicest of foods. Then, as dessert, she called for a cup of sour wine, removed a pearl earring, dropped the pearl in the wine and, as it dissolved, drank. With a few swallows she had consumed her banquet. This is of course, as many observers have pointed out, an unlikely if not totally impossible tale. Pearls, being almost 90 per cent calcium carbonate, will dissolve in an acid solution; they will dissolve much faster if ground to a powder by a pestle and mortar first. Egyptian vinegar was famed for its strength. If Cleopatra's sour wine (*vinum acer*, or vinegar) was strong enough, and if she allowed enough time – experiment would suggest more than twenty hours for a large whole pearl in cold vinegar – the pearl would indeed dissolve, neutralising the acid. Cleopatra, who acquired a considerable posthumous reputation as an alchemist, may well have known this. Whether the resulting mixture would have been palatable, or indeed drinkable, is another matter. Some historians have suggested that Cleopatra's pearlwine mixture may have been considered an aphrodisiac. More prosaically, Ullman's experiments indicate that the pearl-wine mixture, correctly made, may have acted as an antacid. However, to assume that Cleopatra was actually manufacturing her own post-banquet pick-me-up is probably an assumption too far.[17]

What happened to the other earring? Tradition holds that Antony's friend Lucius Munatius Plancus prevented Cleopatra from dissolving it and, after the queen's death, it was cut in two and placed in the ears of the statue of Venus in the Pantheon at Rome. As both Venus and the pearl came from the sea, and both symbolised love, this was an entirely appropriate donation.

Two other Roman pearl-drinking stories exist. Both Horace and Pliny tell the tale of the spendthrift son of the actor Aesopus who drank a pearl taken from the ear of the wealthy lady Metella. Metella's pearl was, however, smaller than Cleopatra's, and was valued at just a million sesterces. Suetonius tells us that Caligula, a notorious eccentric, drank pearls dissolved in vinegar; he also, apparently, bathed in perfume and fed his guests on bread and meat made of gold. These multiple tales do not, of course, mean that Cleopatra's story must be immediately dismissed as an urban myth. Cleopatra may have inspired, or been inspired by, the son of Aesopus, while Caligula may have been inspired by Cleopatra. Nor does the need to boil, crush or steep the pearl in acid necessarily render the story invalid. Cleopatra, acknowledged mistress of the public spectacle, could have stage-managed her act and Antony, flushed with wine and love, is unlikely to have noticed. It is quite obvious that Cleopatra could simply have swallowed the pearl whole, although swallowing, and presumably retrieving the pearl later, would have turned the grandest of gestures into a cheap trick. We know that Cleopatra did wear pearls, as her later coins show her wearing either a lengthy rope of pearls wrapped twice around her neck or, less likely, a shorter pearl necklace and a pearl-embroidered dress. Pearls had no place in traditional Egyptian jewellery, which employed brightly coloured semiprecious stones set in gold, but a Roman fashion for ostentatious pearl-wearing had started in 61, when, following his victory over Mithridates, Pompey commissioned his own portrait to be rendered in pearls. Suetonius tells us that Julius Caesar invaded Britain to collect freshwater pearls, and that back in Rome, as part of an enforced austerity drive, he attempted to restrict the wearing of pearls to those 'of a designated position and age'.[18] Pliny, who clearly disapproved of pearls and all they stood for, records the tale of Lollia Paulina who wore pearl and emerald jewellery worth forty million sesterces and carried the receipts at all times to impress strangers!

On balance, it seems unlikely that the world's most expensive banquet was consumed in quite the way that Pliny describes. This does not matter overmuch; it is what we have come to expect from Cleopatra tales. What does matter is that Pliny apparently believed the tale and used it to spread the propaganda of a Cleopatra who was cunning, recklessly extravagant, and selfish (she alone consumes the 'banquet'): unnatural and worrying traits for a Roman man to encounter in any woman. At the same time, her easy outwitting of Antony does not bode well for his future. A subsequent story, also told by Pliny, sees Cleopatra poisoning the flowers in her crown before challenging Antony, who is refusing to eat or drink anything that has not been tasted by a slave, to drink a flower-wine mixture. This story has a more sinister ending: Cleopatra stops the trusting Antony from drinking her poisoned flowers and 'she ordered a prisoner who had been led in to drink it and he promptly died'.[19] Again, Cleopatra has outwitted the innocent Antony with consummate ease.

Cleopatra feasted with Antony, but she bargained with him too. She would gladly agree to the execution of the traitor Serapion who, having fled Cyprus, had taken refuge in the Phoenician city of Tyre. She would also part-finance Antony's Parthian campaign. But he, in return, must agree to protect her crown and her land. This protection included the removal of the sister who posed a constant threat to Cleopatra and Caesarion and who, as Cleopatra might well have argued, had almost certainly sided with Serapion and Cassius. Dragged from her sanctuary, Arsinoë was murdered on Antony's order, then buried in Ephesus, possibly in the imposing city-centre tomb, today known as the Octagon, which has yielded the remains of an anonymous woman in her twenties. At the same time Antony disposed of a troublesome young man who was claiming to be the long-lost, undrowned Ptolemy XIII.

Cleopatra returned to Egypt and Antony followed a month later. He was to spend the winter of 41/40 relaxing in Alexandria and, perhaps, like Caesar before him, considering the possibility of generating revenue from Egypt. In Alexandria he found that he enjoyed all the popularity that Caesar had lacked. The Alexandrians had not forgotten how Antony had allowed Archelaos an honourable burial, or how he had used his influence to dissuade Auletes from massacring innocent citizens, and they were impressed by his current demeanour. While Caesar had forced himself on Alexandria with all the subtlety of a miniature Roman invasion, Antony appeared as a private individual, happy to abandon his Roman toga for a Greek *chlamys*, a military-style cloak, pinned on one shoulder, which could be worn either alone or over other garments. If the classical authors are to be believed, Cleopatra and Antony enjoyed a carefree, almost childish winter. Together they formed a drinking society, 'The Inimitable Livers' (*amimetobioi*, corrupted by a wag named 'Parasite', on an Alexandrian statue base, to 'The Inimitable Lovers'), which met every night to drink, feast, dice, hunt and, a particular favourite, wander the streets of Alexandria in disguise, playing tricks on the hapless citizens. Plutarch believed that the new society was simply an excuse for Cleopatra to spend all her time with Antony: she could not bear, or could not risk, letting him out of her sight even for an evening. An alternative interpretation is that the Inimitable Livers was a group of Dionysiac initiates who met regularly, not for random debauchery but to perform sacred religious rites that required the consumption of alcohol. Certainly Cleopatra's amethyst ring, which reportedly bore the inscription *methe* (drunkenness), can be accepted as referring to mystical rather than actual inebriation, as the amethyst itself was associated with temperance. Velleius gives a flavour of the long Alexandrian evenings spent carousing when he tells how Plancus was persuaded to perform at one of Cleopatra's banquets: with his naked body painted blue, a crown of reeds on his head and a fish's tail swinging behind, Plancus played the part of the sea god Glaucus.[20]

Plutarch tells us that already, by their second evening together, Cleopatra had 'recognised in the jests of Antony much of the soldier and the common man, and adopted this manner also towards him, without restraint now, and boldly'. Antony was a famous joker. He jested with his men, and roared with laughter when they in turn played tricks on him. He had even attempted to joke with the serious Fulvia, but she had proved less than receptive to his humour:

> *Antony tried, by sportive ways and youthful sallies, to make even Fulvia more light-hearted. For instance, when many were going out to meet Caesar after his victory in Spain, Antony himself went forth. Then, on a sudden, a report burst upon Italy that Caesar was dead and his enemies advancing upon the country, and Antony turned back to Rome. He took the dress of a slave and came by night to his house, and on saying that he was the bearer of a letter to Fulvia from Antony, was admitted to her presence, his face all muffled. Then Fulvia, in great distress, before taking the letter, asked whether Antony was still alive; and he, after handing her the letter without a word, as she began to open and read it, threw his arms about her and kissed her.[21]*

The Ptolemies, too, were fond of a good joke. Athenaeus tells of a trick played by Ptolemy II on Sosibios.[22] Ptolemy had instructed his treasurers that when Sosibios asked for his salary, he was to be told that it had already been paid. This they did and Sosibios brought his complaint of underpayment before the king. Ptolemy looked at the records and slowly read out the names of those who had definitely been paid: Soter, Sosigenes, Bion and Apollonos. As he explained to Sosibios, by taking elements from each name – **SO**ter, so**SI**genes, **BI**on, Apollon**OS** – he could prove that Sosibios had indeed received his salary. Presumably the unpaid Sosibios was duty-bound to find this amusing. Cleopatra's own sense of humour – aimed directly at the boyish Antony – had an equally unsophisticated twist:

> He [Antony] was fishing once, and had bad luck, and was vexed at it because Cleopatra was there to see. He therefore ordered his fishermen to dive down and secretly fasten to his hook some fish that had been previously caught, and pulled up two or three of them. But the Egyptian saw through the trick, and pretending to admire her lover's skill, told her friends about it, and invited them to be spectators of it the following day. So great numbers of them got into the fishing boats, and when Antony had let down his line, she ordered one of her own attendants to get the start of him by swimming onto his hook and fastening on it a salted Pontic herring. Antony thought he had caught something, and pulled it up, whereupon there was great laughter, as was natural, and Cleopatra said: 'Commander, hand over your fishing-rod to the fishermen of Pharos and Canopus; your sport is the hunting of cities, realms, and continents.'[23]

In 40, Cleopatra gave birth to twins whom she named Alexander and Cleopatra. Antony had already left Alexandria. He would not make any effort to see either Cleopatra or his Egyptian children for three and a half years, although it seems that he did employ spies to keep him up to date with events in Egypt. This lengthy split is far from the behaviour of a lovesick swain and suggests that Antony may have considered the months spent with Cleopatra as little more than a brief holiday away from his ordinary life. Cleopatra, who had used Antony to help her fulfil her duty to produce more children, may well have felt the same way.

In late February or early March 40, the Parthians launched a dual attack on the Roman territories of Syria and Asia Minor. Antony rushed from Alexandria to Tyre, where he received the devastating news that many of the Roman client kings had defected to the cause of the Parthians. The still-loyal Herod of Judaea had been forced to flee to Egypt and, arriving in Pelusium, had been escorted by boat to Alexandria. Here he turned down Cleopatra's offer of troops and borrowed a ship to travel to Rhodes, from where he made his way to Rome.

Worse was to come. While Antony had been focusing his attention on his eastern territories and, perhaps, on Cleopatra, Octavian had achieved what must have seemed an impossibility. He had convinced his troops that he, not Antony, was the real hero of Philippi and was slowly but surely eroding Antony's support in Rome. Lucius Antonius, consul in 41, had been doing all he could to protect his older brother's interests, and had worked with the energetic Fulvia to discredit Octavian and subvert his supporters. Fulvia and Lucius had raised their own army, with Fulvia personally forming two legions from her husband's veterans, and had declared war on Octavian. They had a great deal of popular support – country dwellers were angry that Octavian had displaced them to settle 100,000 of his veterans on their land – but without Antony's active help they were never going to succeed and Antony, many hundreds of miles away in Alexandria, was unable or unwilling to intervene. After some negotiations, and some desultory fighting, Lucius had found himself besieged in the hill town of Perusia (Perugia), where conditions soon became so desperate that the slaves, denied any part of the heavily rationed food supplies, were forced to eat grass and leaves. Twenty miles from Perusia, the smoke from their fires clearly visible to Lucius, camped troops loyal to Antony; their leaders, however, refused to take any action against

Octavian without a direct order from Antony, and Antony remained silent. The slingshots that Octavian's troops now fired over the town walls were inscribed with demoralising obscene graffiti:

I'm aiming for Fulvia's cunt!
Baldy Lucius Antonius and Fulvia, open your arses! [24]

In late February 40, the starving Lucius surrendered. Octavian executed the council of Perusia (permitting just one man, who had previously made a public condemnation of Caesar's assassins, to live) and allowed his troops to sack the city, but the relieved soldiers were allowed to go free, as was Lucius. Meanwhile, Fulvia had already fled Italy. Antony met his wife in Athens, where a bitter quarrel ended with Antony abandoning the seriously ill Fulvia. She died soon after their meeting, allowing Antony, who must have known that Fulvia had always acted in his best interests, to shift responsibility for the entire débâcle on to his late wife.

Fulvia's death left Antony free to marry Cleopatra, but marriage to a foreigner, no matter how pro-Roman, was not necessarily the most sensible move at this most sensitive of times. In early October 40 the Treaty of Brundisium (Brindisi) saw the reorganisation of the triumvirate. Antony was required to prove his loyalty to Octavian by relinquishing his control of Gaul and by making a diplomatic marriage with his recently widowed half-sister Octavia. Their wedding was celebrated just weeks after the birth of Antony's Egyptian twins. Octavia, a good and dutiful Roman wife, was to give Antony two daughters, Antonia Maior (future grandmother of the emperor Nero) and Antonia Minor (future grandmother of the emperor Claudius). Early in 38 the couple settled in Athens, where Antony was again hailed as the New Dionysos, consort of the goddess Athena Polias, while the modest Octavia became his earthly consort, the 'Divine Benefactress'. As Antony relaxed into the luxurious lifestyle of an eastern monarch, his soldiers, under the command of Publius Ventidius, began the first, successful stage of his Parthian campaign. Antony himself travelled eastwards in 38 and captured the city of Samosata (Samsat) on the Euphrates.

Silver tetradrachm of Mark Antony: one of many issues showing Antony on one face and Cleopatra on the other, possibly produced at Antioch.

From 40 to 30, Cleopatra ruled an increasingly prosperous Egypt. It is in this last decade of her reign that we can catch a fleeting glimpse of some of the humdrum, day-to-day, unremarkable work that must have filled Cleopatra's hours. A papyrus decree issued on 23 February 33, for example, deals with the privileges to be granted to the family of Antony's great friend Publius Candidus [Crassus]. The family is to be allowed to export grain and import wine tax-free, and lands and servants are also to be exempt. On the bottom of the document is the single Greek word *ginestho*, 'let it be so', written in what some but by no means all experts believe might be Cleopatra's own handwriting.[25] This papyrus, once stored in the Alexandrian archives, was later recycled into a cartonnage mummy case and buried with a Roman mummy. The mummy case was recovered in the Faiyum cemetery of Abusir el-Melek in 1903–5 and was eventually dismantled, revealing the hidden document. Theoretically, anyone in Ptolemaic Egypt was free to petition the king or queen, and archaeologists have recovered a whole archive of relatively trivial correspondence from the Memphite Serapeum, dated between 200 and 150 and addressed to 'King Ptolemy and Queen Cleopatra'. We have already seen, in Chapter 1 (pages 22–3), Ctesicles' petition about his wayward daughter addressed directly to Ptolemy III; this may be compared with a petition written *c*. 220 'to King Ptolemy' by Philista, a lady who has been scalded by a careless Egyptian bath attendant. In practice, it seems unlikely that the monarch would have dealt personally with such matters, and we know that Philista's complaint was actually reviewed by the *strategos* Diophanes.[26]

In the spring/summer of 37 Antony, Octavia and Octavian met at Tarentum (Taranto), where an agreement was reached to renew the triumvirate for a further five years. In addition, Antony agreed to supply Octavian with two squadrons (120 warships) that he could use against Sextus, whose pirate ships were causing an intolerable disruption to trade. Octavian, in return, was to provide Antony with four legions (20,000 men) that he could use against the Parthians. To seal the agreement, Antony's son by Fulvia, the nine-year-old Marcus Antonius (Antyllus), was betrothed to Octavian's two-year-old daughter, Julia. Satisfied, Antony and Octavia set sail together for Corfu. Here they parted, and Antony sent the pregnant Octavia to live under her brother's protection in Rome.

Antony had handed over his 120 ships, but had not received the promised troops. Belatedly, he realised that he could not rely on Octavian. He travelled to Antioch, then summoned his military ally and financial backer Cleopatra. Or, as Plutarch puts it:

… the dire evil which had been slumbering for a long time, namely, his passion for Cleopatra, which men thought had been charmed

away and lulled to rest by better considerations, blazed up again with renewed power as he drew near to Syria. And finally, like the stubborn and unmanageable beast of the soul, of which Plato speaks, he spurned away all saving and noble counsels and sent Fonteius Capito to bring Cleopatra to Syria.[27]

Cleopatra spent the winter of 37/6 in Antioch, locked in negotiations with Antony. Egypt had enjoyed four years of stability and growing prosperity and, personal relationships aside, she was in a far stronger bargaining position than she had been in Tarsus. She could provide the fleet and provisions that Antony needed, but in exchange she asked for the return of the lost eastern empire of Ptolemy II Philadelphos. Antony agreed: not necessarily because he had been driven mad by his infatuation with Cleopatra, but because he needed Cleopatra's help and, in his view, the return of the lands was fully in line with Roman policy, which was happy to allow a certain amount of autonomous government by tried and trusted client monarchs. Octavian's reaction, and the propaganda that he was later able to make out of Antony's donation of whole provinces to Cleopatra without consulting the Senate, suggest that not everyone agreed.

Almost overnight, Cleopatra was given control of Cyprus, Crete, Cyrenaica (Libya), large parts of Coele-Syria, Phoenecia, Cilicia and Nabataea. The only land missing was Judaea, which had recently been declared the property of the newly installed king Herod. Even without Judaea, Cleopatra was the wealthiest monarch in the world, and she was able to increase her wealth further by striking deals with the Jews and the Nabataeans for the lease of land and the right to extract bitumen from the shore of the Dead Sea. Herod even agreed to collect taxes on her behalf.

Antony now acknowledged the twins, who went through a naming or renaming ceremony to become Alexander Helios (sun) and Cleopatra Selene (moon):

... he heightened the scandal by acknowledging his two children by her, and called one Alexander and the other Cleopatra, with the surname for the first of Sun, and for the other of Moon. However, since he was an adept at putting a good face upon shameful deeds, he used to say that the greatness of the Roman empire was made manifest, not by what the Romans received, but by what they bestowed; and that noble families were extended by the successive begettings of many kings. In this way, at any rate, he said, his own progenitor was begotten by Heracles, who did not confine his succession to a single womb, nor stand in awe of laws like Solon's for the regulation of conception, but gave free course to nature, and left behind him the beginnings and foundations of many families.[28]

Cleopatra and Selene were two well-established Ptolemaic names and, as the moon was associated with Isis in her role as Queen of Heaven, both were highly suitable for Cleopatra's daughter. Alexander was also a Ptolemaic name, one which carried memories of Alexander the Great; while Helios, the sun, was not only the traditional twin of the moon, it was a name that associated the young Alexander with the Egyptian solar cults, both traditional (the cult of Re and the cult of Horus, son of Isis and Osiris/Dionysos) and new (the cult of Serapis). Outside Egypt Helios was linked with Apollo, Octavian's own divine inspiration.

Once again Cleopatra and Antony were lovers. Whether this was a part of the bargain, or whether there was genuine passion on both sides, is impossible to determine. The following year, in late summer 36, Cleopatra was to bear a second son, Ptolemy Philadelphos, whom she named, following her reacquisition of the Ptolemaic empire, after the illustrious Ptolemy II. Returning from Antioch in triumph, Cleopatra proclaimed a new era. The year from 1 September 37 to 31 August 36 was now to be known as 'Year 16 that is Year 1' and this double dating system would continue until 'Year 22 that is Year 7', the year of Cleopatra's death. The glorious new age was accompanied by new titles. Phoenician coins now show an obverse portrait of Basilissa Cleopatra Thea Neotera (The Younger Queen Cleopatra Thea, or, Queen Cleopatra the Younger Goddess), with a reverse portrait of Antony. Cleopatra Thea is an obvious reference to our Cleopatra's great-great-aunt Cleopatra Thea, queen of Syria. In 37 a contract from Heracleopolis, Egypt, makes reference to Thea Neotera Philopator kai Philopatris (the Father-Loving and Homeland-Loving Younger Goddess).[29] Caesarion's title, the 'father-Loving and Mother-Loving God' remains unchanged.

In May 36, Antony resumed his Parthian campaign, starting with a long and tiring march northwards through Syria, then east-wards through Armenia. The campaign began well but quickly turned into a humiliating disaster, with the loss of over 30,000 men – approximately two-fifths of his army. Antony, left with just twenty-five legions under his command, was forced to make a weary winter retreat to Syria. Once again Cleopatra was summoned from Egypt, and once again she hesitated, perhaps because she had just given birth, or because she needed time to collect supplies, or because she needed time to consider her position. For Antony's Parthian humiliation had coincided with Octavian's defeat of Sextus, and Octavian had further strengthened his position by forcing Lepidus into retirement and seizing his remaining territories. The balance of power had shifted and Octavian was beginning to pose a serious challenge to Antony's authority. In January 35, Cleopatra met Mark Antony in the obscure Phoenician port of Leuce Come (White Village). She brought supplies of warm clothing and food, but not enough money to pay the troops. A few weeks later both Antony and Cleopatra retired to Alexandria.

Octavia, meanwhile, had been living the virtuous life of a true Roman matron, caring for her own and Antony's various children, and dividing her time between Athens and Rome. In the spring of 35 she left Rome for Greece on the first leg of a journey, planned by her brother, to bring 2,000 troops (not the 20,000 promised) and seventy ships from Octavian to Antony, plus a contribution of money, cattle and gifts from her own purse. Disconcerted, Antony ordered Octavia to stay in Rome (according to Dio) or Athens (Plutarch), but to send the soldiers on. Plutarch tells us that this very public rejection of Octavia was Cleopatra's fault; that she had used all her feminine wiles to persuade Antony not to receive his wife:

> *Cleopatra perceived that Octavia was coming into a contest at close quarters with her, and feared lest, if she added to the dignity of her character and the power of Caesar her pleasurable society and her assiduous attentions to Antony, she would become invincible and get complete control over her husband. She therefore pretended to be passionately in love with Antony herself, and reduced her body by slender diet; she put on a look of rapture when Antony drew near, and one of faintness and melancholy when he went away. She would contrive to be often seen in tears, and then would quickly wipe the tears away and try to hide them, as if she would not have Antony notice them. And she practised these arts while Antony was intending to go up from Syria to join the Mede [attack the Parthians]. Her flatterers, too, were industrious in her behalf, and used to revile Antony as hard-hearted and unfeeling, and as the destroyer of a mistress who was devoted to him and him alone. For Octavia, they said, had married him as a matter of public policy and for the sake of her brother, and enjoyed the name of wedded wife; but Cleopatra, who was queen of so many people, was called Antony's beloved, and she did not shun this name nor disdain it, as long as she could see him and live with him; but if she were driven away from him she would not survive it ...*[30]

Plutarch's explanation is most unlikely, as is Dio's claim that Cleopatra used witchcraft to turn Antony against Octavia. It is more reasonable to assume that, with his relationship with Octavian fast breaking down, Antony's political marriage had become an irrelevance. He had decided that the way ahead lay with Cleopatra. This was not the first time that Antony had discarded a no longer useful wife. But his rejection of the virtuous Octavia in favour of an illicit alliance with a foreigner did not go down well in Rome, where Octavia, still considering herself married, continued to look after Antony's children in his house. Octavia was as strong in her own way as Fulvia had been. As a conspicuously wronged wife, she had an important role to play in her brother's propaganda and, as Antony's reputation plummeted to an all-time low, Octavia's grew from strength to strength. In 33 Octavian, happy to make political capital out of his virtuous sister, gave her *sacrosanctitas* (sacrosanctity: the right to be protected), the highest honour that could be awarded to a married Roman woman. For the time being at least, she eclipsed her sister-in-law Livia as Rome's most prominent woman.

Cleopatra and Antony spent the winter of 35/4 in Alexandria. The following spring Cleopatra travelled with Antony as far as the Euphrates, then made a lengthy royal progress home through her new territories, stopping at Apamea on the Orontes, Emesa, Damascus and Jerusalem, where she again met Herod and, according to Josephus, made an unsuccessful attempt to seduce him:

> *When she was there, and was very often with Herod, she endeavoured to have criminal conversation with the king; nor did she affect secrecy in the indulgence of such sort of pleasures; and perhaps she had in some measure a passion of love to him; or rather, what is most probable, she laid a treacherous snare for him, by aiming to obtain such adulterous conversation from him: however, upon the whole, she seemed overcome with love to him. Now Herod had a great while borne no good-will to Cleopatra, as knowing that she was a woman irksome to all; and at that time he thought her particularly worthy of his hatred, if this attempt proceeded out of lust;*

he had also thought of preventing her intrigues, by putting her to death, if such were her endeavours. However, he refused to comply with her proposals, and called a counsel of his friends to consult with them whether he should not kill her, now he had her in his power; for that he should thereby deliver all those from a multitude of evils to whom she was already become irksome, and was expected to be still so for the time to come; and that this very thing would be much for the advantage of Antony himself, since she would certainly not be faithful to him ...[31]

No other historian tells this tale, which is, to say the least, highly unlikely. In fact Cleopatra and Herod had much in common and would have done well to set aside their territorial dispute and join forces. However, Cleopatra's blatant interference in Jewish politics, and her friendship with his forceful mother-in-law Alexandra, did not endear her to Herod. In 36 Alexandra had written to Cleopatra, asking her to influence Herod's choice of high priest. Cleopatra had referred the matter to Antony, and Alexandra's seventeen-year-old son, Aristobulus, had been duly given the position. When Aristobulus was (most predictably) murdered within a year of his appointment, Alexandra again wrote to Cleopatra asking her to help avenge her son's murder. Cleopatra again referred the matter to Antony, and Herod was summoned to Rome to account for his deeds. Returning home, Herod had resolved his domestic problems by having the more troublesome members of his family either jailed or killed.

In 34 Antony captured King Artavasdes of Armenia, along with most of his family and his treasure. This was hardly the major eastern victory that he had anticipated. Nevertheless, that autumn Antony re-entered Alexandria dressed in the golden robe of Dionysos, crowned with ivy leaves and carrying a *thyrsos* wand. Before his chariot walked Artavasdes, his wife and two sons, festooned with either silver or golden chains. Cleopatra received Antony sitting on a golden throne on a silver dais before the temple of Serapis, but his captives refused to pay homage to her. Dio, rather chillingly, tells us:

> *the barbarians addressed no supplications to her, nor made obeisance to her, though much coercion was brought to bear upon them and many hopes were held out to them to win their compliance, but they merely addressed her by name; this gave them a reputation for high spirit, but they were subjected to much ill-treatment on account of it.*[32]

Octavian, watching from Rome, was not amused. Antony's Dionysiac celebration too closely resembled a triumph, a strictly Roman sacred celebration. Antony, it seemed, considered Alexandria a capital to rival Rome.

Soon after Antony's triumphal return came the elaborate public celebration known today as the 'Donations of Alexandria'. The ceremony was held in the packed gymnasium, where the royal couple appeared before their people on a silver dais. Cleopatra, splendid in the robes of the New Isis, sat on a golden throne, while Antony sat on a silver throne beside her. The royal children were given lesser thrones slightly beneath their parents. Antony delivered a lengthy speech, ostensibly in honour of Julius Caesar, during which he outlined ambitious plans for his eastern lands. Cleopatra was officially recognised as the 'Queen of Kings and her Sons who are Kings'. Her co-ruler Caesarion, now formally acknowledged by Antony as the legitimate son of Caesar, took his rightful place as pharaoh of Egypt, 'King of Kings', yet was still expected to sit below his mother and stepfather. The younger children had been dressed in the national clothing of the rulers of Persia (Alexander Helios), Cyrenaica (Cleopatra Selene) and Macedonia (Ptolemy Philadelphos). The message was again clear and unsubtle. Cleopatra and Caesarion were the joint rulers of Egypt and the associated territories of Cyprus, Libya and Coele-Syria.

In addition, Caesarion was the true heir to Rome and her western territories. Alexander Helios was destined, somewhat optimistically, given that Egypt did not yet own the bulk of these lands, to rule all territories to the east of the Euphrates, including Armenia and Parthia. Cleopatra Selene was to rule Cyrenaica and Crete, while Ptolemy Philadelphos was given parts of Syria and Cilicia, plus all Roman lands to the west of the Euphrates. The three young children would acknowledge allegiance to Cleopatra and Caesarion, while Antony, as head of the royal family, would effectively rule the world. Nothing could have been calculated to displease Octavian more. For the first time, he started to criticise Antony in pubic.

Octavian and Antony were still in correspondence. A private letter from Antony to Octavian survives in Suetonius:

> *What has come over you? Do you object to me sleeping with Cleopatra? But we are married; and it is not even as if this is anything new – the affair started nine years ago. And what about you? Are you faithful to [Livia] Drusilla? My congratulations if, when this letter arrives, you have not been to bed with Tertulia, or Terentilla, or Rufilla, or Salvia Titisenia – or all of them. Does it really matter so much where, or with whom, you perform the sexual act?*[33]

Here, more than ever, the translation of the original Latin affects our understanding of Antony's message. The verb *ineo*, translated as 'sleeping with', is a rather crude term often used to describe animal mating. Octavian would have understood that Antony was not being over-polite about his relationship with Cleopatra, and some modern authorities have stressed this point by using the translation 'screwing' or 'fucking' the queen.[34] But the interesting phrase from our point of view is *uxor mea est*, which can with equal validity be translated as a statement, either 'she is my wife' or – as in Robert Graves's translation quoted above – 'we are married', or as a question – 'is she my wife?'

Either way, it seems that Antony, legally still married to Octavia, considers himself somehow married to Cleopatra. It has been argued that this might mean a theoretical, divine marriage, the union of Dionysos/Osiris with Aphrodite/Isis. Certainly, any mortal marriage that the already married Antony might undertake and, indeed, any marriage with a foreigner could have had no validity under Roman law.

It is generally assumed that Cleopatra would have wished to be legally married to Antony.[35] Quite why modern historians should make this assumption – reducing the powerful Cleopatra to the status of a weak mistress who longs to be an 'honest woman' – is not clear. She is unlikely to have been over-concerned about her children's legitimacy as, in Egypt and her territories, their position as children of the world's most powerful queen goddess would have been unchallenged. In any case, under Egyptian law, there was no formal civil or religious wedding ceremony and a marriage simply required that a couple should live together for the purpose of begetting children. Cleopatra might therefore have legitimately considered herself married to Antony and Caesar, even if they did not consider themselves married to her. The Romans, who looked long and hard at Cleopatra, never saw a wife. They saw an unnatural, immodest woman who preyed on other women's husbands. From this developed the myth of the sexually promiscuous Cleopatra, and claims of torrid affairs with Gnaeus Pompey, Pompey the Great, Ptolemies XIII and IV (incest!), Caesar, Antony, Herod and countless others, including slaves. A harsh legacy indeed for a woman who probably had no more than two, consecutive, sexual relationships.

CHAPTER SEVEN

Death of a Dream

For Rome, who had never consented to fear any nation or people, did in her time fear two human beings: one was Hannibal and the other was a woman.

W. W. Tarn, *Cambridge Ancient History*[1]

With the relationship between Octavian and Antony damaged beyond any hope of repair, a fierce propaganda war erupted in Rome. Octavian accused Antony of murdering Sextus Pompey, of bringing Rome into disrepute by unlawfully imprisoning the king of Armenia, of seizing Egypt and other foreign territories. He demanded his fair share of the spoils. Antony in turn accused Octavian of stealing a pregnant bride (Livia Drusilla) from her husband, unlawfully removing Lepidus from office and misappropriating lands belonging to both Lepidus and Sextus. He, too, demanded his fair share of the spoils. Octavian's campaign received a major boost when Antony's friend Plancus, whom we last met naked and dancing as a blue fish in Alexandria (page 156), joined forces with his nephew Marcus Titius and defected. Plancus and Titius were able to reveal the secrets of

Antony's will, held for safe-keeping with the Vestal Virgins. Octavian seized the document and read extracts (or rather, he read what he claimed to be extracts from Antony's will) before the Senate. Antony's affirmation that Caesarion was indeed the true heir of Caesar was considered highly provocative. His legacies to his children by Cleopatra were considered both illegal and a sign of his degeneracy; he should not have ranked his foreign-born bastards as equals with his Roman children. His sentimental wish that, wherever in the world he died his body be carried in state through the Roman Forum, then sent to Egypt for burial, was greeted with hoots of derision.

Tales of Antony's unnatural subservience to Cleopatra spread like wildfire. Cleopatra had demanded, and received, the vast libraries of Pergamon; she had recruited Roman soldiers into her bodyguard; she had made Antony rub her feet like a slave at an official banquet (and everyone knew what foot-rubbing led to!); she had sent letters which distracted Antony while he presided in court. Cleopatra had only to appear and Antony would drop everything and run after her. Antony was, like Caesar before him, planning to abandon Rome and establish a new capital in Egypt. He was assuming un-Roman, foreign ways; he called his headquarters 'the palace'. He sometimes wore an oriental dagger at his belt, and was often seen reclining on a gilded couch or a chair. He even pissed in a gold chamber pot! Worst of all, as Dio tells us:

> *He posed with her [Cleopatra] for portrait paintings and statues, he representing Osiris or Dionysos and she Selene or Isis. This more than all else made him seem to have been bewitched by her through some enchantment. For she so charmed and enthralled not only him but also the rest who had any influence with him that she conceived the hope of ruling even the Romans; and whenever she used an oath her strongest phrase in swearing was by her purpose to dispense justice on the Capitol.*[2]

Officially, Octavian found this laughable. As far as he was concerned, the only link between Antony and the world-conquering Dionysos was his excessive drinking. If Antony was to be Dionysos, let him be the savage Dionysos Omestes, eater of flesh, who stole from the wealthy to give to his sycophantic followers. Octavian, the moderate Roman, would challenge him as Apollo.

With Octavian's propaganda becoming increasingly effective, Antony was forced to publish a pamphlet (*De Sua Ebrietate*, 'On His Sobriety', now lost[3]) defending himself against charges of drunkenness. It was his turn to launch a spate of personal attacks. Octavian was a man of despicably humble origins; he had been Caesar's catamite; he had betrothed his daughter to a barbarian; he was a coward who dared not fight; he removed the hairs on his legs by singeing them with red-hot walnut shells. At a time of shortages, when the people of Rome were hungry for bread, Octavian had hosted a private banquet, 'The Feast of the Divine Twelve' (*cena dodekatheos*), at which he and his eleven guests, blasphemously disguised as gods and goddesses, had consumed a vast amount of food. Octavian was indeed Apollo; not the archer god of light and learning, but his darker aspect, Apollo Tortor, the tormentor.

Cleopatra and Antony spent the winter of 33/2 assembling a fleet in Ephesus. Here they were joined by the current consuls, Gaius Sosius and Gnaeus Domitius Ahenobarbus, old friends of Antony who brought with them as many as 300 senators – confirmation that by no means everyone in Rome had been swayed by Octavian's rhetoric. Cleopatra's presence was not universally welcomed; the senators liked to believe they were supporting Antony against Octavian rather than Egypt against Rome, and they felt that there was no room for a woman in a war cabinet. But Antony, recognising Cleopatra's experience and intelligence, and of course the fact that she was making a substantial financial contribution to his campaign, argued that she should stay. Now, as the impecunious Octavian struggled to finance a fleet,

Cleopatra, Antony and their forces travelled to the island of Samos, where they boosted morale by holding an impressive festival of music and drama:

> For just as all the kings, dynasts, tetrarchs, nations, and cities between Syria, the Mareotic Lake, Armenia, and Illyria had been ordered to send or bring their equipment for the war, so all the dramatic artists were compelled to put in an appearance at Samos; and while almost all the world around was filled with groans and lamentations, a single island for many days resounded with flutes and stringed instruments; theatres there were filled, and choral bands were competing with one another. Every city also sent an ox for the general sacrifice, and kings vied with one another in their mutual entertainments and gifts. And so men everywhere began to ask: 'How will the conquerors celebrate their victories if their preparations for the war are marked by festivals so costly?'[4]

In May 32 Cleopatra and Antony transferred their troops to the Greek mainland and took up residence in Athens. Dio tells us that the Athenians, who had earlier respected Octavia, extended the same courtesy to Cleopatra, and a statue of the queen as Isis was erected on the Acropolis. It was now, while living in Athens, that Antony formally divorced Octavia, sending representatives to remove her from his house in Rome. Finally, in late 32, came a move to Patras in the northwestern Peloponnese. The fleet was by now moored in over a dozen different harbours along the west coast of Greece, stretching from Actium in the north to Methone in the south. Had they invaded Italy at this time, they might well have triumphed. But Antony believed that the Romans would unite against a 'foreign invasion' if Cleopatra remained in command of her troops, while Cleopatra's Egyptian troops would not necessarily follow his command if their queen went home. So together Antony and Cleopatra waited for Octavian's forces to leave Italy so that they might fight their battle on neutral territory.

In late 32 Antony was formally stripped of all his titles by the Roman Senate. Then, at last, Octavian donned ritual garments, stood before the temple of Bellona on the Campus Martius, hurled a wooden javelin against an invisible foreign enemy and, invoking the most ancient of rites (rites which he appears to have rewritten for the occasion), declared war on Cleopatra. The charge against her was the remarkably vague 'for her acts'. Theoretically, the ancient rites demanded that Octavian should seek compensation from Cleopatra before hurling his javelin: this part of the ritual was, however, ignored. It is hard to see what Cleopatra's heinous anti-Roman 'acts' might have been.[5] Throughout the civil war she had acted as a faithful Roman vassal, supplying assistance to Pompey in 49; preparing a fleet for Antony and Octavian in 42; responding to various summonses to Alexandria (Caesar, 48), Tarsus (Antony, 42) and Antioch (Antony, 37). The truth is, of course, that Octavian had realised that his troops would agree to fight a foreign enemy, but would not fight Antony, who was still, despite all the negative propaganda, a popular figure. As Antony was likely to stand by Cleopatra, he would, by his own deeds, become a true quasi-foreign enemy of Rome.

Plutarch tells us that the omens, published by Octavian and therefore highly suspect, did not look good for the couple. Pisaurum (modern Pesaro, Umbria), a city colonised by Antony, was swallowed by an earthquake, a selection of heroic and divine statues linked with Antony was destroyed, and marble statues were seen to ooze blood or sweat for many days. In Rome the schoolboys formed parties, the Antonians and the Caesarians, which fought for two days before the Caesarians emerged victorious. In Etruria a two-headed serpent eighty-five feet in length appeared from nowhere and did a great deal of damage before it was killed by a bolt of lightning. It is interesting to contrast these omens with the prophecies recorded in the *Sibylline*

Oracles, a collection of twelve books of predictions formally attributed to various Sibyls between 200 BC – AD 400, but actually deriving from other sources. Book 3 of the *Oracles* was written by Egyptian Jewish scholars. The bulk of their prophecies date to the reign of Ptolemy VI and look forward to the arrival of a 'king from the sun' – an Egyptian (Ptolemaic?) messiah. But a passage written much later, shortly before the battle of Actium, equates Cleopatra with 'The Mistress' (*despoina*), an eastern saviour intent on destroying Rome at the dawn of a golden age:

> *Of Asia, even thrice as many goods*
> *Shall Asia back again from Rome receive...*
> *O virgin, soft rich child of Latin Rome,*
> *Oft at thy much-remembered marriage feasts*
> *Drunken with wine, now shalt thou be a slave*
> *And wedded in no honourable way.*
> *And oft shall mistress shear thy pretty hair,*
> *And wreaking satisfaction cast thee down*
> *From heaven to earth...*[6]

Later still, after the battle, Cleopatra is transformed into an eschatological adversary, an anti-saviour who will indeed rule the world, but who will bring about its destruction.

Suddenly there was action of the most unwelcome sort. Marcus Vipsanius Agrippa, Octavian's highly experienced admiral, took the Egyptian naval base of Methone, on the tip of the Peloponnese. From this base Octavian's ships were able to work their way along the coast, attacking Cleopatra's supply ships and targeting Antony's dispersed fleet. Meanwhile, Octavian's army had taken Corecyna (Corfu), landed unopposed on the Greek mainland and marched south to strike camp at low-lying, swampy Actium on the Gulf of Ambracia. Cleopatra and Antony fled north to Actium and struck camp on the opposite side of the gulf to Octavian. Soon after, their joint fleet was trapped by Octavian's ships in the bay. Conditions in their camp deteriorated quickly: the supply lines had been cut, many of the men were suffering from a distressing combination of malaria and dysentery, and morale was at rock bottom. High-profile supporters, Ahenobarbus included, were deserting in droves and Antony was forced to execute a fleeing Roman senator as a warning. In August Antony's ships made a serious but unsuccessful attempt to escape the blockade.

Plutarch – who, historians believe, gained much of his information from a deserter who joined Octavian in time to take part in the sea battle – tells us that Cleopatra and Antony had raised an army of not fewer than 500 warships, 100,000 legionaries and armed infantry and 12,000 cavalry. They were supported by an impressive list of kingly allies: Bocchus of Libya, Tarcondemus of Upper Cilicia, Archelaos of Cappadocia, Philadelphos of Paphlagonia, Mithridates of Commagene and Sadalas of Thrace. Polemon of Pontus sent an army, as did Malchus of Nabataea, Amyntas of Lycaonia, Galatia, the king of the Medes, and Herod, the king of the Jews. Cleopatra supplied at least sixty Egyptian ships and commanded her own fleet. Octavian, with a mere 250 ships, 80,000 infantry and approximately 12,000 cavalry, was outnumbered, but his fleet was both better armed and better prepared, and although Octavian himself was a far from seasoned campaigner, Admiral Agrippa had all the experience that he lacked. Aware of Agrippa's reputation, Antony's friend and general Crassus, a man who, as we have already seen, had a considerable financial interest in Egypt, advised that the fleet should be abandoned and that the troops should march northwards to fight in better circumstances in Macedon. Dio tells us that Cleopatra, reluctant to abandon her ships, disagreed with Crassus, and that Antony sided with her. Her plan, formulated after observing a series of bad omens (swallows nesting on her ships and around her tent; milk and blood dripping from beeswax; several statues of herself and Antony in the guise of gods being struck down by thunderbolts), was to flee to Egypt and regroup:

> *In consequence of these portents and of the resulting dejection of the army, and of the sickness prevalent among them, Cleopatra herself became alarmed and filled Antony with fears. They did not wish, however, to sail out secretly, nor yet openly, as if they were in flight, lest they should inspire their allies also with fear, but rather as if they were making preparations for a naval battle, and incidentally in order that they might force their way through in case there should be any resistance. Therefore they first chose out the best of the vessels and burned the rest, since the sailors had become fewer by death and desertion; next they secretly put all their most valuable possessions on board by night.[7]*

Dio is worth quoting at length here, because he makes it quite clear that Cleopatra and Antony were united in their plan to take the fleet to Egypt. The fact that they loaded sails on to their warships makes it fairly certain that their troops, too, knew that something unusual was afoot.

After some minor skirmishes, more defections from Antony's camp, a bizarre and quickly foiled attempt to kidnap Antony (reported by Plutarch), several days of bad weather and a couple of lengthy and inspirational speeches from the two leaders, the sea battle flared up on 2 September 31. Antony's ships emerged from the Gulf of Ambracia and faced out to sea in three divisions, protecting Cleopatra's fleet, which was held in reserve behind the central division. From the beginning things went badly. Octavian's ships kept out of range, drawing Antony's fleet further and further out to sea so that they might become dispersed. Antony's ships were hopelessly undercrewed and unable to fight efficiently. Antony himself commanded the right division facing

Octavian's left division, commanded by Agrippa. Here things went according to plan and there was some brisk fighting, but the central and left divisions underperformed, allowing Octavian to take an early advantage. At some point the battleships from the central and left divisions stopped participating in the battle and retreated into the gulf. Soon after, possibly at a prearranged signal, Cleopatra's sixty ships hoisted their sails, broke through Octavian's line and sailed away at full speed. Antony abandoned his large flagship, transferred his flag to a quinquereme, and chased after Cleopatra with about forty of his personal squadron:

> … *Antony made it clear to all the world that he was swayed neither by the sentiments of a commander nor of a brave man, nor even by his own, but, as someone in pleasantry said that the soul of the lover dwells in another's body, he was dragged along by the woman as if he had become incorporate with her and must go where she did. For no sooner did he see her ship sailing off than he forgot everything else, betrayed and ran away from those who were fighting and dying in his cause, got into a five-oared galley, where Alexas the Syrian and Scellius were his only companions, and hastened after the woman who had already ruined him and would make his ruin still more complete. Cleopatra recognized him and raised a signal on her ship; so Antony came up and was taken on board, but he neither saw nor was seen by her. Instead, he went forward alone to the prow and sat down by himself in silence, holding his head in both hands.*[8]

It is perhaps inevitable that Plutarch would interpret this as the cowardly or devious Cleopatra running away from the battle. He was faced with the unenviable task of showing Antony in a sympathetic light while making it clear to his readers that Octavian is the real hero of Actium, and he achieved this by making Cleopatra into the villain of his piece. It is less easy to understand how so many modern historians, with full access to Dio, have made the same assumption.

Octavian thought of chasing after Cleopatra's ships, but quickly realised that he would be unable to catch her and so continued with the battle. Antony's fleet fought on, but their situation was hopeless. Octavian's own memoir tells us that the sea battle ended at 4 p.m. with some 5,000 of Antony's men lost and 300 of his ships taken; Tarn has used these figures to calculate that between ten and fifteen of Antony's ships must have sunk.[9] Meanwhile, Antony's ground forces had started the long march north but had been caught by Octavian's troops. Tempted by generous bribes, the bulk of Antony's soldiers defected, bringing a swift and relatively painless end to the confrontation. Crassus was able to escape under cover of nightfall and make his way back to Antony. Octavian, who already had enough ships, burned many of Antony's vessels lest they fall into the wrong hands. His failure to capture Cleopatra's war chest, now safely on its way to Egypt, meant that he would be embarrassingly short of money to pay his victorious veterans. Nevertheless, in celebration of his success, Octavian dedicated ten complete ships from Antony's captured fleet to Apollo, and founded the city of Nicopolis. The battle of Actium, hardly the greatest of victories, was to be remembered as a triumph for Octavian, Agrippa and Apollo, and as the beginning of the end for Cleopatra, Antony and Egypt.

It is hard not to feel sympathy for Antony, sitting day after day on deck with his head in his hands. Without knowing exactly what did happen at Actium, it is impossible to imagine the thoughts going through his mind, but although he and Cleopatra (and their treasure chest) lived on to fight another day, he must have realised that he was running out of men prepared to fight for his cause. Only after the ship had docked at Taenarum (modern Cape Matapan, the southernmost point of the Peloponnese) did Cleopatra and Antony meet. Soon after, encouraged by Cleopatra's ladies-in-waiting, they were dining and sleeping together again.

Separated from Cleopatra again, Antony made his way across the

Mediterranean to the Greek town of Paraetonium (modern Mersa Matruh) on the Egyptian–Cyrenaican border. Here he was horrified to find that a garrison of previously loyal troops had defected to Octavian. Their general, Lucius Pinarius Scarpus, not only refused to receive Antony, but executed Antony's messengers and all those among his own troops who were inclined to support him. Faced with this betrayal, Antony contemplated suicide, but was persuaded by friends to rejoin Cleopatra in Alexandria instead.

Cleopatra, worried about the very real danger of civil unrest, had gone straight to Alexandria. Arriving ahead of the news from Actium, she was able to fool her people by entering the harbour in triumph, with garlands draped over the front of her boat and musicians playing victory songs. Then, or so Dio tells us, having lulled her people into a false sense of security, she embarked upon a remarkable killing spree designed to rid the city of all potential enemies. The hostage king of Armenia and his family were executed and many prominent citizens were murdered and their property seized. Temple and state assets, too, were confiscated, until Cleopatra had amassed a huge war chest, which she apparently intended to use to finance her escape and – if at all possible – pay for an army to regain her throne. That Cleopatra needed to maximise her assets makes sense, even though she had apparently managed to save her treasure from the disaster of Actium. The killing spree, however, seems highly implausible, given that she was likely to need the support of the people of Alexandria in the very near future.

It still seemed reasonable to make extravagant plans. One idea, to flee by boat to Spain, meet up with the last remnants of Pompey's rebels and provoke a revolt against Octavian, was dropped when it became obvious that Agrippa's ships, still patrolling the Mediterranean, would make a sea crossing far too dangerous. Instead, determined to flee to India via the Red Sea, Cleopatra ordered that her fleet be transported overland via the Wadi Tumilat to the Gulf of Suez. This was not as desperate a move as it might now seem; the dynastic

Egyptians had regularly transported boats from the Nile overland to the Red Sea. But the plan had to be abandoned when the first boats were captured and burned by the Nabataean king, Malchus, who, still smarting from Antony's cavalier treatment of his land, wished to demonstrate his loyalty to Octavian. Antony arrived in Alexandria to find Cleopatra's partially completed mausoleum packed with all kinds of treasure and protected by piles of flammable material. If attacked, she intended to torch the mausoleum and destroy her fortune. The very thought must have filled Octavian with horror. He needed Cleopatra's wealth to compensate his underpaid veterans, who had been teetering on the verge of mutiny since the battle of Actium.

Severely depressed, Antony spent some time living in solitude on the Alexandrian peninsula of Lochias, where he built the Timoneion, a shrine named after the legendary recluse Timon of Athens. His return to Cleopatra's palace saw the disbanding of the Inimitable Livers in favour of a new society, 'The Partners in Death' (*synapothanoumenoi*), a smaller, more close-knit group of friends who chose to face the inevitable by carousing more than ever.

The winter of 31/30 saw the sixteen-year-old Caesarion and his fourteen-year-old stepbrother Antyllus officially come of age. Caesarion was enrolled into the Alexandrian *ephebes*, the list of young male citizens, while Antyllus donned the purple-hemmed *toga virilis* that showed the world that he was a citizen of Rome. Dio correctly identifies this as a propaganda exercise: a means of reminding the conservative Egyptians that the dynastic line would continue through their adult male king, and the population as a whole that the two sons could replace Cleopatra and Antony should the worst happen. Antyllus, Antony's oldest son and principal heir, had already appeared on a gold coin alongside his father. Now a stela dated to Year 22, which is Year 7 of the female king Cleopatra 'and of the king Ptolemy called Caesar, the Father-Loving, Mother-Loving God' (21 September 31; just nineteen days after the battle of Actium), shows Caesarion dressed as a traditional Egyptian king as he makes offerings of lettuce and wine to the ithyphallic fertility god Min and his consort Isis, and offerings of wine to the earth god Geb and his temple companion the crocodile-headed Sobek. The stela, recovered from Koptos and now in the British Museum, confirms that life outside Alexandria was continuing much as before. It details two contracts drawn up by a guild of thirty-six linen manufacturers concerning the expenses of the local sacred bull.

Plutarch tells us that it was at this time that Cleopatra started to experiment with various poisons:

> *Cleopatra was getting together collections of all sorts of deadly poisons, and she tested the painless working of each of them by giving them to prisoners under sentence of death. But when she saw that the speedy poisons enhanced the sharpness of death by the pain they caused, while the milder poisons were not quick, she made trial of venomous animals, watching with her own eyes as they were set upon another. She did this daily, tried them almost all; and she found that the bite of the asp alone induced a sleepy torpor and sinking, where there was no spasm or groan, but a gentle perspiration on the face, while the perceptive faculties were easily relaxed and dimmed, and resisted all attempts to rouse and restore them, as is the case with those who are soundly asleep.*[10]

Octavian, still in Asia Minor, received a stream of messages from Egypt. Plutarch tells us that Cleopatra begged to be allowed to abdicate in favour of her children, while Antony asked that he might be allowed to retire as a private person to Athens. Antony never received a reply, but Cleopatra was informed that Octavian would consider her request if she either killed or at least renounced Antony. These most sensitive of negotiations were conducted through Thyrsus, Octavian's freedman. Cleopatra had so many private conversations with Thyrsus that Antony, made tense and irritable by his situation, became suspicious of his motives, had him flogged and returned him to Octavian with a terse message: 'If you don't like what I have done, you have my freedman Hipparchus; hang him up and give him a flogging, and we shall be quits.'[11] As Antony grew increasingly suspicious of Cleopatra's motives, she responded with flattery, throwing a lavish celebration for his birthday while virtually ignoring her own. However, Dio adds that, unknown to Antony, Cleopatra had already sent Octavian a golden sceptre and a golden crown, together with the royal throne that represented her kingdom. Now Cleopatra, reading Octavian well, attempted to bribe him with vast amounts of money (presumably the treasure stored in her mausoleum), while Antony, reading Octavian less well, sought to remind him of their friendship and their shared adventures. Desperate, he surrendered Publius Turullius, one of Caesar's assassins, and offered to take his own life if, in return, Cleopatra might be saved. Octavian put Turullius to death, but made no formal reply. Next Antony sent Antyllus to Octavian with a large gift of gold. Octavian took the money, but sent the boy back without an answer.

The summer of 30 saw Egypt under double attack. Cornelius Gallus had assumed command of Scarpus's Paraetonium troops and now launched land and sea assaults from the west. Antony hastened to negotiate, feeling that he might be able to persuade the soldiers (who had once been his) to change sides, but it was in vain: Dio tells us that Gallus had his trumpeters play a fanfare to drown out Antony's words. Then, from the east, Octavian crossed the Sinai land bridge and captured Pelusium. An uncomfortable, persistent rumour that Cleopatra had actually given Pelusium to Octavian in return for clemency for herself and her children does not square with the story that Cleopatra had the wife and children of Seleucos, the unsuccessful defender of Pelusium, put to death. Octavian marched westwards across the Delta, crossing the Nile branches to strike camp near the hippodrome, immediately outside Alexandria's Canopic Gate, and

Antony returned just in time to defend the city against his advance cavalry. Rushing into the palace, sweaty and bloody from the battle, he presented his bravest soldier to Cleopatra. She rewarded the soldier with a valuable gift of golden armour; he repaid her generosity by defecting to Octavian that night, taking the precious armour with him.

Trapped and impotent in Alexandria, Antony resorted to bribery. Leaflets promising generous rewards were tied to arrows and shot into Octavian's camp. As it was obvious to everyone that Antony would never be in a position to honour his promises, no one was tempted by the offer. Next Antony challenged Octavian to single combat, but Octavian refused to be drawn. Finally, he resolved to meet Octavian in battle. That night, Antony's gods left him. They could be heard passing though the gates of Alexandria, making their way towards Octavian.

> *During this night, it is said, about the middle of it, while the city was quiet and depressed through fear and expectation of what was coming, suddenly certain harmonious sounds from all sorts of instruments were heard, and the shouting of a throng, accompanied by cries of Bacchic revelry and satyric leapings, as if a troop of revellers, making a great tumult, were going forth from the city; and their course seemed to lie about through the middle of the city toward the outer gate which faced the enemy, at which point the tumult became loudest and then dashed out. Those who sought the meaning of the sign were of the opinion that the god to whom Antony always most likened and attached himself was now deserting him.*[12]

Graeco-Roman gods were prone to desert those who were about to lose in battle. The disaster at Troy was preceded by desertion, and Domitian would later dream that Minerva had left him because 'she could no longer protect him because she had been disarmed by

Jupiter'.[13] Abandoned by Dionysos-Osiris, Antony would become mortal, and vulnerable, once again.

On the morning of 1 August the godless Antony led his troops through the city gate towards the hippodrome, while his Egyptian fleet sailed eastwards to meet the Roman ships. To his horror his fleet surrendered straight away, raising their oars to salute Octavian. His cavalry, having witnessed the loss of the fleet, immediately deserted. His infantry remained loyal, but it was a one-sided battle and, heavily defeated, Antony retreated into Alexandria, wrestling with the unbearable thought that Cleopatra may have betrayed him. Almost immediately, he heard the rumour that Cleopatra had committed suicide. Antony knew that his time had come. He unbuckled his breastplate and asked his faithful slave Eros to help him to die. Eros drew his sword, but stabbed himself rather than his master. As Eros collapsed at his feet, Antony stabbed himself in the stomach. Plutarch, unable to resist a dramatic moment, tells us that he cried out as he fell, 'Cleopatra, I am not grieved to be bereft of you, for I shall straightway join you; but I am grieved that such a leader as I am has been found to be inferior to a woman in courage.'[14] At this vital point, as Antony lay fatally wounded, Cleopatra's secretary, Diomedes, arrived with the news that the queen was not, after all, dead.

Together with her lady-in-waiting Charmian, her hairdresser Eiras and, perhaps, an anonymous eunuch who is mentioned by Dio but not by Plutarch, Cleopatra had barricaded herself in the mausoleum that housed her treasure. The tomb and its attached temple of Isis are now lost beneath the waters of the Mediterranean, but we can deduce from Plutarch's description of Cleopatra's final days that this was a substantial two-storey structure: a windowless ground floor with a stairway leading up to a windowed, galleried upper floor. Still under construction at her death, it would be completed by Octavian when he authorised the burial of Egypt's last queen. Now Antony, weak from loss of blood, was taken to the tomb, hauled up the walls and dragged inside through an upper-floor window so that he might die in Cleopatra's arms. Octavian entered Alexandria unopposed to find Cleopatra trapped in her mausoleum with Antony's body. A system of stone portcullises and stout doors sealed the ground floor and ensured that no one could enter or leave. This was a serious problem; there was a very real danger that Cleopatra might burn both herself and her treasure. Octavian wished to keep Cleopatra alive so that she could be exhibited in his Roman triumph and, far more importantly, he wished to keep her fabulous treasure intact.

Octavian's top priority had to be to extract Cleopatra from her flammable tomb. He sent his persuasive friend Gaius Proculeius to the mausoleum to negotiate and, if at all possible, to persuade Cleopatra to return to her palace. Conversing through a grille in the locked door, Cleopatra refused to move and again asked that her children be spared. Proculeius made no promises, but told her to be of good cheer and to trust Octavian. The next day Cornelius Gallus was sent to talk through the mausoleum door. With Cleopatra distracted, the resourceful Proculeius used a ladder to gain access to the upper part of the mausoleum. Accompanied by two servants, he climbed through the window that had earlier admitted Antony. The three crept downstairs towards Cleopatra, but were spotted by one of Cleopatra's women, who, according to Plutarch, let out a shriek: 'Wretched Cleopatra, you are taken alive!' Cleopatra turned, saw Proculeius and, drawing a dagger from her girdle, stabbed herself, inflicting a non-fatal wound. Proculeius disarmed her and had the presence of mind to shake her clothing to see if she was hiding any poison in her garments.

Octavian was at last able to recover the treasure that would allow him to pay his debts. Such was the feeling of relief that interest rates in Rome plunged from 12 to 4 per cent.[15] Back in Alexandria, Cleopatra was put in the care of a freedman, Epaphroditus, who was instructed to use utmost vigilance to keep her alive. Dio tells us that, following Antony's funeral, Cleopatra moved from her tomb to her palace, where she fell ill from grief and the effects of her stab wound. Plutarch does not mention the move but he agrees about the illness: he tells us that Cleopatra was sick from grief and that her breasts had become inflamed by constant beating. This had led to a fever, which Cleopatra welcomed. She had stopped eating and was looking forward to death. Octavian could only persuade her to start eating again by threatening her children.

Cleopatra and Octavian met for the first time, probably on 10 August and presumably in her palace. Plutarch tells us that Octavian found the sick Cleopatra in the most miserable of conditions; that she threw herself at his feet; that she was dishevelled, with sunken eyes and a trembling voice; and that she bore obvious bruising on her bosom. Nevertheless, beneath the mask of grief, it was still possible for Octavian to detect vestiges of a spirited woman. Cleopatra lay on her bed, Octavian sat beside her, and Cleopatra launched into a flood of self-justification, blaming everything on her fear of Antony. As it became obvious that Octavian was not convinced by her tale she changed tack and started to beg for mercy. Finally she presented Octavian with a complete list of her treasures. When Seleucus, one of her servants, intervened to point out that Cleopatra's list was in fact incomplete and that she had kept some treasure back, Cleopatra was quick to explain that she had retained some gifts for Octavia and Livia, who, she hoped, might intercede on her behalf. Convinced that she had in fact attempted to keep some treasure for herself, Octavian deduced that Cleopatra was far from suicidal.

Dio tells a very different story. His Cleopatra is still very much the alluring woman who captivated Caesar and Antony, and who is now hoping to captivate Octavian in the same way. She receives Octavian in a splendid apartment, where she reclines on a couch dressed in the most becoming of mourning garments. The room is decorated with portraits of Octavian's adoptive father, Caesar. Seizing the initiative, she starts the conversation by reminding Octavian of her links with his adoptive father. She even reads aloud extracts from Caesar's love letters. Thankfully Octavian, a good Roman husband, is able to resist her feminine wiles. He does not look her in the eye, but merely begs her to be of good cheer. Realising that things are not going too well, Cleopatra starts to plead with Octavian to let her die to join Antony. When this, too, fails to generate a response, she tells Octavian that she is now happy to place her trust in Octavian and Livia. Again, it seems, her intention is to convince Octavian that she is not suicidal.

It is difficult for the modern reader to work out just who is bluffing whom here. The obvious answer is that Cleopatra, who wishes to die, is bluffing Octavian, who wishes to keep her alive. The pre-planned and somewhat clumsy revelation about her hidden treasure is therefore a ruse designed to convince Octavian that she still hopes to live. Alternatively, it may be Octavian who is bluffing. He wishes Cleopatra to die, but does not want to be seen to kill her.[16] Having determined that Cleopatra should die by her own hand, he is nevertheless concerned to ensure that posterity will remember him as a good man who did everything he could to save the queen's life. He knows that Cleopatra has already made two suicide attempts – by stabbing and by starvation – and can surely, if so inclined, prevent her from making a third simply by locking her up. Would Cleopatra have wished to die by her own hand? Suicide is barely mentioned in Egyptian myths and writings, where the only clear evidence for self immolation comes from the trial records which confirm that some of those found guilty of murdering Ramesses III were permitted to kill themselves rather than face public execution. But suicide was, under the appropriate circumstances, a Greek virtue, and Greek mythology includes a surprising number of females who hang or stab themselves following the loss of a loved one (Ariadne, Calypso and Thisbe) or as a sacrifice in order that others might live (Alcestis, Iphigenia). These deaths are all seen as rational responses to unkind fate. Cleopatra, killing herself after the death of Mark Antony, and with her children's future to consider, fits well into this mould. There was, of course, good Ptolemaic precedent for suicide. Cleopatra's uncle Ptolemy, king of Cyprus, had taken poison rather than be captured by the Romans.

Plutarch tells us that Cleopatra's suicide was triggered by a secret (or deliberately leaked?) message from a member of Octavian's staff, telling her that Octavian had resolved to send the queen and her children to Rome within the next three days. Realising that her time had run out, Cleopatra requested that she be allowed to visit Antony's tomb (which was almost certainly her own mausoleum) to pour libations for him. She was carried to the tomb, where she embraced Antony's remains and uttered a beautifully composed speech, which is likely to owe more to Plutarch's literary talents than to Cleopatra's own spontaneous oratory:

'Dear Antony, I buried you but lately with hands still free; now, however, I pour libations for you as a captive, and so carefully guarded that I cannot either with blows or tears disfigure this body of mine, which is a slave's body, and closely watched that it may grace the triumph over you. Do not expect other honours or libations; these are the last from Cleopatra the captive. For though in life nothing could part us from each other, in death we are likely to change places; you, the Roman, lying buried here, while I, the hapless woman, lie in Italy, and get only so much of your country as my portion. But if indeed there is any might or power in the gods of that country (for the gods of this country have betrayed us), do not abandon your wife while she lives, nor permit a triumph to be celebrated over myself in my person, but hide and bury me here with you, since out of all my innumerable ills not one is so great and dreadful as this short time that I have lived apart from you.'[17]

Returning to the palace, Cleopatra bathed, dressed and dined in splendour, enjoying as part of her final meal a basket of figs sent in from the county. The meal over, she gave a sealed tablet to Epaphroditus, for delivery to Octavian. Then she dismissed her servants, keeping only Charmian and Eiras by her side, and retired for the night. The decision to die in front of her female servants made good practical sense, as even the dead needed a chaperone. One of the horrors of a female suicide was that the body might be glimpsed naked, or partially naked, by strangers. Reading Cleopatra's message, a final request to be buried beside Antony, Octavian realised that the queen was about to kill herself. Soldiers ran to the palace and pushed past the guards, who stood, oblivious, outside her room. Opening the doors, they found Cleopatra lying dead on a golden couch. Eiras lay dying at her feet, while Charmian, already feeling the influence of the poison, was desperately trying to straighten the diadem on her mistress's brow. Dio tells us that Octavian summoned *psylli* (Libyan snake-charmers famous for curing snakebites by sucking out the venom) to minister to Cleopatra, but they were too late.

Here we have the classic sealed-room mystery. Cleopatra, Eiras and Charmian are found dead or dying, with only (possibly) a couple of puncture marks on the queen's body to suggest how they died. Why, then, is it so widely accepted that Cleopatra had chosen death by snake? Dio tells what he knows of Cleopatra's passing:

> No one knows clearly in what way she perished, for the only marks on her body were slight pricks on the arm. Some say she applied to herself an asp which had been brought in to her in a water-jar, or perhaps hidden in some flowers. Others declare that she had smeared a pin, with which she was wont to fasten her hair, with some poison possessed of such a property that in ordinary circumstances it would not injure the body at all, but if it came into contact with even a drop of blood would destroy the body very quietly and painlessly; and that previous to this time she had worn it in her hair as usual, but now had made a slight scratch on her arm and had dipped the pin

*in the blood. In this or in some very similar way she perished, and
her two handmaidens with her. As for the eunuch, he had of his own
accord delivered himself up to the serpents at the very time of Cleopatra's arrest, and after being bitten by them had leaped into a coffin
already prepared for him.*[18]

Plutarch gives more detail. He has already prepared us for the possibility of Cleopatra's suicide by detailing her experiments with poison,
but he, too, seems less than convinced by the story of the snake:

*It is said that the asp was brought with those figs and leaves and lay
hidden beneath them, for thus Cleopatra had given orders, that the
reptile might fasten itself upon her body without her being aware of
it. But when she took away some of the figs and saw it, she said:
'There it is, you see,' and baring her arm she held it out for the
bite. But others say that the asp was kept carefully shut up in a water
jar, and that while Cleopatra was stirring it up and irritating it with
a golden distaff it sprang and fastened itself upon her arm. But the
truth of the matter no one knows; for it was also said that she carried
about poison in a hollow comb and kept the comb hidden in her
hair; and yet neither spot nor other sign of poison broke out upon her
body. Moreover, not even was the reptile seen within the chamber,
though people said they saw some traces of it near the sea, where the
chamber looked out upon it with its windows. And some also say that
Cleopatra's arm was seen to have two slight and indistinct punctures;
and this Caesar [Octavian] also seems to have believed. For in his
triumph an image of Cleopatra herself with the asp clinging to her
was carried in the procession. These, then, are the various accounts of
what happened.*[19]

As many historians have observed, suicide by snakebite is not the easy
matter that it might first appear, particularly when one snake is
expected to kill three people. At best it would be a risky business with

a high chance of failure. One cannot, after all, force a reluctant snake to bite and, even if the snake does bite, not every bite injects poison and not every poisoned bite kills. And, as most of the poison is injected with the first bite, it is unlikely that one snake would kill three adults with three consecutive strikes. In Cleopatra's case, the preliminaries would have been fraught with the additional danger of detection. If we accept Octavian's often expressed desire to keep Cleopatra alive, we must assume that she was effectively on 'suicide watch': an order for a snake would have had to be smuggled out of the palace, and the snake would have had to be smuggled back in. Although relatively slender, the Egyptian cobra, *Naja haje*, the principal suspect, can grow to just over six feet in length. An adult cobra, or three, would have needed an exceptionally large fig basket or water jar.

However, in the absence of any obvious weapon, death by snake-bite was accepted by everyone as a symbolically suitable means of female royal suicide. Egypt is currently home to some thirty-nine varieties of snake and there seems no reason to assume that things were very different in antiquity.[20] The dynastic Egyptians had a love-hate relationship with these snakes. They knew all too well that snakes could kill, but they also knew that snakes played an important role in pest control. A snake living beside the granary was infinitely preferable to a nest of rats. This ambivalent attitude is best expressed in the pantheon, home to both good and bad snakes. The serpent Apophis was pure evil: every night he attacked the boat of the sun god Re as it sailed through the dark and dangerous underworld. Fortunately Re had the tightly coiled good snake god Mehen to protect him. Female snake deities were considered to be exemplary mothers. We have already met Wadjyt, 'The Green One', the cobra goddess of the Nile Delta, who appears as the uraeus that decorates and protects the royal crown. Meretseger, 'She Who Loves Silence', guarded the dead of the Theban cemetery. Renenutet, a deadly hooded cobra, was the goddess of the harvest. She protected granaries and families and, as a divine nurse, cared for both babies and the king. Isis, herself a famously good mother, occasionally appeared as the snake Isis Thermoutharion. Alexandria even had its own protective snake deity. *The Alexander Romance* tells how the workmen who built the city were pestered by a snake. Alexander had the snake killed, then built a sanctuary on the spot where it had died. Soon the sanctuary filled with snakes, which squirmed into the neighbouring houses. These were known as the Agathoi Daemones, 'The Good Spirits'.

The Macedonian royal family, too, took a keen interest in snakes. We have already read the story of Nectanebo II assuming the form of a snake to father Alexander the Great (page 132). A variant on this tale is told by Plutarch:

> *A serpent was once seen lying stretched out by the side of Olympias as she slept, and we are told that this, more than anything else, dulled the ardour of Philip's attentions to his wife, so that he no longer came often to sleep by her side, either because he feared that some spells and enchantments might be practised upon him by her, or because he shrank from her embraces in the conviction that she was the partner of a superior being. But concerning these matters there is another story to this effect: all the women of these parts were addicted to the Orphic rites and the orgies of Dionysos from very ancient times, and imitated in many ways the practices of the Edonian women and the Thracian women about Mount Haemus, from whom, as it would seem, the word 'threskeuein' came to be applied to the celebration of extravagant and superstitious ceremonies. Now Olympias, who affected these divine possessions more zealously than other women, and carried them out in wilder fashion, used to provide the revelling companies with great tame serpents, which would often lift their heads from out the ivy and the mystic winnowing-baskets, or coil themselves about the wands and garlands of the women, thus terrifying the men.*[21]

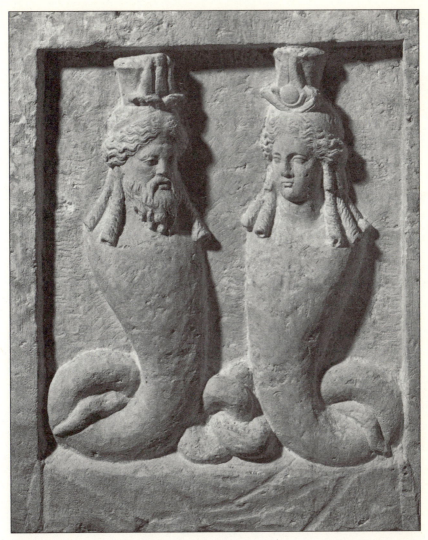

16. A sandstone stela of unknown provenance showing Isis and Dionysos as intertwined snakes. Isis wears an Egyptian-style crown on her Classical style coiffure; Dionysos bears a passing resemblance to Serapis. The pair recall the Agathos Daimon of Alexandria.

17. The 'Alabaster Tomb' of Alexandria: resting place of Alexander the Great?

18. The god Serapis, consort of Isis and patron deity of Alexandria.

19. *A wooden model of Osiris, consort of Isis and king of the dead. Osiris has the body of a wrapped mummy. He wears the crown of Egypt on his unwrapped head, and carries the crook and flail which signify his authority.*

20. *The Egyptian goddess Isis. The queen wears a sheath dress and a short wig. The throne symbol on her head signifies her name Aset or Isis.*

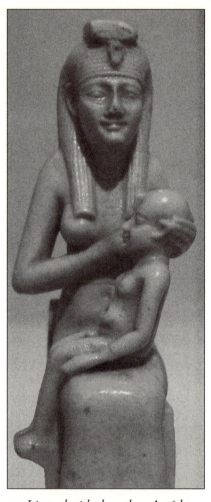

21. *Isis as the ideal mother. A 26th Dynasty faience Isis nurses her infant son Horus. Here the queen wears a long wig and a uraeus.*

22. *Amaryllis, a 1st century* AD *priestess of Isis in Athens, depicted on her funerary stela. Amaryllis wears the knotted robe associated with the goddess.*

23. *Isis carries the sistrum, or sacred rattle, which has the power to stimulate the gods.*

24. *Cleopatra stands in a supportive position behind her son Ptolemy Caesar (Caesarion). She wears the tight sheath dress, long wig, and complicated crown (a modius double plumes, cow horns and solar disk) worn by many Egyptian queens before her. Caesarion appears as an entirely typical Egyptian king.*

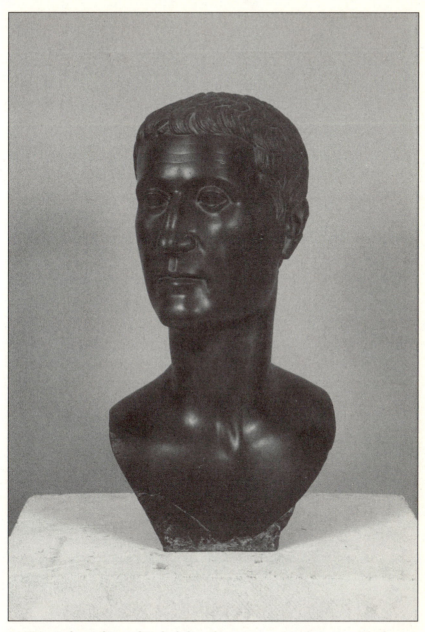

25. *Roman bust of green basalt, believed to represent Mark Antony. The bust was acquired at Canopus in c. 1780, and bought in 1828 at auction by William John Bankes.*

26. Octavian: The Emperor Augustus. Bronze statue recovered from the Aegean Sea.

It is therefore not surprising that, when lost on his way to the oracle of Zeus-Ammon, Alexander was guided on his way by talking snakes. Even the infant Heracles, 'ancestor' of Mark Antony, Alexander the Great and the Ptolemies, had a run-in with a pair of snakes sent by Hera to kill him.

Octavian had allowed Cleopatra to organise Antony's funeral as she wished:

> *though many generals and kings asked for his body that they might give it burial, Caesar [Octavian] would not take it away from Cleopatra, and it was buried by her hands in sumptuous and royal fashion, such things being granted her for the purpose as she desired.*[22]

We are not told what form this burial took. During the first century BC Roman burial customs varied from region to region, with inhumation being preferred in the eastern empire and cremation in the west. Antony, as a western Roman, may therefore have expected to be cremated, and indeed Plutarch writes of Cleopatra 'embracing the urn which held his ashes', and again, 'she wreathed and kissed the urn'.[23] Plutarch may, of course, have been succumbing to his own cultural expectations. The fact that Cleopatra was able to visit Antony in his tomb a mere twelve days after his death suggests that he had not been mummified, as mummification was a lengthy practical and sacred ritual, taking seventy days. However, the rock-cut tombs of southern Egypt, with their eclectic mix of Egyptian, Greek and Roman styles, confirm just how appealing the elaborate traditional burial customs were to Egyptians of non-Egyptian heritage. Alexander the Great is purported to have been embalmed, and the fact that the tombs of the

Ptolemies were places of pilgrimage suggests, without proving, that they too were mummified. In Alexandria, the early excavators, Evaristo Breccia and Achille Adriani, found hundreds of mummified bodies in the cemeteries of Ras el-Tin and Anfushy. All these mummies were badly decomposed and all are now lost. But the tombs have yielded coins of both Cleopatra and Augustus (Octavian), proving that inhumation preceded by mummification was practised in Alexandria at the time of Cleopatra's death. It is interesting that no mummies are recorded for the other necropoleis of Alexandria, including the most recently excavated Gabbari cemetery, which has produced hundreds of simple interments.

Now Octavian made plans for Cleopatra's funeral:

Caesar [Octavian], although vexed at the death of the woman, admired her lofty spirit; and he gave orders that her body should be buried with that of Antony in splendid and regal fashion. Her women also received honourable interment by his orders.[24]

The joint tomb of Cleopatra and Antony is today, like all the other Ptolemaic royal tombs, lost beneath the waters of the Mediterranean Sea.

CHAPTER EIGHT

Cleopatra's Children

The story we are writing, and the great name of Cleopatra which figures in it, have plunged us into those reflections which displease a civilized ear. But the spectacle of the ancient world is something so overwhelming, so discouraging for imaginations that believe themselves unlicensed, and for spirits that imagine they have attained the last limits of fairy-like magnificence, that we could not refrain from registering here our complaints and regrets that we were not contemporary with Sardanapalus, with Tiglath-Pileser, with Cleopatra, Queen of Egypt, or even of Heliogabalus, Emperor of Rome and Priest of the Sun.

Théophile Gautier, *Une Nuit de Cléopâtre*[1]

In the end, Cleopatra did process through the streets of Rome. A statue of the queen lying on her deathbed with a snake suitably attached was carried in Octavian's triple triumph, celebrated in 29, to commemorate his defeat of various barbarians, his victory at Actium and his conquest of Egypt. Soon after, the Augustan poets Horace, Virgil and Propertius included references to Cleopatra's death in their works, each specifically incorporating not one but two snakes, the 'twin snakes of death', in their tale.[2] Later artists, Shakespeare included, accepted the idea of the two snakes and transferred their bites from the arm to the much more dramatically appropriate breast, so that the image of Cleopatra with one or two asps clasped to her bosom could be contrasted with the image of Cleopatra/Isis the mother goddess nursing her child:

Peace, peace!
Does thou not see my baby at my breast,
That sucks the nurse asleep?[3]

Cleopatra died on 12 August 30.[4] Octavian formally annexed Egypt on 31 August 30. This left an eighteen-day gap when Egypt was, in theory, ruled by the sixteen-year-old Caesarion. A broken statue, said to have been recovered from Karnak in the early twentieth century and now housed in Cairo Museum, shows us Egypt's last king: a confident but unmistakably young man with rounded, almost childish cheeks and Greek-style curls on his forehead. Cleopatra had raised her first army at twenty years of age; Arsinoë IV had commanded hers at fourteen. But Caesarion had no meaningful support and could have no thought of taking up his throne. Belatedly aware that her son's official adult status made him vulnerable, Cleopatra had already sent him away from Alexandria. Together with his tutor, Rhodon, and part of Cleopatra's treasure, Caesarion was to make his way to the southern city of Koptos, travel overland via the desert trade route to the Red Sea port of Myos Hormos, then board a ship for India where, if all went well, he would be reunited with his mother. But all did not go well. Soon after his mother's suicide Caesarion was captured – Plutarch tells us that he was betrayed by Rhodon, who somehow persuaded him to return to Alexandria – and executed. Documentary evidence confirms that there was civil unrest in the Theban area immediately after

Cleopatra's death, but it seems that this was caused by high taxes and should not be interpreted as a pro-Cleopatra or pro-Caesarion uprising.

Antyllus was also dead; decapitated as he sought sanctuary beside a statue of Julius Caesar in Alexandria. He, too, had been betrayed by his tutor, Theodorus, who was tempted by the precious stone (another part of Cleopatra's treasure?) that he knew Antyllus concealed beneath his garments. He snatched the stone from Antyllus's bleeding neck and sewed it into his girdle. But Theodorus was to pay dearly for his betrayal; he was caught, convicted and crucified. Antony's other children were all allowed to survive. Iotape, the daughter of the Median king who had been brought to Egypt as the fiancée of Alexander Helios, was sent back to her family. The ten-year-old twins and four-year-old Ptolemy Philadelphos were taken to Rome, where, carrying heavy golden chains, they were displayed in the public triumph alongside the statue of their dead mother. They were then given to the virtuous Octavia to raise alongside her own children and their half-brother Julius Antonius, younger brother of Antyllus. Julius was to marry Octavia's daughter Marcella, and would eventually be executed for alleged adultery with Octavian's daughter Julia. Alexander Helios and Ptolemy Philadelphos vanish from the historical record soon after entering Octavia's household and, although Dio tells us that they passed into the care of Cleopatra Selene on the occasion of her marriage, it seems perhaps more likely that they did not survive childhood.

Five years after her mother's suicide Cleopatra Selene was provided by Octavian with a large dowry and an eminently suitable husband. She was to marry the Numidian prince Juba II, whom we last met as an infant walking in Caesar's African triumph (page 104). The province of Numidia (Africa Nova: New Africa) lay on the north African coast, sandwiched between the province of Mauretania (modern western Algeria and northern Morocco[5]) to the west and the province of Africa (modern Tunisia) to the east. Juba's father, Juba I, had allied himself with Pompey, and had chosen to fight a duel to the death rather than be captured by Caesar's forces. Taken from his homeland as an infant, Juba II had been raised in Rome, where, restyled Gaius Julius Juba, he had become a model Roman citizen and a close friend to Octavian. He accompanied Octavian on several military campaigns and fought at Actium, but he is best remembered as a serious and scholarly young man, a poet, historian, philologist and geographer who published more than fifty books written in both Greek and Latin. As a keen explorer Juba is credited with discovering the Canary Islands, and naming them after the fierce dogs (*canaria*) that he found there. His claim to have discovered the source of the Nile in the Atlas Mountains of his own land was supported by his recovery of a crocodile from the 'source'; the crocodile was later presented as a votive offering to the temple of Isis in Caesarea.[6]

Soon after the battle of Actium, Juba was sent to rule Numidia as a fully Romanised client-king. In *c.* 25, probably at the time of his marriage, he was relocated to neighbouring Mauretania, a province made prosperous by strong trade links with Italy and Spain. Fertile Mauretania exported grain, pearls, wooden furniture and fruit. A purple dye manufactured from Mauretanian shellfish was used to provide the stripes in the senatorial togas, while highly flavoured garum sauce, so popular in Rome, included large anounts of Mauretanian fish. Juba and Cleopatra Selene ruled from Caesarea, the ancient city of Iol (modern Cherchell), which they renamed to honour Augustus Caesar (Octavian). Architecture and sculpture recovered from Caesarea show a contemporary mixture of Roman architecture and Hellenistic statuary: there were baths, a temple to Augustus and a theatre designed by an acclaimed Roman architect which was later converted into an amphitheatre.

A marble portrait head, excavated from Cherchell in 1901 and now housed in Cherchell museum, shows a veiled, curly haired woman with a prominent nose and jaw who bears a strong resemblance to Auletes. A second head, excavated in 1856, shows a more mature woman with similar facial features, a melon hairstyle, a kiss-curl fringe and a diadem. W. N. Weech, engaged on one of his 'rambles in Mauretania Caesariensis' in 1932, was struck by the anonymous queen's appearance:

> *It is an extraordinarily expressive face – intelligent eyes, arrogant nose, firm mouth. Many of the critics suggest that this represents Cleopatra Selene; if they are right, we must abandon all romantic pictures of a Moon princess, fragrant with the mystic glamour of ancient Nile, endowed with Cleopatra's sorcery and Mark Antony's fire. This is the head of a woman whose will swayed her passions, a maîtresse femme, and Selene must have ruled her Juba with inflexible decision during the thirteen years of their joint reign.*[7]

Whether either of these heads represents Cleopatra Selene or her mother is impossible to determine.

Mauretanian coinage reflects both Roman and Egyptian themes. While Juba's coin portraits generally show a Roman-style king whose name is written in Latin (Rex Juba), Cleopatra Selene's coins display Hellenistic Egyptian motifs with no hint of her Roman heritage. There are crocodiles, *sistra* and Isiac symbols, and Cleopatra Selene's name and title are given in Greek so that she becomes Basilissa Cleopatra, the title used by her mother. Clearly neither Octavian nor the strongly pro-Roman Juba felt threatened by the queen's persistent references to her Egyptian roots.

Cleopatra Selene bore a son named (of course) Ptolemy and, perhaps, a daughter who, we may guess, was named Cleopatra. She died some time between 5 BC and AD 11, her death being commemorated in an epigram by the poet Crinagoras, a friend and client of Octavia:

When she rose the moon herself grew dark
Veiling her grief in the night, for she saw
Her lovely namesake Selene bereft of life
And going down to gloomy Hades.
With her she had shared her light's beauty,
And with her death she mingled her own darkness.[8]

The bereaved Juba married Glaphyra, the widowed daughter of Arche-laos of Cappadocia (who, rumour maintained, was the natural son of Mark Antony), but the marriage proved highly unsatisfactory – the bride was in love with someone else – and they divorced, childless, soon after. Juba appointed his son Ptolemy co-regent in AD 21 and died in AD 23. He was buried at Caesarea alongside Cleopatra Selene in the circular mausoleum known today as the Kubr-er-Rumia (also known as the Tombeau de la Chrétienne).

Ptolemy of Mauretania inherited his father's throne. His personal history is ill-recorded, but it seems that he married a lady named either Urania or Julia Urania, and that he had a daughter, Drusilla, who married Marcus Antonius Felix, procurator of Judaea during the reign of Claudius. In AD 40 Ptolemy was executed on a trumped-up charge by his half-cousin Caligula. Suetonius tells us that his 'crime' was to wear a robe more splendidly purple than Caligula's own.[9] It is perhaps more likely that Ptolemy, 'son of King Juba and descendant of king Ptolemy', was suspected of plotting against Rome, although Caligula, notoriously unstable, hardly needed an excuse to execute people.

Looking back from the historian's perspective, we can see that the death of Cleopatra VII heralded the death of the Hellenistic age and the birth of Imperial Rome, which led in turn to the birth of the modern western world. Octavian, appreciating this point, renamed the eighth month (Sextilis) after himself, because it was both the month when he received the title 'Augustus' and the month in which 'Imperator Caesar [Octavian] freed the commonwealth from a most grievous danger': Alexandria had fallen on 1 August. The vast majority of the Egyptian people were, of course, unaware of this; for them, life continued much as it had before and much as it would for centuries to come. Rule by a Ptolemy or a Roman, a pagan, Christian or Muslim, it made little difference.

Other conquerors had tailored their behaviour to the beliefs of their new country and had continued the tradition of royal rule supported by the gods. But Octavian, confident of his military strength and, perhaps, averse to the idea of hereditary kingship, saw no need to pander to the Egyptians. Thousand years of royal rule came to an abrupt end as he claimed Egypt as his own personal estate. Technically kingless, although the Egyptian priests would continue to give their Roman overlords cartouches and titles, and to depict them in traditional Egyptian style, Egypt was to be administered by the relatively lowly Cornelius Gallus, a prefect of the equestrian rank. Egyptians would not be allowed to serve in the Roman army, or to enter the Senate; Romans wishing to visit Egypt would need to obtain permission from Octavian. Octavian embarked on a tour of his new property, inspecting canals and irrigation ditches. Intent on suppressing the eastern cults and unconcerned about offending the local priests, he refused to visit the Apis bull, announcing to anyone who would listen that he worshipped gods, not cattle. Presumably he neither knew nor cared overmuch that Egypt's priests were already depicting him as a pharaoh participating in the traditional animal cults.

As Rome moved into Egypt, Egyptian culture started to invade Rome. Egyptian artefacts were suddenly all the rage and, in a move guaranteed to confuse the archaeologists of the future, the Romans started to import both genuine and fake Egyptian antiquities. Now sphinxes and obelisks stood, slightly self-consciously, alongside the statues of noble Romans that adorned the public squares. In the Field of Mars in Rome, a Late Period Egyptian obelisk even served as the gnomon for a gigantic sundial:

Augustus [Octavian] used the obelisk in the Campus Martius in a remarkable way: to cast a shadow and so mark out the length of the days and nights. An area was paved in proportion to the height of the monolith in such a way that the shadow at noon on the shortest day would reach to the edge of the pavement. As the shadow shrank and expanded, it was measured by bronze rods fixed in the pavement.[10]

Cleopatra's treasure – now Octavian's treasure – was taken to Rome, where it was used to finance Octavian's political career. The statue of Victory that Octavian erected in the new Senate House was decorated with Egyptian spoils, as were the Capitoline temple of Jupiter, Juno and Minerva and, appropriately perhaps, the temple of the Divine Julius. For Dio, this made a fitting end to a turbulent tale:

Thus Cleopatra, though defeated and captured, was nevertheless glorified, inasmuch as her adornments repose as dedications in our temples and she herself is seen in gold in the shrine of Venus.[11]

CHAPTER NINE

History Becomes Legend

Cleopatra had a jazz band
In her castle on the Nile
Every night she gave a jazz dance
In her queer Egyptian style …

J. Morgan and J. Coogan, 'Cleopatra Had a Jazz Band'[1]

Three hundred years after her death, Cleopatra-Isis was still being worshipped at Philae. Her image would remain on Egypt's coins for decades and on her temple walls for thousands of years. But this version of Cleopatra the queen and wise mother goddess was confined to Egypt. In the wider Mediterranean world the well-oiled Roman propaganda machine continued to manipulate public opinion against Cleopatra long after the battle of Actium.

Octavian was determined that his own personal history should be recorded for posterity in a way that justified his not always heroic actions and confirmed his god-given right to rule; a difficult matter for a self-proclaimed republican to explain. To achieve this, he not only published his own autobiography, he edited, and in some cases burned, Rome's official records. Much of his propaganda – the ephemeral jokes, graffiti, pamphlets, private letters and public speeches – has of course been lost. But enough remains to allow us an understanding of the corruption of Cleopatra's memory.

As Cleopatra had played a key role in Octavian's struggle to power, her story was allowed to survive as an integral part of his. But it was to be diminished into just two episodes: her relationship with Julius Caesar and, more particularly, her relationship with Mark Antony. Caesar, the adoptive father who gave Octavian his right to rule, was to be remembered with respect as a brave and upright man who manipulated an immoral foreign woman for his own ends. Antony, Octavian's rival, was to be remembered with a mixture of pity and contempt as a brave but fatally weak man hopelessly ensnared in the coils of an immoral foreign woman. Cleopatra, stripped of any political validity, was to be remembered as that immoral foreign woman. Almost overnight she became the most frightening of Roman stereotypes: an unnatural female. A woman who worshipped crude gods, dominated men, slept with her brothers and gave birth to bastards. A woman foolish enough to think that she might one day rule Rome, and devious enough to lure a decent man away from his hearth and home. This version of Cleopatra is, of course, the precise opposite of the chaste and loyal Roman wife, typified by the wronged Octavia and the virtuous Livia, just as Cleopatra's exotic eastern land is the louche feminine counterpoint to upright, uptight, essentially masculine Rome. As public enemy number one, Cleopatra was extremely useful to Octavian, who not unnaturally preferred to be remembered fighting misguided foreigners rather than decent fellow Romans.

The most vivid near-contemporary interpretation of Cleopatra is a fictional account. When, in 29, Publius Vergilius Maro started work on his twelve-volume *Aeneid*, he determined to create a modern epic in the style of Homer's *Odyssey* (Books 16) and *Iliad* (Books 712) that would both glorify Rome and celebrate Octavian's rule. Aeneas, son of the goddess Venus and founder of Rome, was to be equated with Octavian, descendant of Venus and of Aeneas and founder of the Roman Empire. Underpinning the first part of *The Aeneid* is the tragedy of Dido and Aeneas. The eponymous hero, fleeing by boat from devastated Troy, is desperate to reach his ancestral homeland but runs into a storm and washes ashore on the North African coast. Here he meets Dido, founder and queen of Carthage, who is compelled by the gods to fall in love with him. The two go through a form of marriage, which Dido recognises as legally binding but Aeneas, it soon transpires, does not. Happy in their love for each other, they forget the outside world. But Aeneas is a strong moral character, obedient to the will of the gods. Faced with the choice between pleasure and duty he chooses duty, and deserts the queen:

> '*I know, O queen, you can list a multitude of kindnesses you have done me. I shall never deny them and never be sorry to remember Dido while I remember myself, while my spirit still governs this body. Much could be said. I shall say only a little. It was never my intention to be deceitful or run away without your knowing, and do not pretend that it was. Nor have I ever offered you marriage or entered into that contract with you.*'[2]

Furious and despairing, Dido curses her former lover, then commits suicide rather than face life alone.

Parallels with the stories of Julius Caesar (a strong man who put duty above pleasure) and of Antony (a lesser man than Aeneas/Caesar/Octavian who was tempted by a foreign queen and found wanting) are obvious. Dido, a woman who willingly enters into a pseudo-marriage and who is ultimately destroyed by her own guilt, is to be equated with Cleopatra. Virgil is, however, relatively sympathetic to Dido, whose life has been deliberately destroyed by the gods. Less sympathetic to Cleopatra is his anachronistic reference to Aeneas's intricate shield, forged by Vulcan, which features Octavian's victory at the battle of Actium:

> On the other side, with the wealth of the barbarian world and war-riors in all kinds of different armour, came Antony ... With him sailed Egypt and the power of the East from as far as distant Bactria, and there bringing up the rear was the greatest outrage of all, his Egyptian wife! ... The queen summoned her warships by rattling her Egyptian timbrels – she was not yet seeing the two snakes there at her back – while Anubis barked and all manner of monstrous gods lev-elled their weapons at Neptune and Venus and Minerva.[3]

Faced with such a glorious image, Virgil's readers might perhaps forget just how weak Octavian's military record actually was.

The subversive Augustan poet Sextus Propertius writes longingly of his feisty mistress Cynthia. He, like Mark Antony, has been ensnared and to a certain extent emasculated by a powerful woman, and he is not afraid of admitting it. Answering the question, 'Why do you wonder if a woman controls my life?' he lists examples of famous, unnaturally dominating women, including the Amazon Penthesilea, Omphale, queen of Lydia, Semiramis and, of course, Cleopatra, 'the whore queen of Canopus'. Later he provides a somewhat tongue-in-cheek tribute to Octavian and the battle of Actium. Clearly Propertius is aware of the irony of a Roman man celebrating a great victory over a mere woman, but, like Virgil before him, he sensibly sees no need to labour this delicate point.[4] In this he is joined by his contemporary Horace, who is happy to reduce Cleopatra to the status of a mad-woman drunk on power, yet who also gives a surprisingly sympathetic account of her death: 'fiercer she was in the death she chose, as though she did not wish to cease being queen'.[5] By restoring some of Cleo-patra's dignity, Horace actually makes her a more credible and worthy foe for Octavian.

Rome's historians, writing later than the poets, preserve a more rounded impression of Cleopatra. She is seductive and unnatural, yes, but we also catch glimpses of an educated, even intelligent woman. But history, in Rome, was not the strict discipline that it is (or should be) today. Sparse historical 'facts' were woven into a coherent narrative with large helpings of personal opinion and guesswork. Stories were selected in order to make a moral or political point. And, of course, the Roman historians concentrated on Cleopatra's interaction with the Roman world while ignoring her life in Egypt. The two most influential of Cleopatra's 'biographers' are Plutarch and Dio; from their works come the Cleopatras described by later classical authors. The Roman writer Suetonius (*The Divine Julius* and *The Divine Augustus*) and the somewhat unreliable Alexandrian Greek Appian (*The Civil Wars*) add further to Cleopatra's tale.

Maestrius Plutarchus (Plutarch), a Greek from Chaironeia in Boeotia, wrote his *Parallel Lives* in *c.* AD 100, using the not always successful device of 'parallels' to allow a comparison between the moral strengths and weaknesses of his Greek and Roman subjects. Among those he studied were Pompey the Great (paired with the Spartan king Agesilaus), Julius Caesar (paired with Alexander the Great) and Mark Antony (paired with Demetrios Poliorcetes of Macedon, son of Antigonos 'the One-Eyed'). Cleopatra's story was, of necessity, interwoven with theirs. Although it is claimed that Plutarch had access to the memoirs (now lost) of Cleopatra's physician Olympus, and that his grandfather had a friend who knew Cleopatra's cook, his sources remain hidden. His methodology, however, is made clear from the outset:

> ... *it is not histories that I am writing, but lives; and in the most illustrious deeds there is not always a manifestation of virtue or vice, nay, a slight thing like a phrase or a jest often makes a greater revelation of character than battles when thousands fall, or the greatest*

armaments, or sieges of cities. Accordingly, just as painters get the likenesses in their portraits from the face and the expression of the eyes, wherein the character shows itself, but make very little account of the other parts of the body, so I must be permitted to devote myself rather to the signs of the soul in men, and by means of these to portray the life of each, leaving to others the description of their great contests.[6]

The *Lives* were popular with Plutarch's fellow Romans, and popular again in medieval times and the Renaissance, when they inspired a whole host of authors and artists. Plutarch's Cleopatra is a confusing creature; he seems unable to make up his mind whether she is essentially good or essentially bad, although he is certain that she is manipulative, and that she has been the ruin of at least one good Roman.

The Greek historian and Roman senator Cassius Dio Cocceianus wrote his highly readable, action-packed eighty-volume *Roman History* in the years between AD 200 and 222. He tells us that he spent a decade researching his magnum opus, and that he consulted all the important references. These, most unfortunately, go unnamed, but almost certainly included the works of the historians Livy and Polybius. Cleopatra's story stretches from Book 42 – Julius Caesar in Egypt – to her suicide in Book 51. Dio's Cleopatra is an erotically powerful, manipulative woman with a fatal allure. Naturally, Antony is unable to resist her. The two deaths are followed by a brief but damning character assessment. Antony is a contradiction: brave yet foolish, both generous and harsh, 'characterised equally by greatness of soul and by servility of mind', while Cleopatra:

> *... was of insatiable passion and insatiable avarice; she was swayed often by laudable ambition, but overweening effrontery. By love she gained the title Queen of the Egyptians, and when she hoped by the same means to win also that of Queen of the Romans, she failed of*

this, and lost the other besides. She captivated the two greatest Romans of her day, and because of the third she destroyed herself.[7]

Plutarch and Dio were non-Roman by birth, yet they were happy to transmit the official Roman worldview. The historian Josephus, or Joseph son of Matthias (*c.* AD 37–100), had a Jewish education and saw things from a slightly different perspective. Josephus had stood against the Romans in the Jewish–Roman war of AD 66–73. Having failed to commit suicide with his fellow soldiers, he was captured by Vespasian's forces and changed his allegiance. Now a loyal Roman citizen, Titus Flavius Josephus settled in Rome, where, in receipt of generous public funds, he published a series of works, each intent on proving that he was both a good Roman and a good Jew. His two-volume *Against Apion* was published in response to an anti-Jewish outburst by the Greek grammarian Apion of Alexandria. Book 2 includes a highly idiosyncratic outline of Ptolemaic history that, of course, includes an unflattering portrait of Cleopatra, who, in Josephus's eyes, commits the double offence of being both anti-Roman and anti-Jewish:

> *… This man [Apion] also makes mention of Cleopatra, the last queen of Alexandria, and abuses us, [the Jews], because she was ungrateful to us; whereas he ought to have reproved her, who indulged herself with all kinds of injustices and wicked practices, both with regard to her nearest relations and husbands who had loved her, and, indeed, in general with regard to all the Romans and those emperors that were her benefactor … she destroyed the gods of her country and the sepulchres of her progenitors, and while she had received her kingdom from the first Caesar, she had the impudence to rebel against his son [Octavian] …*[8]

In AD 640 Egypt fell to the Islamic forces led by the Arab general Amr Ibn-al-As. Almost immediately, Muslim Egypt became isolated from the Christian world. For over a thousand years, until the sixteenth-century Ottoman conquest, western scholars continued to study ancient Egypt second-hand via the only sources available to them: the classical authors and the Bible. Meanwhile, in Egypt, a separate and very different historical tradition was evolving. Medieval Arabic scholars had access to Coptic (Christian), classical, Jewish and Arabic texts, including the Egyptian history written by the seventh-century Coptic Bishop John of Nikiou, which includes a sympathetic account of the good Queen Cleopatra, wife of Julius Caesar.[9] Most importantly, they also had first-hand access to the ancient monuments, and to the scholars and storytellers who preserved Egypt's oral heritage. From this invaluable information the Arab historians were able to develop a parallel understanding of Egypt's past which included a very different version of Cleopatra from that recognised in the West. The traveller and historian Al-Masudi (died c. 956) introduces us to the eastern Cleopatra, who variously appears as Qilopatra, Kilapatra or Aklaupatr:

> *... She was a sage, a philosopher, who elevated the ranks of scholars and enjoyed their company. She also wrote books on medicine, charms and cosmetics in addition to many other books ascribed to her which are known to those who practice medicine.[10]*

This Cleopatra is the 'virtuous scholar' mentioned in Chapter 1 (pages 32–3): a public benefactor who protects her people and presides over academic seminars, where she displays an impressive knowledge of mathematics, science and philosophy. She is credited with the authorship of a series of books ranging from cosmetics (an important and by no means female-orientated science in Egypt) through gynaecology to coins, weights and measures.

As a detailed account of Cleopatra's reign, the Arab history is in many ways flawed: Bishop John believed, for example, that Cleopatra built both the Heptastadion linking Pharos to the mainland and the canal which brought fresh water to Alexandria; others believed that she built the Pharos lighthouse. But looking beneath these specifics, and allowing for the fact that the historians may well have confused the lives of several Ptolemaic queens, plus other scholarly women, it does confirm that the lingering memory of Cleopatra within Egypt was a positive and appreciative one – a memory which focused on her political and administrative achievements rather than her love life. Unfortunately, the works of the Arabic historians, written in Arabic and until recently not widely available in translation, have been to a large extent overlooked by western Egyptologists.

Meanwhile, in the West, the Roman version of Cleopatra continued to evolve, reflecting contemporary images and ideals of womanhood. She became a beauty rather than a monster and, as beauty was unthinkingly equated with goodness, her story became that of an unconventional life redeemed by loyalty to a man. At the same time, her firm association with a snake led to a hazy identification with the Biblical Eve. The Christian Church, of course, forbade suicide. But in a world accustomed to stories of Christian martyrs finding redemption through suffering and death, Cleopatra's story was an acceptable variant. In 1380 Geoffrey Chaucer included the *legend* of Cleopatra the martyr in his *Legend of Good Women,* and her transformation into a virtuous queen who lived only for the love of a man was complete.

Plutarch's *Parallel Lives,* translated into French by Jacques Amyot (1559), then from the French into English by Sir Thomas North (1579, 1595, 1603), served as the inspiration behind William Shakespeare's *Julius Caesar* (c. 1600), *Antony and Cleopatra* (c. 1606) and *Coriolanus* (c. 1607). The parallels between Plutarch and *Antony and Cleopatra* are obvious. Plutarch says

> …she disdained to set forward otherwise, but to take her barge in the river of Cydnus; the poop whereof was of gold, the sails of purple, and the oars of silver, which kept stroke in rowing after the sound of the

music of flutes, howboys, cithernes, viols, and such other instruments
as they played upon in the barge. And now for the person of her self,
she was laid under a pavilion of cloth of gold of tissue, apparelled and
attired like the goddess Venus, commonly drawn in picture: and hard
by her, on either hand of her, pretty fair boys apparelled as painters
do set forth god Cupid, with little fans in their hands, with the which
they fanned wind upon her …

Shakespeare's Domitius Enobarbus says

I will tell you.
The barge she sat in, like a burnished throne,
Burned on the water: the poop was beaten gold;
Purple the sails, and so perfumèd that
The winds were love-sick with them. The oars were silver,
Which to the tune of flutes kept stroke, and made
The water which they beat to follow faster,
As amorous of their strokes. For her own person,
It beggared all description: she did lie
In her pavilion, cloth-of-gold of tissue,
O'erpicturing that Venus where we see
The fancy outwork nature. On each side her
Stood pretty dimpled boys, like smiling cupids,
With divers-coloured fans, whose wind did seem
To glow the delicate cheeks which they did cool,
And what they undid did.[11]

Placing drama and popular appeal above loyalty to his source, Shakespeare dropped some of Plutarch's disapproval, borrowed slightly from Horace, and allowed his queen to become a genuine heroine ruined by uncontrollable passion. Female rule, in Shakespeare's day, was seen as neither unnatural nor undesirable, and Shakespeare's play, written when memory of the reign of Elizabeth I was still vivid, reflects this.

His was by no means the first of the modern Cleopatras, nor would it be the last, but his Cleopatra has had the greatest effect on the public imagination, inspiring a wealth of Cleopatra-themed art: novels, plays, poetry, paintings, sculptures, operas, ballets, songs, tragedies, comedies and epic films. These in turn have inspired a wealth of Egypt-themed marketing, with an anachronistic Cleopatra being used to sell everything from cigarettes to sandals.[12]

The cultural historian Mary Hamer speaks for many when she tells of her confusion when first faced with a Cleopatra who was not Shakespeare's: 'I learned to stop using Shakespeare as a norm and to ask what Cleopatra had meant before he wrote.'[13] It is more disconcerting to realise that several 'academic' publications have been unable to cast aside Shakespeare's vision and have been seduced into quoting Shakespeare as if he were a primary historical source.[14] To understand that this has happened due to a shortage of contemporary descriptions of Cleopatra is only partially to excuse the offence.

That modern representations of Cleopatra distort history to reflect the prejudices and assumptions of their creators perhaps goes without saying. Some of these distortions are obvious and naïve. Medieval and Renaissance artists, for example, were happy to abandon any attempt at realism and depict Cleopatra as a pale blonde because the pale blonde was their ideal of beauty. Others are more subtle or manipulative. Nineteenth-century artists gave Cleopatra a vaguely Egyptian-oriental appearance, and used her as a metaphor for the penetration and ownership of the (feminine) East by the (masculine) West. In many instances their aggressively seductive Cleopatras appear to invite their own destruction. Twentieth-century film-makers spoke grandly of historical accuracy and serious drama, yet produced a succession of Cleopatras designed to appeal to the audiences whose repeated visits to the cinema would make their films a success.[15] Theda Bara's 1917 vampish Cleopatra, much admired in its day, quickly became laughable. The cinematic Cleopatra had to evolve into a woman who would appeal both to the men who had enjoyed Miss Bara's barely-there costumes and to the newly educated, newly enfranchised working women who were now able to pay for their own cinema tickets. Claudette Colbert made a smart, amusing and very modern Cleopatra for the pre-war audience. Elizabeth Taylor, a sultry temptress on screen and off, brought glamour to an austere world and became for many the 'real' Cleopatra. Doubtless, soon the studios will present us with an updated Cleopatra – an action woman for the twenty-first century. Underlying all these films, hidden beneath the glitter and the wigs, lie issues of censorship and political correctness and disturbing messages about colonialism, racism, motherhood and the rights of women to control their own sexuality. Just how much sex, violence and plain, dull history can be shown in a film that has to earn its way at the box office? How much can history be rewritten to lend more immediate dramatic impact to the story? Is there anything wrong with distorting characters and changing locations in the name of art and entertainment? Those, and there are many, who learn their ancient history solely from *Troy* (Petersen, 2004), *Alexander* (Stone, 2004) and *Cleopatra* (Mankiewicz, 1963) are not necessarily aware of these issues but are heavily affected by them.

Joseph Mankiewicz based his *Cleopatra* on Carlo Maria Franzero's *The Life and Times of Cleopatra*, a book in which the author relied upon his 'Latin instinct' rather than simple scholarship to interpret Cleopatra's life. A brief excerpt is enough to give the flavour of the book:

> *Was she, as a young girl, taken to the Temple of Thebes and deflowered, in the old custom, on the altar of Amon-Re. Did she, in the corrupt atmosphere of the Palace and of her city, allow herself a few amorous adventures? And most important of all – was she a sensual woman, as Josephus calls her, 'a slave to her senses'? The answer is perhaps simple and eternal: there is no beautiful and intelligent and gifted woman who is not also a woman of the senses.*[16]

A better choice would have been the *Life and Times of Cleopatra Queen of Egypt* by Arthur Weigall. Weigall's 1914 book, written for a popular audience, was the first to attempt to break away from Shakespeare and set the queen in her own context. Cleopatra was to be viewed as an Egyptian politician rather than a Roman mistress. Indeed, the introduction to the book specifically warns against seeing Cleopatra through purely Roman, or purely modern eyes, and Weigall advises his readers, as they pace the courts of the Ptolemies, against succumbing to 'the anachronism of criticising our surroundings from the standard of twenty centuries after Christ'.[17] He takes great pains to explain and excuse Cleopatra's unconventional eastern lifestyle to his conventional middle-class western readers, who, he assumes, will be shocked by the queen's antics, yet he cannot resist dedicating his first chapter to a consideration of the queen's character and looks. As a quotation from Weigall started this book, it is perhaps appropriate that he should have the last word:

> ...*Having shut out from his memory the stinging words of Propertius, and the fierce lines of Horace ... the reader will be in a position to judge whether the interpretation of Cleopatra's character and actions, which I have laid before him, is to be considered as unduly lenient, and whether I have made unfair use of the merciful prerogative of the historian, in [sic] behalf of an often lonely and sorely tried woman, who fought all her life for the fulfilment of a patriotic and splendid ambition, and who died in a manner 'befitting the descendant of so many kings'.*[18]

Who Was Who

The Ptolemaic Royal Family:
from Alexander the Great to Ptolemy of Mauretania

It is thought that the genes we inherit may have more to do with the make-up of our personalities than our environment ... We have some knowledge of Cleopatra's forebears – not at all a promising start!

Julia Samson, *Nefertiti and Cleopatra*[1]

By 69, the year of Cleopatra's birth, her increasingly dysfunctional family had ruled Egypt for two and a half centuries. They had created and lost an empire whose influence was felt throughout the Mediterranean world and far beyond, ruling from a purpose-built city widely acknowledged as the world's most advanced seat of learning and culture. And, in marked contrast to Egypt's native kings, whose private affairs went unrecorded, they had lived recorded lives of extraordinary complexity and violence. Reviewing the personal histories of Cleopatra's immediate forebears, a confusing mixture of Ptolemies, Arsinoës, Berenices and Cleopatras, it becomes increasingly difficult to regard the Ptolemies as real people with anything approaching real feelings. To be born a Ptolemy was to be born into a family where survival of the ruthless was the cardinal rule and self-preservation a matter of overwhelming importance. Those Ptolemies who did survive had strong, larger-than-life personalities and, their deeds suggest, extremely thick skins. But repeated tales of murder, adultery, rebellion, lynchings, incest and uncontrollable ambition are the stuff of third-rate crime fiction and television soap operas; they fascinate and repel in equal measure, but do not necessarily inspire the sympathy that they should. Reading of so many untimely and unnatural deaths in so short a period somehow blunts our appreciation of the reality – one is tempted to say the horror – of Ptolemaic family life. Yet read these stories we must, albeit in abbreviated form, as they form the immediate background to Cleopatra's own story. And, as the Ptolemies owed their throne to Alexander the Great, it seems appropriate to start with his brief reign as king of Egypt.[2]

Alexander III the Great, King of Egypt 332–323
Son of Philip II of Macedon and Olympias of Epiros

In the winter of 332/1 Egypt surrendered to Alexander the Great without a struggle, ending almost two centuries of intermittent Persian rule. History tells us that the Egyptians welcomed Alexander as a liberator and cheered him on his way to Memphis. This history, written by Greeks and therefore heavily pro-Greek, is hardly unbiased, but the number of recorded rebellions and harsh reprisals during the Persian periods does suggest that the Egyptians, who hated any form of foreign domination, had a particular dislike of the Persians.

Alexander had ambitious plans for his new land. Already Alexandria had been established, and there had been some bureaucratic reorganisation. But there was no need to hurry. Time was on Alexander's side, and there were other battles yet to fight, other Persian territories to conquer. In May 331 Alexander marched northwards from Memphis to confront his old enemy, Darius III. He died in Babylon on 10 June

323, his unexpected death variously attributed to fever, to excessive drinking and to poison.

Philip III Arrhidaeos, King of Egypt 323–316
Son of Philip II of Macedon

With Alexander dead, his half-brother assumed nominal control of an empire stretching from Macedon to India, becoming uncrowned king of Egypt by default. Philip Arrhidaeos was the son of a Thessalian woman of humble birth; unkind rumour held that she was little better than a dancing girl, and everyone agreed that her son was, at best, half-witted. Half-witted or not, Arrhidaeos had managed to survive the violent family struggle which followed the assassination of his father, Philip, and which saw the elimination of all other potential rivals to the throne. Supported by his forceful wife, Adea, Arrhidaeos ruled his empire for just six years, his reign ending with an invasion of Macedon led by the dowager Olympias of Epiros. With Olympias triumphant, Arrhidaeos was executed and Adea, offered the choice of a dagger, a noose or poison, hanged herself.

Alexander IV, King of Egypt 316–304
Posthumous son of Alexander III the Great and Roxanne

Alexander the Great was just thirty-three years old and childless when he died. However, his Sogdian (Iranian) wife, Roxanne, was pregnant with a child who, if a boy, was destined to share the throne with Alexander's half-brother, Philip Arrhidaeos. The child was indeed a boy, and at Arrhidaeos's untimely death the throne passed unchallenged to his nephew, Alexander IV. The younger Alexander would never see Egypt; both he and Roxanne were murdered in Macedon in 310. The remains of a 'young prince', discovered in a silver funerary urn in the Macedonian royal cemetery of Vergina, may well be those of

Alexander IV. For the last six years of Alexander's 'reign', as recorded in Egypt's official lists, Ptolemy son of Lagos acted as uncrowned king.

Ptolemy I Soter I (Saviour), King of Egypt 304–284
Son of Lagos of Eordaea and Arsinoë

Ptolemy I was born in Macedon in 367. His father, Lagos, was a man of respectable but unexceptional Macedonian descent who had made a good marriage; his mother, Arsinoë, was second cousin to Philip II. Like many of Egypt's commoner-born kings, Ptolemy was not over-proud of his humble origins. Soon after the death of Alexander III he would spread the rumour that his mother had been one of Philip's many mistresses and that he himself was half-brother to the late, great king.

As a Macedonian general, Ptolemy witnessed Alexander defeat Darius III of Persia at the battle of Issus in November 333. A year later he was present when Alexander took Egypt, and he was almost certainly present when Alexander marched to the Siwa Oasis. Other military successes followed. In 329 he captured Bessus, satrap of Bactria and assassin of Darius III, and in 327 he campaigned in India, commanding a third of Alexander's army.

In 323 Ptolemy took control of Egypt, governing first on behalf of Philip Arrhidaeos, then on behalf of Alexander IV. It was Ptolemy who, in Philip's name, supervised the temple improvements at Karnak and Hermopolis Magna, and in Alexander's name built at the Elephantine temple of Khnum. He extended Egypt's territories to create a buffer zone around his land and masterminded the kidnapping and subsequent display of Alexander's body in Alexandria. In 304 the situation was regularised. In a coronation ceremony held at Alexandria, General Ptolemy was transformed into King Ptolemy I Soter I. As Ptolemy's Greek profile – hook-nosed, sharp-chinned, sunken-eyed and topped with a mop of unruly curls – started to appear on her coins, Egypt became an independent realm with Alexandria as her capital.

Alexander's enormous empire was by now irretrievably fragmented and his own dynastic line had ended. The Wars of the Successors (321–285) left the Mediterranean world dominated by three rival Macedonian-based kingdoms: the Antigonid empire of Macedon and mainland Greece, ruled by the descendants of Antigonos 'the One-Eyed'; the Seleucid empire of Syria and Mesopotamia, ruled by Seleucos I; and the Lagid or Ptolemaic empire of Egypt and Libya, whose territories included Cyprus and much of Palestine (including much of the modern states of Israel, Jordan, Lebanon and southern Syria; a region known as Coele-Syria, or 'Hollow Syria'). There would be frequent small-scale skirmishes – borders would expand and contract, alliances form and break, loyalties wax and wane – but the situation would remain more or less constant until a new superpower emerged to challenge the status quo.

Ptolemy was an imaginative economist and a competent scholar. Keen to promote Alexandria as an international centre of learning, he established the Museion and its world famous library. Outside Alexandria new temples were raised to ancient gods at Terenuthis (Hathor), Naukratis (Amen), Kom el-Ahmar (Osiris) and Tebtynis (Soknebtynis). The vast and highly efficient Egyptian bureaucracy was left more or less untouched, but the new city of Ptolemais Hormou was founded to counteract the influence of the ever-rebellious ancient southern capital, Thebes.

His personal life was less well organised. Already divorced from his first wife, the Persian princess Artakama, he had married Eurydice of Macedon some time between 322 and 319. Eurydice bore her husband four or five children: two sons (Ptolemy Ceraunos and Meleager; both destined to rule Macedon), two daughters (Lysandra and Ptolemais) and a third possible daughter (Theoxena). A simultaneous relationship with Berenice I yielded three children. Eventually Eurydice was divorced and Ptolemy married his long-term mistress.

Berenice I
Daughter of Magas (?) and Antigone, wife of Ptolemy I

Berenice, widow of Philip II of Macedon, already had a son, Magus, who was to become king of Cyrenaica. Initially the mistress of Ptolemy I, she displaced Eurydice, married Ptolemy and became queen of Egypt. She bore Ptolemy two daughters (Arsinoë II and Philotera) and a son (Ptolemy II).

Ptolemy II Philadelphos (Brother-Loving), King of Egypt 285–246
Son of Ptolemy I and Berenice I

Ptolemy II had ruled alongside Ptolemy I as co-regent for three years; it was obvious that he was his father's chosen successor. Nevertheless, his accession did not go unchallenged. There were those who felt, with some justification, that Berenice's children should not have precedence over Eurydice's offspring. Having secured his throne, Ptolemy's reign developed into one of internal peace and sporadic foreign campaigns which initially saw an expansion, followed by a setback, of Egypt's territories.

Back home, Ptolemy made significant improvements to the state bureaucracy and the banking system, refining the taxation structure until it became one of the most sophisticated, and punitive, in the world. Some of the revenue raised was used to complete his father's unfinished building projects, including the Museion of Alexandria and the Pharos lighthouse. His own building works included the naos (inner sacred area) of the Philae temple of Isis, improvements to the Karnak temple complex (the temple of the goddess Mut and the Opet temple), and an extension to the birth house at the Dendera temple of Hathor. He restored the canal, silted up since Persian days, which linked the eastern Delta to the Gulf of Suez, and founded the city of Arsinoë – just one of many cities that he founded or renamed Arsinoë – at its southern end. Land reclamation and improvements to irrigation in the Faiyum led to a significantly increased agricultural yield, and the papyrus and grain industries flourished.

Ptolemy II used the memory of his deceased parents and his sister-wife, Arsinoë II, to promote the legitimacy of his dynasty and provide his people, both Greeks and Egyptians, with a unifying royal cult. But perhaps his greatest legacy was the commissioning of a history of Egypt, to be written in Greek for a Greek readership by the Egyptian priest Manetho of Sebennytos. Manetho's work, now lost but surviving in valuable fragments in later histories, forms the basis of our modern division of Egyptian history into a sequence of ruling dynasties.

Arsinoë I

Daughter of Lysimachos of Thrace, wife of Ptolemy II

Arsinoë I bore Ptolemy II two sons (Ptolemy III Euergetes and Lysimachos) and a daughter (Berenice II) before she was banished from court, accused of plotting against her husband. She took up permanent residence in the southern Egyptian city of Koptos.

Arsinoë II

Daughter of Ptolemy I and Berenice I, sister-wife of Ptolemy II

The sixteen-year-old Arsinoë had been married to the elderly Lysimachos of Thrace, becoming stepmother to Arsinoë I. Several years later, hoping to promote the cause of her own two sons, she masterminded the death of Lysimachos's heir, Agathocles, husband of her half-sister

Lysandra. This tore the royal family apart, and Lysimachos died in battle in 281, fighting his dead son's supporters. Arsinoë next married her half-brother Ptolemy Ceraunos. But Ceraunos, self-proclaimed king of Macedon, had her sons by Lysimachos murdered, and Arsinoë fled first to Samothrace and then to her brother's court in Egypt. Ceraunos ruled Macedon for two years before dying in battle; his brother Meleager succeeded him but was deposed after a mere two months.

Arsinoë II next married her younger brother, Ptolemy II. She was queen of Egypt for less than seven years, yet had an enormous influence on the developing role of the queen. Deified after her death, her statue stood in all of Egypt's temples.

Ptolemy III Euergetes I (Benefactor), King of Egypt 246–221
Son of Ptolemy II and Arsinoë I

The ending of the Third Syrian War (246–241) saw Ptolemy III, having captured the port of the enemy capital, Antioch, ruling an eastern Mediterranean empire whose influence stretched from the River Euphrates to Cyrenaica, as far north as Thrace and as far south as northern Nubia.

Ptolemy III was a successful and hard-working king whose building achievements include the founding of the temple of Horus at Edfu and the construction of the Alexandria Serapeum, but the end of his reign was marred by an unprecedented series of native uprisings, a response to the high levels of taxation and the growing economic differences between the Egyptian peasants and the immigrant Greeks.

Berenice II
Daughter of Magus of Cyrenaica, wife of Ptolemy III

The classical authors admired Berenice II as a strong and

independently wealthy consort who, not content with ruling Egypt in her husband's absence, rode into battle alongside him. Less admirable, and equally unlikely to be true, is the rumour that the hot-tempered Berenice had murdered her first fiancé, the Macedonian prince Demetrios the Fair, because she had found him in bed with her mother, Apame. Ptolemy III and Berenice II seem to have been genuinely fond of each other and their marriage produced six children. Berenice was murdered during her son's reign.

Ptolemy IV Philopator (Father-Loving), King of Egypt
221–205
Son of Ptolemy III and Berenice II

The reign of Ptolemy IV heralded the beginning of the end of the Ptolemaic empire. The eldest son of Ptolemy III, Ptolemy IV has gone down in history as a pleasure-seeking drunkard who chose to stand silent as the highly influential, multi-talented athlete, priest and courtier Sosibios purged the royal family, murdering Ptolemy's brother Magas, his uncle Lysimachos and his mother, Berenice II. Guided by Sosibios, Ptolemy took his younger sister, Arsinoë III, as his queen, but his affections lay with his mistress Agathoclea, who was herself the daughter of his father's mistress. This formidable lady bore him at least one child before (allegedly) poisoning first Ptolemy IV and then Arsinoë III.

Private life aside, Ptolemy's reign was by no means all bad. He successfully and most surprisingly armed his people and defended his country against an attempted takeover by Antiochos III of Syria. In winning the battle of Raphia on 22 June 217 he became the first Ptolemy to use native Egyptian troops. He improved and extended many temples, and completed the temple of Horus at Edfu. An enthusiastic scholar, he endowed a temple and cult to Homer at Alexandria. He even composed a tragedy, *Adonis*. Nevertheless, he was a deeply unpopular king, and his reign saw continuing native revolts that included the emergence of an Egyptian counter-pharaoh, Harwennefer, who ruled from Thebes in 206–200.

Arsinoë III
Daughter of Ptolemy III and Berenice II, sister-wife of Ptolemy IV

The mother of Ptolemy V was murdered soon after her husband's unnatural death.

Ptolemy V Epiphanes (Manifest God), King of Egypt 205–180
Son of Ptolemy IV and Arsinoë III

Ptolemy V had been named co-regent alongside his father as a baby. He became solo king at just six years of age. But the purge that had followed his father's succession, and his mother's murder, meant that there was no one suitable to act as regent on his behalf. His father's (almost certainly forged) will named Sosibios and Agathocles, brother of Agathoclea, as guardians. When Sosibios died suddenly, Agathocles became sole guardian – until, that is, in 203 his entire family was murdered; torn apart by an angry mob determined to avenge their king and queen.

The mob may have supported the young Ptolemy V, but away from Alexandria the Egyptian people remained deeply unhappy with their Macedonian rulers and with the expensive after-effects of their seemingly endless military campaigns. Ptolemy IV had armed the Egyptian people to defeat Antiochos III in the battle of Raphia; they now realised just how powerful they could be. In 200 the Theban counter-pharaoh Harwennefer was succeeded by a second counter-pharaoh, Ankhwennefer, who held power in southern Egypt until 186. Meanwhile, a simultaneous rebellion in the Delta threatened the security of Alexandria. In order to secure his throne, Ptolemy reached an agreement with the Egyptian priesthood. The details of this agreement were carved on the bilingual Rosetta Stone, used in Champollion's decipherment of the hieroglyphic script.

A sensible diplomatic marriage to the ten-year-old Cleopatra I, daughter of Antiochos III of Syria, ensured that Ptolemy V remained on good terms with his most influential neighbour. But his reign saw the loss of many foreign territories and the empire contracted until it essentially comprised Cyprus, Cyrenaica and a handful of Aegean outposts. Greek immigration into Egypt, a constant stream since the reign of Ptolemy I, now slowed to a trickle and, deprived of constant renewed contact with their homeland, the Greeks within Egypt finally started to accept a more assimilated culture.

Following a threat to levy heavy taxes on Egypt's Greek elite – the money was needed to finance military campaigns that, it was hoped, would restore the lost territories – Ptolemy V was poisoned by his generals in 180.

Cleopatra I
Daughter of Antiochos III of Syria, wife of Ptolemy V

Cleopatra I bore two sons (Ptolemy VI and Ptolemy VIII) and a daughter (Cleopatra II). Although a foreigner (Cleopatra, nicknamed 'the Syrian', was of Macedonian-Persian descent), she managed to achieve what few members of the Ptolemaic dynasty could: a position of importance and respect within the royal family, both within Alexandria and the wider Egypt. After her husband's death her influence grew even stronger as she acted as both regent and guardian for the five-year-old Ptolemy VI. While she lived, Egypt sensibly showed little interest in foreign affairs and remained on good terms with her native Syria. But Cleopatra I died a mere four years after Ptolemy V.

Ptolemy VI Philometor (Mother-Loving), King of Egypt 180–164, 163–145
Son of Ptolemy V and Cleopatra I

The orphaned Ptolemy VI, still too young to rule alone, came under the control of the eunuch Eulaeus and the Syrian ex-slave Lenaeus. It is not clear how such a curious couple came to be chosen as regents, although we may speculate that Cleopatra I died unexpectedly, before she had appointed a suitable guardian. Eulaeus and Lenaeus decided that the young king should marry his slightly older sister Cleopatra II. Soon after, in a move which was presumably intended to strengthen national unity but which had precisely the opposite effect, they announced that the kingship was to be a triumvirate, with the two young Ptolemies (VI and VIII) plus Cleopatra II as co-rulers.

Their next decision – in hindsight an extremely foolish one – was an attempt to reclaim Egypt's lost territories by provoking a new Syrian war. This almost brought about the collapse of the Ptolemaic dynasty. Egypt suffered a humiliating invasion, Ptolemy VI was captured by his uncle Antiochos IV, Eulaeus and Lenaeus disappeared, and the people of Alexandria proclaimed the twelve-year-old Cleopatra II and her younger brother, Ptolemy VIII, their queen and king. For a time Egypt had two rival courts, based at Memphis (Ptolemy VI under the control of Antiochos IV) and Alexandria (Ptolemy VIII and Cleopatra II), but the situation was untenable and the triumvirate was resumed at Alexandria. Antiochos, angered by the defection of Ptolemy VI, marched west; only direct Roman intervention prevented Alexandria from falling to the Syrians. Antiochos departed from Egypt in 168, leaving the siblings ruling from Alexandria, and Egypt greatly indebted to Rome.

The people outside Alexandria were unhappy. In 164, with Ptolemy VI distracted by civil unrest, Ptolemy VIII seized the throne and, as his brother fled first to Rome and thence to Cyprus, ruled alongside Cleopatra II from Alexandria. The Alexandrian mob quickly turned against their new king, and in 163 Ptolemy VI, with the full support of Rome, was invited home to rule with Cleopatra II. Increased stability brought increased prosperity to Egypt, and there was an impressive programme of temple restorations. In 145, having regained many of Egypt's lost territories, Ptolemy VI died in battle in Syria.

Ptolemy Eupator ([Born] of a Noble Father)
Son of Ptolemy VI and Cleopatra II

Died while still crown prince.

Ptolemy VII Neos Philopator (New Father-Loving), King of Egypt 145
Son of Ptolemy VI and Cleopatra II

Murdered in his mother's arms by his new stepfather, his uncle Ptolemy VIII, on their wedding day.

Ptolemy VIII Euergetes II (Benefactor): 'Physcon' (Pot-Belly) or 'Kakergetes' (Malefactor), King of Egypt 170–163, 145–116
Son of Ptolemy V and Cleopatra I

The young Ptolemy VIII ruled Egypt alongside his brother, Ptolemy VI, and his sister, Cleopatra II. Following the Syrian invasion, Ptolemy VIII and Cleopatra II ruled Egypt together from Alexandria. The triumvirate was briefly resumed before Ptolemy VIII succeeded in dislodging his brother and once again ruled from Alexandria with Cleopatra II. In 163 the people of Alexandria summoned Ptolemy VI to rule alongside Cleopatra II, and the exiled Ptolemy VIII became the highly unpopular king of Cyrenaica. Ptolemy VIII persistently and unsuccessfully petitioned Rome, demanding support for his right to rule Cyprus as well as Cyrenaica. The Romans sympathised, but gave little practical help. They acknowledged Ptolemy as their friend, however, and following an attempted assassination in 156, Ptolemy repaid this friendship by making a will leaving 'his kingdom' to Rome should he die without a legitimate heir.

In 145 the death of Ptolemy VI allowed Ptolemy VIII to return from Cyrenaica, marry his widowed sister and murder her son and heir. A purge of the Museion and Library of Alexandria followed, with most of the scholars forced to flee. As Alexandria's reputation as a centre of intellectual excellence plummeted, the displaced scholars gained their revenge by recording unflattering portraits of their abnormally short and grotesquely fat king.

In 144 Cleopatra II gave birth to her brother's son, Ptolemy Memphites. A year later Ptolemy fathered a son, Ptolemy IX, by his step-daughter-niece, Cleopatra III. A marriage followed, but there had been no divorce. Cleopatra II refused to be sidelined by her daughter, and the three found themselves locked together in an uncomfortable ménage. When, in 131, Ptolemy VIII was once again forced to flee Egypt, he took Cleopatra III with him but left Cleopatra II behind. Safely settled in Cyprus, he sent for his fourteen-year-old son, Memphites, and had him murdered. Thus he ensured that the children of Cleopatra III would inherit his throne.

In 130 Ptolemy VIII returned to Egypt, forcing Cleopatra II to flee to Syria. She returned in 124, and brother and sister were reconciled. Ptolemy VIII died in 116. He left Egypt to his sons by Cleopatra III, but stipulated that the five Greek towns of Cyrenaica should pass as a separate kingdom to Ptolemy Apion, his son by his mistress Eirene.

Cleopatra II

Daughter of Ptolemy V and Cleopatra I, wife of Ptolemy VI and Ptolemy VIII

Cleopatra II bore Ptolemy VI four children: the short-lived Ptolemy

Eupator, Ptolemy VII, Cleopatra III and Cleopatra Thea. During her first husband's reign she became widely respected as a supporter of the Jews, whom she encouraged to settle in Egypt. Following the death of Ptolemy VI, she married her brother Ptolemy VIII and bore his son, Ptolemy Memphites. Both Ptolemy VII and Ptolemy Memphites were to be murdered by Ptolemy VIII.

Humiliated by her husband's marriage to her daughter Cleopatra III, Cleopatra refused to accept a divorce. Mother and daughter shared the queenship – and a husband – as Cleopatra the Sister and Cleopatra the Wife. When Ptolemy VIII was exiled to Cyprus, Cleopatra II ruled Egypt alone. But, while Cleopatra II had the support of the Greeks of Alexandria, Ptolemy VIII, thanks to a policy of promoting native-born Egyptians, had the support of the people outside Alexandria. Neither could truly rule Egypt without the other.

In 130 Euergetes returned to Egypt, forcing Cleopatra II to flee to safety in Syria. She returned in 124, and Cleopatra II, Cleopatra III and Ptolemy VIII united to rule an Egypt crippled by civil unrest. Cleopatra II died a few months after her husband-brother in 116.

Ptolemy Memphites (of Memphis)
Son of Ptolemy VIII and Cleopatra II

Ptolemy Memphites was born at the time of his father's coronation at Memphis and presented to the Egyptian priesthood. Fourteen years later he was murdered by his father. It was rumoured that his dismembered body was sent home to his mother in a chest.

Cleopatra III
Daughter of Ptolemy VI and Cleopatra II, wife of Ptolemy VIII

Cleopatra III bore her first son by her uncle Ptolemy VIII before she married him. She would eventually bear him two sons and three daughters, and would be rewarded for her loyalty with her own personal divinity.

In 116, following the death of Ptolemy VIII, a triumvirate of Cleopatra II, Cleopatra III and Ptolemy IX briefly ruled Egypt. The death of Cleopatra II left Cleopatra III regent for her two sons, Ptolemy IX and Ptolemy X. Under the terms of her husband's will, she was to decide which son should become her co-ruler. This brought the royal family to the brink of collapse. The three ruled together in complete disharmony, with first one brother and then the other being forced to take refuge in Cyprus. Finally, in 107, Ptolemy IX fled, falsely accused of plotting to murder his mother. Cleopatra III and Ptolemy X ruled Egypt together until the sixty-year-old Cleopatra III died in 101, almost certainly murdered by her younger son.

Ptolemy IX Soter II (Saviour): 'Lathyros' (Chickpea), King of Egypt 116–107, 88–81
Son of Ptolemy VIII and Cleopatra III

Ptolemy IX married his forceful sister Cleopatra IV and then, after a divorce forced upon him by his mother, his other sister, Cleopatra Selene. Forced to flee in 107, he established himself as ruler of Cyprus. After a thwarted attempt to retake Egypt, he lived peacefully on Cyprus until 88, when he returned to Alexandria to rule Egypt.

Ptolemy X Alexander I, King of Egypt 107–88
Son of Ptolemy VIII and Cleopatra III

In 100 Ptolemy X murdered his mother and married his niece, Berenice III. He ruled Egypt for a decade of declining prosperity until the people of Alexandria took exception to his favourable treatment of the Jews and he was forced to flee, leaving the throne vacant for his exiled brother Ptolemy IX. In revenge, he willed the Egyptian empire to the

Romans. They did not take up the bequest, but they never forgot it. Ptolemy X is rumoured to have melted down the gold coffin of Alexander the Great in order to pay his troops. He died in 88, attempting to take Cyprus from his brother.

Cleopatra Berenice III Thea Philopator (Father-Loving Goddess), Queen of Egypt 81–80

Daughter of Ptolemy IX and Cleopatra IV, wife of Ptolemy X and Ptolemy XI

Berenice III was initially married to her uncle, Ptolemy X. She inherited her father's throne in 81, changed her name to Cleopatra Berenice and, encouraged by Rome, married her illegitimate stepson Ptolemy XI. Cleopatra Berenice III was popular with the people of Alexandria but not with her husband: he had her murdered soon after their marriage.

Ptolemy XI Alexander II, King of Egypt 80

Son of Ptolemy X

Ptolemy XI had the support of the Roman general Sulla but was over-ambitious. He murdered his popular wife, Berenice III, and was in turn killed by the people of Alexandria.

Ptolemy XII Neos Dionysos (New Dionysos): 'Auletes' (Flute Player), King of Egypt 80–58, 55–51

Son of Ptolemy IX, Brother of Ptolemy of Cyprus

Following the unexpected death of Berenice III, the elder of the two illegitimate sons of Ptolemy IX took the throne of Egypt as Ptolemy XII.

Ptolemy XII was faced with the unenviable task of preserving a dying dynasty. The Romans, coveting Egypt's unfailing fertility, were deciding how best to strip the Ptolemies of their throne. Ptolemy knew that he had to remain on friendly terms with Rome, but this policy turned his people against him. In 58, when the Romans annexed Cyprus, a wave of panic swept Egypt. As the people of Alexandria took to the streets, Ptolemy fled to Rome to appeal for military aid. Berenice IV now ruled Egypt in her father's absence. Ptolemy XII was able to bribe the governor of Syria to support him against his daughter. A Roman army took Alexandria in 55 and Ptolemy XII was restored to his throne. Heavily in debt, he levied stringent taxes, which left his people hungry and desperate. Ptolemy XII died a natural death in 51.

Ptolemy of Cyprus, King of Cyprus 80–58
Son of Ptolemy IX, brother of Ptolemy XII

The younger of the two illegitimate sons of Ptolemy IX took the throne of Cyprus as King Ptolemy. In 58 the Romans annexed Cyprus, driving Ptolemy to commit suicide.

Cleopatra V Tryphaena (Opulent One)
Wife and perhaps sister or half-sister of Ptolemy XII

A woman of obscure origins, Cleopatra V Tryphaena was the mother of Berenice IV, and possibly the mother of Cleopatra VI Tryphaena, Cleopatra VII, Arsinoë IV, Ptolemy XIII and Ptolemy XIV. She may have acted briefly as co-regent alongside Berenice IV.

Berenice IV, Queen of Egypt 58–55
Daughter of Ptolemy XII and Cleopatra V Tryphaena

Berenice married an insignificant cousin, Seleucos, then had him murdered within a week of their wedding. Her second husband, Archelaos, lasted longer; the couple ruled for two years with the full support of the people of Alexandria. A Roman army took Alexandria in 55. Archelaos was killed and Ptolemy XII, returning home in triumph, had his daughter executed.

Cleopatra VI Tryphaena (Opulent One)
Daughter of Ptolemy XII and (probably) Cleopatra V Tryphaena

The obscure sister of Cleopatra VII who may be identical with Cleopatra Tryphaena V. Cleopatra VI ruled briefly alongside Berenice IV before disappearing from the historical record in 57.

Cleopatra VII Thea Philopator (Father-Loving Goddess), Queen of Egypt 51–30
Daughter of Ptolemy XII and (probably) Cleopatra V Tryphaena, probably wife of Ptolemy XIII and Ptolemy XIV

The subject of this book.

Arsinoë IV, Queen of Egypt 47
Daughter of Ptolemy XII

Proclaimed Queen of Cyprus by Julius Caesar, Arsinoë ruled Alexandria briefly during the civil war. Captured by the Romans, she was displayed in Caesar's Egyptian triumph, then exiled to Ephesus. In 41 she was dragged from the temple and executed on the orders of Mark Antony.

Ptolemy XIII, King of Egypt 51–47
Son of Ptolemy XII, husband of Cleopatra VII

Ptolemy XIII inherited his throne alongside his sister Cleopatra VII. For the first year and a half of their joint reign Cleopatra was the effective monarch, while her brother was pushed into the background. The first decree with Ptolemy's name preceding Cleopatra's was issued on 27 October 50. In the summer of 49 Cleopatra's name disappeared from all official documents as the queen and her supporters fled Egypt. Later that year Ptolemy turned a blind eye to the murder of Pompey. Ptolemy had expected to be granted sole rule of Egypt but Caesar, angered by Pompey's murder, decided that he was to rule alongside his sister Cleopatra VII. Ptolemy XIII drowned in 47, at the end of the Alexandrian Wars.

Ptolemy XIV, King of Egypt 47–44
Son of Ptolemy XII, husband of Cleopatra VII

Proclaimed king of Cyprus by Caesar, Ptolemy became king of Egypt following the death of his elder brother, Ptolemy XIII. He had an undistinguished reign and died soon after the birth of Cleopatra's son, Caesarion.

Ptolemy XV Caesar Theos Philopator Philometor (Father-Loving, Mother-Loving God): 'Caesarion' (Little Caesar), King of Egypt 44–30
Son of Cleopatra VII and (allegedly) Julius Caesar

Following the death of Ptolemy XIV, Caesarion ruled Egypt alongside his mother. Cleopatra VII died on 12 August 30 and Octavian formally annexed Egypt on 31 August 30. This left an eighteen-day period when Caesarion ruled alone. But he had no meaningful support and could have had no thought of taking up his throne. Soon after his mother's suicide, Caesarion was betrayed and executed.

Alexander Helios
Son of Cleopatra VII and Mark Antony, twin of Cleopatra Selene

Following Cleopatra's suicide, the ten-year-old twins and four-year-old Ptolemy Philadelphos were taken to Rome to be raised by their father's wife, Octavia. The boys vanished from the historical record soon after entering Octavia's care.

Cleopatra Selene
Daughter of Cleopatra VII and Mark Antony, twin of Alexander Helios, wife of Juba of Mauretania

Cleopatra Selene was raised in Rome by Octavia and married the Numidian prince Juba II. She bore a son named Ptolemy and, perhaps, a daughter who, we may guess, was named Cleopatra. She died a natural death some time between 5 BC and AD 11.

Ptolemy Philadelphos (Brother/Sister-Loving)
Son of Cleopatra VII and Mark Antony

Following his mother's suicide, Ptolemy Philadelphos was taken to Rome to be raised alongside his brother and sister. He vanished from the historical record soon after.

Ptolemy of Mauretania
Son of Cleopatra Selene and Juba II of Mauretania

Ptolemy inherited his father's throne in AD 23. Seventeen years later he was executed by his half-cousin Caligula.

Chronology of Ancient Egypt

All dates given are BC. The dating of the earlier dynasties is by no means certain. This chronology is based on the dates suggested in J. Baines and J. Malek (1984), *Atlas of Ancient Egypt*, Phaidon, Oxford.

LATE PREDYNASTIC/EARLY DYNASTIC PERIOD (DYNASTIES 0–2): *c.* 3100–2649

OLD KINGDOM (DYNASTIES 3–6): *c.* 2649–2150

FIRST INTERMEDIATE PERIOD (DYNASTIES 7–11): *c.* 2150–2040

MIDDLE KINGDOM (DYNASTIES 11–14): *c.* 2040–1640

SECOND INTERMEDIATE PERIOD (DYNASTIES 15–17): *c.* 1640–1550

NEW KINGDOM (DYNASTIES 18–20): *c.* 1550–1070

THIRD INTERMEDIATE PERIOD (DYNASTIES 21–25): *c.* 1070–712

LATE PERIOD (DYNASTIES 25–31): *c.* 712–332

MACEDONIAN DYNASTY 332–304
Alexander III the Great (332–323)
Philip III Arrhidaeos (323–316)
Alexander IV (316–304)

PTOLEMAIC DYNASTY (304–30)
Ptolemy I Soter I (304–284)
Ptolemy II Philadelphos (285–246)
Ptolemy III Euergetes I (246–221)
Ptolemy IV Philopator (221–205)
Ptolemy V Epiphanes (205–180)
Ptolemy VI Philometor (180–164, 163–145)
Ptolemy VIII Euergetes II (170–163, 145–116)
Ptolemy VII Neos Philopator (145)
Ptolemy IX Soter II (116–107, 88–81)
Ptolemy X Alexander I (107–88)
Cleopatra Berenice III (81–80)
Ptolemy XI Alexander II (80)
Ptolemy XII Neos Dionysos (80–58, 55–51)
Berenice IV (58–55)
Cleopatra VII Thea Philopator (51–30)
Ptolemy XIII, King of Egypt (51–47)
Ptolemy XIV, King of Egypt (47–44)
Ptolemy XV Caesar (44–30)

Notes

Introduction

1 Weigall (1914, revised 1924): v.

2 The most influential queen consorts were Meritneith, Khentkawes, Ankhnesmerypepi II, Tetisheri, Ahhotep, Ahmose-Nefertari, Tiy and Nefertiti; the three queens regnant were Sobeknofru, Hatshepsut and Tawosret. Egyptologists are currently divided about a possible fourth queen regnant who may have ruled Egypt at the end of the Amarna period. The Old Kingdom Queen Nitocris, described by Manetho as 'the most noble and lovely woman of her time, fair-skinned, with red cheeks', is likely to have been a legendary figure. Although the 19th Dynasty chronology known as the Turin Canon does allocate 'Neitaqerti' a brief reign of two years one month and one day, it is likely that 'Neitaqerti' is a misrecorded fragment of a male king's name.

3 Manetho, the acknowledged father of Egyptian history, compiled his list of Egypt's kings during the reign of Ptolemy II. He divided the kings into dynasties – lines of connected rulers – but stopped at Nectanebo, the last king of the 30th Dynasty. His list was later expanded to include Egypt's Persian rulers as the 31st Dynasty, but Manetho's own age remained excluded.

4 The Egyptian falcon-headed god Horus was the son of the Goddess Isis and her murdered husband, the God Osiris. He represented the living king of Egypt, while Osiris represented all of Egypt's dead kings. Outside

Egypt Horus was equated with the Greek god Eros, who in later Greek mythology was recognised as the son of Aphrodite.

5 Not everyone agrees. Carlo Maria Franzero, whose 1957 book *The Life and Times of Cleopatra*, The Philosophical Library, New York, inspired Joseph L. Mankiewicz's 1963 film *Cleopatra*, said of the ruined temple of Venus Genetrix, 'The site of those three beautiful columns seemed to give me the key to the mystery of Cleopatra': 9–10.

6 See, for example, Hughes-Hallett (1990), a work that has inspired others to investigate the phenomenon of the modern Cleopatra.

7 The *Guardian*, having published 'Antony and Cleopatra: Coin Find Changes the Faces of History' on 14 February, was forced to make a correction two days later, agreeing that Cleopatra was not in fact descended from Alexander the Great, and that the battle of Actium was not actually fought off the coast of Egypt. Other less scrupulous newspapers left their errors uncorrected, their readers misinformed. And so the Cleopatra myth grows.

Chapter 1: Princess of Egypt

1 E. R. Bevan (1927), *The House of Ptolemy*, Methuen Publishing, London: 359.

2 Antiochos VIII, Antiochos IX and Antiochos X.

3 Strabo, *The Geography*, 17:1:11. Translated by H. L. Jones.

4 Lucian, *Slander, A Warning*, 16. Dionysiac cross–dressing is discussed in detail in E. Csapo (1997), 'Riding the Phallus for Dionysus: Iconology, Ritual, and Gender-Role Deconstruction, *Phoenix*, 51: 3–4: 253–95. Lucian describes his King Ptolemy as one 'who was nicknamed Dionysos': experts are undecided whether he means Ptolemy IV or, more likely in my opinion, Ptolemy XII.

5 Greek law itself was a complicated and diverse mass of rules, with the cities of Naukratis, Alexandria and Ptolemais Hormou applying their own laws, and Greeks living outside these cities being subject to a version of the laws of their home city-states.

6 Herodotus, *The Histories*, 2: 35–6. Translated by A. de Sélincourt.

7 Quoted in Ray (2002): 138.

8 The exact number of nomes varied from time to time, and nomes were occasionally combined and created as economic and political circumstances dictated.

9 Figures suggested in Rowlandson (1998): 5.

10 B. P. Grenfell and A. S. Hunt, eds (1901), *The Amherst Papyri*, H. Frowde, London, 2: 12.2 .

11 Theocritos, *Odes* 15: 44–71. After A. S. F. Gow (1952), *Theocritus*, Cambridge University Press, Cambridge: 'Nowadays no ruffian slips up to you in the street Egyptian-fashion and does you a mischief – the tricks those packets of rascality used to play, one as bad as another with their nasty tricks, a cursed lot.'

12 *Papyrus Enteuxis*, 26. Translation adapted from A. S. Hunt and C. C. Edgar (1963), *Select Papyri*, Heinemann, London, 2: 233: 268.

13 Theocritos translation after R. Hunter (2003), *Theocritus: Ecomium of Ptolemy Philadelphus, Text and Translation with Introduction and Commentary*, University of California Press, Berkeley: 88–91.

14 The misguided equation of ancient Egypt with slavery, promoted by the biblical story of the Exodus, has made discussion of Cleopatra's racial origins into an even more sensitive area. For an introduction to Afrocentric history, see M. Bernal (1987, 1991), *Black Athena: The Afroasiatic Roots of Classical Civilization*, Free Association Books, London. For a counter argument, see M. R. Lefkowitz and G. M. Rogers eds (1996), *Black Athena Revisited*, University of North Carolina Press, Chapel Hill. See also M. Hamer (1996), 'Queen of Denial', *Transition*, 72: 80–92.

15 Cicero, *Letters to Atticus*, 15: 15. Translated by E. O. Winstedt (1918), Heinemann, London and New York; Appian, *Roman* History, 5: 1. Both are quoted in Hughes-Hallett (1990): 72.

16 Plutarch, *Life of Antony*, 26. Translated by B. Perrin.

17 Technically not a triumvirate, this period is nevertheless often described as the 'first triumvirate' to distinguish it from the second, genuine

triumvirate of Octavian, Lepidus and Antony, which was established following Caesar's assassination.

18 An English translation of H. Petermann's Latin translation of an Armenian translation of the original Greek text of Eusebius's *Chronicle* is available on www.attalus.org/translate/seusebius1.html.

19 Plutarch, *Life of Antony*, 3: 2. Translated by B. Perrin.

20 As just one other king, the long-lived 18th Dynasty Amenhotep III, married a daughter, the true nature of these father–daughter unions must be open to question. Only one royal daughter, Bint-Anath, consort to Ramesses II, produced a child, and the paternity of Bint-Anath's daughter is never stated. The lack of children suggests that these marriages may have been unconsummated unions designed to ensure that the father had a consort, and the daughter achieved the highest female status in the land.

21 Auletes either built or completed existing projects at Athribis (the enlargement of the sanctuary of Triphis), Akhmim (a ritual building of unknown purpose), Dendera (the replacement of the 30th Dynasty Hathor temple), Koptos (the gateway to the Geb temple), Karnak (the gateway to the Ptah temple and various small buildings), Deir el-Medina (the enclosure wall for the Hathor temple), Edfu (the expansion of the Horus temple), Philae (the decoration of the first gateway of the Isis temple and the transfer of the kiosk of Nectanebo I), Biggeh (work at the Osiris temple) and, perhaps, Kom Ombo (the enclosure wall and a new gateway), and the walls of his temples were covered in his own propaganda.

Chapter 2: Queen of Egypt

1 Boccaccio, *On the Lives of Famous Women*, Johann Zainer, Ulm, 1473. Translated by Guido A. Guarino, quoted in Flamarion (1997): 128–31: 128.

2 Stela 13. H. W. Fairman (1934), in R. Mond and O. H. Myers (1934), *The Bucheum*, 2 vols, Egypt Exploration Fund, London, 2. See also W. W. Tarn (1936), 'The Bucheum Stelae: A Note', *Journal of Roman Studies*, 26: 2: 187–9. The stela is currently housed in the Carlsberg Glyptotek, Copenhagen.

3 There is even an outside possibility that the anonymous king might be Auletes. This is discussed further in R. S. Bianchi, 'Images of Cleopatra Reconsidered', and S.-A. Ashton, 'Cleopatra: Goddess, Ruler or Regent?', both papers in Walker and Ashton, eds (2003): 13–23 and 25–30.

4 Dates calculated from the information given on Tayimhotep's funerary stela. In Rome, Augustan law would soon fix the legal minimum age for marriage at twelve for girls and fourteen for boys.

5 Hatshepsut's images are discussed further in J. A. Tyldesley (1996), *Hatshepsut: The Female Pharaoh,* Viking Penguin, London. Hatshepsut excepted, images of queens dressed as kings are extremely rare, although both Berenice II and Berenice IV have been associated with male images.

6 ' ...she based the external trappings of her monarchy on the precedents provided by famous ancient Egyptian female monarchs, Hatshepsut among them, as was clearly demonstrated in her representations and the accompanying inscriptions at the temple of Hathor at Dendera': R. S. Bianchi, 'Cleopatra VII', in D. B. Redford (2001), *The Oxford Encyclopaedia of Ancient Egypt*, Oxford University Press, Oxford and New York: 273–4.

7 This papyrus was discovered as part of a cartonnage mummy case (cartonnage being made from layers of linen or papyrus held together by plaster or glue and moulded to shape). It is now housed in Berlin Museum (C Ord Ptol 73). A. S. Hunt and C. C. Edgar (1934), *Select Papyri II*, Loeb Classical Library, Harvard University Press, Cambridge, Mass., and Heinemann, London: 209.

8 W. Schubart and D. Schäfer (1933), *Spätptolemäische Papyri aus amtlichen Büros des Herakleopolites*, Weidmann, Berlin: 1,834.

9 The visit to Thebes appears in many histories, but is not supported by contemporary documentation and so must be open to a certain amount of doubt. Strabo and Appian record the visit to 'Syria' without further definition.

10 Plutarch, *Life of Pompey*, 77–80. Translated by B. Perrin; Cassius Dio, *Roman History*, 42: 4. Translated by E. Cary.

11 Alternatively, the Ptolemy of circle nine may be the inhospitable captain of Jericho who killed his guest Simon Maccabaeus.

12 Plutarch, *Life of Caesar*, 49. Translated by B. Perrin.

13 Suetonius, *Divine Julius*, 45. Translated by R. Graves.

14 Ibid., 52.

15 Cicero, quoted ibid., 49.

16 Ibid., 50–51.

17 The other Cleopatra heads are housed in the Antikensammlung, Berlin, the Louvre, Paris (a Hellenistic-style Cleopatra probably carved by an Egyptian craftsman) and the Cherchell Museum, Algeria. For further details of Cleopatra's images, see the various papers in Walker and Ashton, eds (2003).

18 The coin images – the official face of Cleopatra – can be compared with images on clay seal impressions found among a diverse collection of sealings from the Ptolemaic temple of Horus at Edfu and today housed in the Royal Ontario Museum, Toronto. The sealings were originally attached to papyrus documents that vanished long ago. One sealing shows a queen – Cleopatra VII? – wearing a vulture headdress, solar crown and a long, full wig. Another replicates the Cypriot Cleopatra/Isis coin but Caesarion, somewhat bizarrely, has vanished from the scene.

19 For a discussion on approaches to Cleopatra's beauty, see E. Shohat 'Disorientating Cleopatra: A Modern Trope of Identity', in Walker and Ashton, eds (2003): 127–38.

20 Grant (1972): 66.

21 The Berlin head is just one among many representations of Nefertiti. Few of the others display the same stark symmetrical beauty. See J. A. Tyldesley (2005, revised edition), *Nefertiti: Egypt's Sun Queen*, Penguin Books, London.

22 Plutarch, *Life of Antony*, 27. Translated by B. Perrin.

23 Cassius Dio, *Roman History*, 42: 34. Translated by E. Cary.

24 It is possible to catch a glimpse of 'real' people going about their daily business, but to do this we have to look principally at the graffiti and doodles left by dynastic Egypt's unofficial artists. During the Ptolemaic age the situation changed slightly as the elite started to commission art

that was less idealised and, to modern eyes, more realistic. This change is not apparent in royal art. See R. S. Bianchi (1988), 'The Pharaonic Art of Ptolemaic Egypt', in *Cleopatra's Egypt: Age of the Ptolemies*, Brooklyn Museum, New York: 55–80.

25 The extent to which priestly decrees outlined how pose, material, scale and placement should be used in these propaganda pieces is discussed further in Stanwick (2002): 6–14.

26 As her fertility was important to the queen, it was necessary that she be depicted as eternally young. When we do find an image of an older queen it therefore comes as something of a shock. The 18th Dynasty Queen Tiy and her daughter-in-law Nefertiti lived in an age of artistic experimentation, and both were depicted as older women. In contrast, it was always considered acceptable to depict men at all stages of life.

27 The significance of the triple uraeus is discussed, with further references, in R. Bianchi, 'Images of Cleopatra VII Reconsidered', in Walker and Ashton, eds, (2003): 13–23. See also S.-A Ashton (2005), 'The Use of the Double and Triple Uraeus in Royal Iconography', in A. Cooke and F. Simpson eds, *Current Research in Egyptology II*, BAR International Series 1,380, Oxford: 1–9.

28 A title which, given the uncertainty over Cleopatra's marital status, might more appropriately apply to Arsinoë II.

Chapter 3: Alexandria-next-to-Egypt

1 R. T. Kelly (1912), *Egypt*, Adam and Charles Black, London: 5. Kelly is describing his first visit to Egypt in 1883.

2 Plutarch, *Life of Alexander*. 26. Translated by B. Perrin.

3 Historian Michel Chauveau (2000: 57) has suggested that 'Rhakotis' may have been not a proper town name but simply the misunderstood Greek form of the Egyptian *Rá-qed* or 'building site'.

4 Arrian, *Anabasis of Alexander*. Translated by E. J. Chinnock 1893. Arrian lived *c.* AD 86–146.

5 Pseudo-Callisthenes, *The Alexander Romance*. This is at best an unreliable source, but in the matter of the two architects there is little reason to doubt its accuracy.

6 Suetonius, *Divine Augustus*, 18. Translated by R. Graves.

7 Cassius Dio, *Roman History*, 51: 61.5. Translated by E. Cary.

8 Historians have looked in Egypt (Alexandria, Memphis and Siwa), in Macedonia and beyond. See, for example, A. M. Chugg (2004), *The Lost Tomb of Alexander the Great*, Richmond, London, where the author argues that the body of St Mark, currently housed in the St Mark's Basilica, Venice, is actually the body of Alexander the Great.

9 Flavius Josephus, *Against Apion*, 2: 53–6. A version of the drunken elephant story is told in 3 Maccabees 5–6, where the king involved is Ptolemy IV.

10 Discussed in more detail in Fraser (1972): 93–131.

11 Strabo, *The Geography*, 17: 8. Translated by H. L. Jones.

12 H. A. R. Gibb (1929), *Ibn Battuta: Travels in Asia and Africa 1325–1354*, George Routledge and Sons, London: 47–50.

13 Athenaeus, *Deipnosophists*, 12: 184. Translated by C. D. Yonge.

14 Ibid., 11: 67. Athenaeus wrote his *Deipnosophists* (*Banquet of the Learned*) during the third century AD. The text, essentially a lengthy conversation, ranges over a variety of topics dear to the author's heart, including sex (both 'natural' and 'unnatural'), luxury, food and drink, and is packed full of quotations from earlier authorities.

15 Ibid., 13: 37.

16 Ibid., 7: 2–3.

17 Ibid., 5: 25–36.

18 This can be compared to the Ptolemaic town of Kerkeosiris, which, with a population of approximately 1,500 in the second century BC, had three Egyptian shrines to Thoth, two to Isis, two to Taweret and one each to Petesouchos, Orsenouphis, Harpsenesis, Anubis, Bast and Amen, plus Greek shrines to Zeus and the twin gods Castor and Pollux. Figures given in Bowman (1990): 171.

19 Pliny the Elder, *Natural History*, 34: 42. Translated by H. Rackham. This, together with other uses of magnetism in temples, is discussed in Empereur (1998): 92–5.

20 Pliny the Elder, *Natural History*, 36: 14. Translated by H. Rackham.

21 Philo, *The Embassy to Gaius*, 149–51. Translated by F. H. Coulson (1962), Loeb Classical Library, Harvard University Press, Cambridge, Mass., and Heinemann, London.

Chapter 4: Cleopatra and Julius Caesar

1 G. H. Macurdy (1932), *Hellenistic Queens: Study of Womanpower in Macedonia, Seleucid Syria, and Ptolemaic Egypt*, Johns Hopkins University Studies in Archaeology 14, Johns Hopkins Press, Baltimore: 189.

2 Lucan (Marcus Annaeus Lucanus), *Pharsalia* (*The Civil War*), 10: 110ff. Translated by E. Ridley (1896), *The Pharsalia of Lucan*, Longmans, Green, and Co., London.

3 Suetonius, *Divine Julius*, 35. Translated by R. Graves.

4 Recorded in Caesar's *The Alexandrian Wars*, which was most probably written by Aulus Hirtius.

5 Ibid., 23. Translated by W. A. McDevitte and W. S. Bohn.

6 Cassius Dio, *Roman History*, 42: 44. Translated by E. Cary.

7 Suetonius, *Divine Julius*, 52. Translated by R. Graves.

8 Appian, *The Civil Wars*, 3: 2: 90.

9 Athenaeus, *Deipnosophists*, 5: 37–40. See T. W. Hillard (2002), 'The Nile Cruise of Cleopatra and Caesar', *Cambridge Quarterly*, 52: 2: 549–54.

10 Lucan, *Pharsalia* (*The Civil War*), 10: 192–331. Translated by J. D. Duff (1928), Loeb Classical Library, Harvard University Press, Cambridge, Mass., and Heinemann, London. Lucan did not finish his Book 10, and so never described the actual voyage.

11 Plutarch, *Life of Caesar*, 49: 10; *Life of Antony*, 54: 6.

12 Cassius Dio, *Roman History*, 47: 31.5; Suetonius, *Divine Julius*, 52: 2–3.

13 This piece is discussed in J. P. V. D. Balsdon's 1960 review of H. Volkmann's *Cleopatra*, in *Classical Review*, 10: 1: 68–71. There are difficulties in translating the stela date, as both the Roman and Egyptian calendars were operating incorrectly at the time and it is possible to argue with some validity that this date should be read as September rather than June.

14 D. Devauchelle (2001), 'La stèle du Louvre IM8 (Sérapéum de Memphis) et la prétendue date de naissance de Césarion', *Enchoria*, 27: 41: 56 (27).

15 See D. Todman (2007), 'Childbirth in Ancient Rome: From Traditional Folklore to Obstetrics', *Australian and New Zealand Journal of Obstetrics and Gynaecology*, 47: 82–5.

16 Cassius Dio, *Roman History*, 43: 27.3. Translated by E. Cary.

17 Cicero, *Letters to Atticus*, 15: 15.2. Translated by L. P. Wilkinson, quoted and discussed in Grant (1972): 96.

18 See E. Gruen (2003), 'Cleopatra in Rome: Facts and Fantasies', in D. Braund and C. Gill eds, *Myth, History and Culture in Republican Rome*, University of Exeter Press, Exeter, 256–74.

19 Cicero, *Letters to Atticus*, 14: 8.1.

20 Ibid., 14: 20.2.

21 See, for example, Chauveau (2002): 32–3; J. Carcopino, *Passion et politique chez les Césars* (1958) :37. Carcopino has suggested that Mark Antony may have been Caesarion's father. Just one further piece of evidence can be cited in support of a late birth date for Caesarion. We have already noted the bronze Cypriot coin which shows Cleopatra suckling the infant Caesarion (page 61). Unfortunately, there is no firm date for this coin. If we imagine that it is a literal representation of Caesarion and his mother, we might also imagine that it was produced soon after Caesarion's birth, at a time when Cleopatra ruled Cyprus. The first firm evidence for Cleopatra ruling Cyprus dates to 43. But, as Caesar is reported to have gifted Cyprus to Egypt in 48, it could equally well be argued that the coin was struck as early as 47, following Cleopatra's union with Ptolemy XIV.

22 Speculation about this 'second child' abounds. See, for example, R. Ellis (2006), *Cleopatra to Christ*, Edfu Books, Cheshire, which identifies the phantom daughter of Cleopatra and Caesar as the grandmother of Jesus.

Chapter 5: The New Isis

1 Mond and Myers advertise for assistance in the *Geographical Journal* (1936), 87: 1: 95.

2 Flavius Josephus, *Antiquities of the Jews*, 15: 89. Translated by W. Whiston (1895, updated and republished 2001).

3 Tyldesley (2006).

4 The palette, recovered from Hierakonpolis, is today displayed in Cairo Museum.

5 Herodotus, *The Histories*, 2: 41. Translated by A. de Sélincourt (1954).

6 See R. E. Witt (1971): 20: 'Isis was all things to all men. That was what made her so formidable a foe to Jesus and oecumenical Paul.' Other serious rivals were Mithras and, to a lesser extent, Dionysos.

7 Plutarch's version, adapted to fit with traditional Egyptian accounts of the same myth, has been used as the basis of this retelling which is adapted from J. A. Tyldesley (2004), *Tales from Ancient Egypt*, Rutherford Press, Bolton: 16–25.

8 Cleopatra's Egyptian titulary is discussed in J. Tait (2003), 'Cleopatra by Name', in Walker and Ashton, eds (2003): 3–7.

9 A. B. Edwards (1877), *A Thousand Miles up the Nile*, George Routledge and Sons, London. The quotation is taken from page 122 of the 1888 edition.

10 The history of this curious piece has been reconstructed in A. Rammant-Peeters (1998), 'L'Affaire Cléopâtre: ou comment la photographie servit de véhicule à l'imagination du XIX siècle', in W. Clarysse, A. Schoors and H. Willems, eds, *Egyptian Religion the Last Thousand Years: Studies Dedicated to the memory of Jan Quaegebeur*, Peeters, Leuven: 1,449–57.

11 Lucius Apuleius, *Metamorphoses,* or, *The Golden Ass,* 11: 47. Translation adapted from W. Adlington (1566; 1639 published edition), 'Imprinted at London in Fleatstreate at the sign of the Oliphante, by Henry Wykes'. Compare with the translation given by R. Graves (1950, revised edition 1990), *The Golden Ass,* Penguin Books, Harmondsworth.

12 Plutarch, *Isis and Osiris,* 5: 382. Translated by F. C. Babbitt (1936), *Moralia V,* Loeb Classical Library, Harvard University Press, Cambridge, Mass., and Heinemann, London.

13 Diodorus Siculus, *Library of History,* I: 83.8. Translated by C. H. Oldfather.

14 The cult temples, situated in the cities, may be contrasted with the mortuary temples which were built in the desert as part of the king's own funerary provision.

15 Translated by Ashton (2003): 105.

16 Translated by J. Quagebeur (1988), 'Cleopatra VII and the Cults of the Ptolemaic Queens', in *Cleopatra's Egypt, Age of the Ptolemies,* Brooklyn Museum, New York: 41–54: 43.

17 Translation adapted from J. D. Ray (1976), *The Archive of Hor,* Egypt Exploration Society, London: 11–12 (text 1.11–18).

Chapter 6: Cleopatra and Mark Antony

1 Grant (1972): 84.

2 Seneca, *Quaestiones Naturales,* 4a2.16.

3 Flavius Josephus, *Against Apion,* 2: 60. Translated by W. Whiston.

4 Offering formulae were magical lists of food and other goods that the deceased might require in the tomb. The lists acted as an *aide mémoire* to the living who brought food to the tomb and the reading out of the list would cause the goods to magically and invisibly appear for the spirit of the deceased.

5 J. P. Lesley (1868), 'A Classified Catalogue of Antiquities Collected by Mr Harris, and Now in his Museum in Alexandria, in Notes on Some of the

Historical and Mythological Features of the D'Orbiney Papyri',
Proceedings of the American Philological Society 10: 80: 543–82: 565.

6 M. Lichtheim (1990), *Ancient Egyptian Literature 3: The Late Period*,
University of California Press, Berkeley and London: 63.

7 Plutarch, *Life of Antony*, 9: 3–4. Translated by B. Perrin.

8 See P. Walcot (1998), 'Plutarch on Sex', *Greece and Rome*, 45: 2: 166–87.

9 Discussed in more detail in K. Welch (1995), 'Antony, Fulvia, and the
Ghost of Clodius in 47 BC', *Greece and Rome*, 42: 2: 182–201. Fulvia had
also previously been married to Gaius Scribonius Curio.

10 Plutarch, *Life of Antony*, 10: 3. Translated by B. Perrin.

11 Appian, *The Civil Wars*, 4: 5.8. They may well have met in Alexandria, but
it seems unlikely that Antony would have fallen so violently in love.

12 Plutarch, *Life of Antony*, 25: 3–4. Translated by B. Perrin.

13 Cassius Dio, *Roman History*, 48: 27.5. Translated by E. Cary.

14 Quoting Socrates the Rhodian: Athenaeus, *Deipnosophists*, 4: 29.

15 Plutarch, *Life of Antony*, 28. Translated by B. Perrin.

16 Pliny the Elder, *Natural History*, 19.59: 119–21.

17 For a fascinating account of experiments with pearls and sour wine, see B.
L. Ullman (1957), 'Cleopatra's Pearls', *Classical Journal*, 52: 5: 193–201.
'When I boiled a pearl for thirty-three minutes the vinegar boiled off
when I was reading a detective story. I can still smell that vinegar. The
pearl seemed not to be affected, though I thought it looked a trifle
peaked.' I am grateful to the author for saving me the necessity of
sacrificing my own somewhat insignificant pearl earrings in the interest of
science.

18 Suetonius, *Divine Julius*, 43.

19 Pliny the Elder, *Natural History*, 21.12. The story of Lollia Paulina is told
in 9: 117.

20 Discussed in A. Wright (2002), 'Velleius Paterculus and L. Munatius
Plancus', *Classical Philology*, 97: 2: 178–84. It is apparent that Velleius is

deliberately setting out to blacken Plancus's name and the accuracy of his story must therefore be questioned.

21 Plutarch, *Life of Antony*, 10: 4. Translated by B. Perrin.

22 Athanaeus, *Deipnosophists*, 11: 85. Translated by C. D. Yonge.

23 Plutarch, *Life of Antony*, 29. Translated by B. Perrin.

24 H. Volkmann (1958), translated by C. J. Cadoux, *Cleopatra: Politics and Propaganda*, Elek Books, London: 72.

25 P. van Minden (2000), 'An Official Act of Cleopatra (with subscription in her own hand)', *Ancient Society*, 30: 29–34. The papyrus is today housed in Berlin Museum.

26 For further Ptolemaic correspondence, consult Rowlandson (1998).

27 Plutarch, *Life of Antony*, 36. Translated by B. Perrin.

28 Ibid., 36. 13. Translated by B. Perrin.

29 Cleopatra's new title, 'Philopatris', has sparked huge debate among academics, with some arguing that the 'homeland' which Cleopatra loves is either Egypt or Alexandria and others that she is referring to her family's traditional homeland of Macedonia. See, for example, Bingen (2007): 57–62.

30 Plutarch, *Life of Antony*, 53. 3. Translated by B. Perrin.

31 Flavius Josephus, *Antiquities of the Jews*, 15: 97. Translated by W. Whiston.

32 Cassius Dio, *Roman History*, 49: 40: 4. Translated by E. Cary.

33 Suetonius, *Divine Augustus*, 69. Translated by R. Graves.

34 See, for example, A. Meadows in Walker and Higgs (2001): 29. R. Holland (2004), *Augustus: Godfather of Europe*, Sutton Publishing, Stroud: 241, uses 'fucking' but omits the vital *uxor mea est*.

35 To take just one of many possible examples, 'Cleopatra was naturally hoping to persuade him [Antony] to divorce Octavia officially under Roman law'. ibid.: 235.

Chapter 7: Death of a Dream

1 W. W. Tarn, writing in the *Cambridge Ancient History* (1934, 10: III), defines Cleopatra by her gender and fails to name her.

2 Cassius Dio, *Roman History*, 50: 5. Translated by E. Cary.

3 K. Scott (1929), 'Octavian's Propaganda and Antony's *De Sua Ebrietate*', *Classical Philology*, 24: 2: 133–41.

4 Plutarch, *Life of Antony*, 56. Translated by B. Perrin.

5 M. Reinhold (1981), 'The Declaration of War against Cleopatra', *Classical Journal*, 77 :2; 97–103.

6 *The Sibylline Oracles* are more correctly known as *The Pseudo-Sibylline Oracles*. For a full translation, including this quoted extract, see M. S. Terry (1899), *The Sibylline Oracles. Translated from the Greek into English Blank Verse*, Hunt and Eaton, New York. For more discussion, see J. J. Collins 'Sibylline Oracles (Second Century BC – Seventh Century AD)', in J. Charlesworth, ed. (1982), *The Old Testament Pseudepigrapha*, Darton, Longman and Todd, New York, 1: 223–316.

7 Cassius Dio, *Roman History*, 50: 15. Translated by E. Cary.

8 Plutarch, *Life of Antony*, 66–7. Translated by B. Perrin.

9 W. W. Tarn (1931), 'The Battle of Actium', *Journal of Roman Studies*, 21: 173–99. See also G. W. Richardson (1937), 'Actium', *Journal of Roman Studies*, 27: 2: 153–64. The assumption is that a quinquereme at Actium would carry a minimum of 420 men, while a trireme would carry 200–300 and a larger ship might carry as many as 600.

10 Plutarch, *Life of Antony*, 71: 4–5. Translated by B. Perrin.

11 Ibid., 73: 2.

12 Ibid., 75: 3. The story of Antony's abandonment by his gods inspired Constantine Cavafy's hauntingly beautiful poem 'The God Abandons Antony': see *The Poems by C. P. Cavafy* (1971), translated by J. Mavrogordato, Hogarth Press, London.

13 Suetonius, *Life of Domitian*, (*The Twelve Caesars*), 11. Translated by R. Graves.

14 Plutarch, *Life of Antony*, 76. Translated by B. Perrin.

15 Whitehorne (1994): 188.

16 The theory that Octavian murdered Cleopatra has been around for many
years. It was discussed most recently and most publicly in Atlantic
Production's *Who Killed Cleopatra? Revealed* (broadcast 2004). There can
be little doubt that Octavian wanted Cleopatra dead, although the
argument that he wished to end the troublesome Ptolemaic line once and
for all holds little water when we consider that he spared the lives of three
of Cleopatra's children and allowed Cleopatra's daughter to marry and
have children of her own. However, a murder at this late stage, and in
such spectacular style, makes little sense. Octavian had already had plenty
of opportunities to kill Cleopatra – when she was barricaded in her
mausoleum with Proculeius, for example, and later when she was under
his protection in the palace – and, of course, he had no need to hide his
actions. Cleopatra was a defeated enemy and as such could openly and
justifiably be executed.

17 Plutarch, *Life of Antony*, 84. Translated by B. Perrin.

18 Cassius Dio, *Roman History*, 51. Translated by E. Cary.

19 Plutarch, *Life of Antony*, 86. Translated by B. Perrin.

20 Figures given in S. H. el Din (2006), *A Guide to the Reptiles and
Amphibians of Egypt*, American University in Cairo Press, Cairo: 11.

21 Plutarch, *Life of Alexander*, 1: 2. Translated by B. Perrin.

22 Ibid., 82.

23 Ibid., 83, 84.

24 Ibid., 86.

Chapter 8: Cleopatra's Children

1 T. Gautier (1838), *Une Nuit de Cléopâtre*. Translated by L. Hearn (1882),
One of Cleopatra's Nights and Other Fantastic Romances, B. Worthington,
New York.

2 Horace (*Odesi*, 1.37: 25–9), Virgil (*The Aeneid*, 8: 696–7), Propertius
(*Elegies*, 3. 11: 53–4). Virgil uses more twin-snake imagery when relating

the fate of Laocoön and his sons, and again when describing the vision sent to Turnus by Allecto.

3 Shakespeare, *Antony and Cleopatra*, 5: 2.

4 Given modern society's reluctance to accept that glittering celebrities can die, it is not surprising that several theories have evolved to explain that Cleopatra survived. In the 1920s, for example, A. J. Bethell decided that Cleopatra did not die but was sent by Octavian to be the wife of Phraates IV of Parthia: unpublished work quoted in Hughes-Hallett (1990): 108.

5 Not to be confused with the entirely different modern Mauritania on Africa's Atlantic coast.

6 Aristotle was another who believed that the Nile originated in Mauretania. See D. Braund (1984), 'Anth. Pal. 9.235: Juba II, Cleopatra Selene and the Course of the Niel', *Classical Quarterly*, 34: 1: 175–8. Three centuries earlier, Alexander the Great had announced that he had discovered the source of the Nile when he encountered crocodiles in India.

7 W. N. Weech (1932), 'Rambles in Mauretania Caesariensis (continued)', *Greece and Rome*: 2: 65–73: 72.

8 Crinagoras, 18. After A. S. F. Gow and D. L. Page (1968), *The Greek Anthology. The Garland of Philip*, Cambridge University Press, Cambridge.

9 Suetonius, *Life of Gaius (Caligula)* (*The Twelve Caesars*) 35. 2.

10 Pliny the Elder, *Natural History*, 36: 72. Translated by H. Rackham.

11 Cassius Dio, *Roman History*, 51: 22. Translated by E. Cary.

Chapter 9: History Becomes Legend

1 Chorus from 'Cleopatra had a Jazz Band', words by J. Morgan and J. Coogan, music by J. Coogan (1917). The sheet music gives 'has a jazz band' for the chorus but the title of the piece is 'had a jazz band', so I have adjusted the words here.

2 Virgil, *The Aeneid*, 4: 330. Translated by D. West.

3 Ibid., 8: 680.

4 Propertius, *Elegies*, 3: 11 and 4: 6. Discussed in more detail in Wyke (2002): 195–243.

5 Horace, *Epode 9, Ode* 1: 37.

6 Plutarch, *Life of Alexander*, 1. Translated by B. Perrin.

7 Cassius Dio, *Histories*, 51: 15. Translated by E. Cary.

8 Flavius Josephus, *Against Apion*, 2: 7.

9 O. Abd el-Galil (2000), *Tarikh Misr li-Yohana Al-Niqusi*, Dar Ain, Cairo.

10 Al-Masudi, *Muruj*: quoted in el-Daly (2005): 133. El-Daly provides a full exploration of the medieval Arab and Islamic historians.

11 Plutarch, *Life of Antony* 26. W. J. Skeat (1875, revised edition 1892), *Shakespeare's Plutarch*, Macmillan and Co., London. Skeat uses the republished 1612 version of North. It is not clear which version Shakespeare used: *Antony and Cleopatra*, 2: 2.

12 The development of Cleopatra in popular culture is outlined by Hughes-Hallet (1990), Hamer (1993) and Wyke (2002). All three supply more detailed references.

13 Hamer (1993): xv.

14 The 1930 edition of the *Cambridge Ancient History* famously quotes Shakespeare; this was removed from subsequent editions. Samson (1990) gives twenty-five footnotes for the Cleopatra section of her book, over half of them references to Shakespeare. These are by no means the only texts to fall into this trap.

15 Including Gianna Terribili Gonzales (1913); Theda Bara (1917), her stage name being an anagram of 'Arab death'; Claudette Colbert (1934); Vivien Leigh (1945); Elizabeth Taylor (1962). Each of these actresses was, to a greater or lesser extent, required by the studios and the media to live out the role of Cleopatra in her private life. Amanda Barrie, frolicking with Sid James in the discarded Taylor–Burton sets, was a very British Cleopatra in the 1964 camp comedy *Carry on Cleo*. The recent BBC television series *Rome* (2005) included a playful yet determined Cleopatra ruling over a decadent court.

16 C. M. Franzero (1957), *The Life and Times of Cleopatra*, The Philosophical Library, New York. This book was subsequently revised and republished, with the original illustrations replaced by stills from the film, as *Cleopatra Queen of Egypt* (1962), Panther Books, London; this extract is taken from the 1968 edition, page 17. It perhaps goes without saying that there was no 'old custom' of deflowering virgins in the Karnak temple.

17 Weigall (1914, revised edition 1924): vi.

18 Ibid.: 440.

Who was Who

1 Samson (1985): 103.

2 To ensure consistency, all dates in this section have been taken from J. Baines and J. Malek (1984), *Atlas of Ancient Egypt*, Phaidon, Oxford.

Bibliography

Many, many books, scholarly articles and works of fiction have been written about Cleopatra, her family, life and times. As this book is primarily aimed at the general reader, I have listed here the more accessible and up to date, giving preference to those written in English. Most of them provide their own list of further reading. More specialised references are given, where appropriate, as footnotes to the text.

I have deliberately excluded websites dealing with Cleopatra as, by their very nature, these tend to be ephemeral and are of varying accuracy. However, the Ptolemaic genealogies compiled and constantly updated by Chris Bennett offers a valuable exception to this rule (www.geocieties.com/christopherjbennett/index.htm).

Classical Texts

Many of the older translations of classical texts, now in the public domain, are available for free consultation on the Internet.

Appian, *The Civil Wars*, Volumes III and IV of *Roman History*, Translated by H. White (1912–13), Loeb Classical Library, Harvard University Press, Cambridge, Mass., and Heinemann, London

Arrian, *Anabasis of Alexander*. Translated by E. J. Chinnock (1893), George Bell and Sons, London

Athenaeus, *Deipnosophists or Banquet of the Learned*. Translated by C. D. Yonge (1854) 3 vols, Henry G. Bohn, London

Julius Caesar, *The Alexandrian Wars*. Translated by W. A. McDevitte and W. S. Bohn (1869), Harper and Brothers, New York

Cassius Dio, *Roman History.* Translated by E. Cary (1914–27) 9 vols, Loeb Classical Library, Harvard University Press, Cambridge, Mass. and Heinemann, London

Diodórus Siculus, *Library of History* Book I. Translated by C. H. Oldfather (1933), Vol. I, Loeb Classical Library, Harvard University Press, Cambridge, Mass., and Heinemann, London

Flavius Josephus, *Against Apion*. Translated by W. Whiston (1895; updated and republished 2001), *The Works of Josephus, Complete and Unabridged*, Hendrickson Publishers, Peabody, Mass.

— *Antiquities of the Jews*. Translated by W. Whiston (1895; updated and republished 2001), *The Works of Josephus, Complete and Unabridged*, Hendrickson Publishers, Peabody, Mass.

Herodotus, *The Histories*. Translated by A. de Sélincourt (1954), revised with introduction and notes by J. Marincola (1996), Penguin Books, Harmondsworth

Kleiner, D. E. E. (2005) *Cleopatra and Rome*, Harvard University Press, Cambridge, Mass.

Pliny the Elder, *Natural History*. Translated by H. Rackham (1938–40), Loeb Classical Library, Harvard University Press, Cambridge, Mass., and Heinemann, London

Plutarch, *The Parallel Lives: Life of Alexander*. Translated by B. Perrin (1919), Vol VII, Loeb Classical Library, Harvard University Press, Cambridge, Mass., and Heinemann, London

— *The Parallel Lives: Life of Antony*. Translated by B. Perrin (1920), Vol. IX, Loeb Classical Library, Harvard University Press, Cambridge, Mass., and Heinemann, London

— *The Parallel Lives: Life of Caesar*. Translated by B. Perrin (1919), Vol. VII, Loeb Classical Library, Harvard University Press, Cambridge, Mass., and Heinemann, London

— *The Parallel Lives: Life of Pompey*. Translated by B. Perrin (1917), Vol. V, Loeb Classical Library, Harvard University Press, Cambridge, Mass., and Heinemann, London

Strabo, *The Geography*. Translated by H. L. Jones (1917–32), Vols 1–8 (Books 1–17), Loeb Classical Library, Harvard University Press, Cambridge, Mass., and Heinemann, London

Suetonius, *Julius Caesar, Afterwards deified* and *Augustus, Afterwards deified*, part of *The Twelve Caesars*. Translated by Robert Graves, revised with an introduction by Michael Grant (1979), Penguin Books, Harmondsworth

Virgil, *The Aeneid*. Translated by D. West (1990), Penguin Books, Harmondsworth

Further Reading

Arnold, D. (1999), *Temples of the Last Pharaohs,* Oxford University Press, Oxford and New York

Ashton, S.-A. (2003), *The Last Queens of Egypt*, Pearson Education, Harlow

Bingen, J. (2007), *Hellenistic Egypt: Monarchy, Society, Economy, Culture,* edited by R. S. Bagnall, Edinburgh University Press, Edinburgh

Bowman, A. K. (1990), *Egypt After the Pharaohs*, Oxford University Press, Oxford

Burstein, S. M. (2004), *The Reign of Cleopatra*, Greenwood Press, Westport, Conn.

Cabfora, L. (1987), *The Vanished Library: A Wonder of the Ancient World*, University of California Press, Berkeley and Los Angeles

Chauveau, M. (2000), *Egypt in the Age of Cleopatra: History and Society Under the Ptolemies*, translated by D. Lorton, Cornell University Press, Ithaca and London

— (2002), *Cleopatra: Beyond the Myth*, translated by D. Lorton, Cornell University Press, Ithaca and London

Corbelli, J. A. (2006), *The Art of Death in Graeco-Roman Egypt*, Shire Publications, Princes Risborough

El-Daly, O. (2005), *Egyptology: The Missing Millennium – Ancient Egypt in Medieval Arabic Writings*, UCL Press, London

Empereur, J.-Y. (1998), *Alexandria Rediscovered*, translated by M. Maehler, British Museum Press, London

Fantham, E. et al. (1994), *Women in the Classical World*, Oxford University Press, New York and Oxford

Flamarion, E. (1997), *Cleopatra: From History to Legend*, Thames and Hudson, London

Fraser, P. M. (1972), *Ptolemaic Alexandria*, Oxford University Press, Oxford

Garland, R. (2003), *Julius Caesar*, Bristol Phoenix Press, Bristol

Goddio, F. et al. (1998), *Alexandria: The Submerged Royal Quarters*, Periplus Ltd, London

Grant, M. (1972), *Cleopatra: A Biography*, Barnes and Noble Books, New York

— (1982), *From Alexander to Cleopatra: The Hellenistic World*, Weidenfeld and Nicolson, London

Hamer, M. (1993), *Signs of Cleopatra*, Routledge, London and New York

Höbl, G. (2001), *A History of the Ptolemaic Empire*. Translated by T. Saavedra, Routledge, London and New York

Hughes-Hallett, L. (1990), *Cleopatra: Histories, Dreams and Distortions*, Bloomsbury Publishing Ltd, London

Jacob, C. and de Polignac, F. (2000), *Alexandria Third Century BC: The Knowledge of the World in a Single City*. Translated by Colin Clement, Harpocrates, Alexandria

Jones, P. J. (1971), *Cleopatra: A Sourcebook*, University of Oklahoma Press, Norman

Lane Fox, R. (2004 updated edition), *Alexander the Great*, Penguin Books, London

Lefkowitz, M. and Rogers, G. M., eds (1996), *Black Athena Revisited*, North Carolina University Press, Chapel Hill

Matyszak, P. (2003), *Chronicle of the Roman Republic*, Thames and Hudson, London

Mysliewic, K. (2000), *The Twilight of Ancient Egypt: First Millennium BC*. Translated by D. Lorton, Cornell University Press, Ithaca and London

Pomeroy, S. B. (1975, revised edition 1995), *Goddesses, Whores, Wives and Slaves,* Schocken Books, New York

Pomeroy, S. B., Burnstein, S. M., Donlan, W. and Tolbert Roberts, J. (1999), *Ancient Greece: A Political, Social, and Cultural History*, Oxford University Press, New York and Oxford

Ray, J. (2002), *Reflections of Osiris*, Profile Books, London

Rice, E. E. (1999), *Cleopatra*, Sutton Publishing, Stroud

Rowlandson, J., ed. (1998), *Women and Society in Greek and Roman Egypt: A Sourcebook*, Cambridge University Press, Cambridge

Samson, J. (1990, second edition), *Nefertiti and Cleopatra: Queen-Monarchs of Ancient Egypt*, Rubicon Press, London

Shakespeare, W. (1606/7), *Antony and Cleopatra*

Stanwick, P. E. (2002), *Portraits of the Ptolemies: Greek Kings as Egyptian Pharaohs*, University of Texas Press, Austin

Troy, L. (1986), *Patterns of Queenship in Ancient Egyptian Myth and History: Uppsala Studies in Ancient Mediterranean and Near Eastern Civilizations 14*, Boreas, Uppsala

Tyldesley, J. A. (2006), *Chronicle of the Queens of Egypt*, Thames and Hudson, London

Vasunia, P. (2001), *The Gift of the Nile: Hellenizing Egypt from Aeschylus to Alexander*, University of California Press, Berkeley

Walker, S. and Ashton, S.-A. (2006), *Cleopatra*, Bristol Classical Press, Bristol

Walker, S. and Ashton, S.-A., eds (2003), *Cleopatra Reassessed*, British Museum Occasional Papers 103, London

Walker, S. and Higgs, P., eds (2001), *Cleopatra of Egypt: From History to Myth*, British Museum Publications, London

Whitehorn, J. (1994), *Cleopatras*, Routledge, London and New York

Weigall, A. (1914, revised edition 1924), *The Life and Times of Cleopatra Queen of Egypt: A Study in the Origin of the Roman Empire*, G. P. Putnam's and Sons, New York, and Knickerbocker Press, London

Witt, R.E. (1971), *Isis in the Ancient World*, Johns Hopkins University Press, Baltimore and London (originally published as *Isis in the Graeco-Roman World*)

Wyke, M. (2002), *The Roman Mistress; Ancient and Modern Representations*, Oxford University Press, Oxford

List of Illustrations

Family Tree and Maps

Family Tree adapted from Walker S. and Higgs P., eds (2001), *Cleopatra of Egypt: From History to Myth*, British Museum Publications, London.
Cleopatra's World adapted from Walker S. and Higgs P., eds (2001), *Cleopatra of Egypt: From History to Myth*, British Museum Publications, London.
Cleopatra's Egypt adapted from Höbl G. (2001), *A History of the Ptolemaic Empire*. Translated by T. Saavedra, Routledge, London and New York.
Cleopatra's Alexandria adapted from various sources.

Cartouches

 Alexander the Great – Alexandros

 Ptolemy XII – Ptolemy living forever, beloved of Ptah and Isis

 Cleopatra VII – Cleopatra the Father-loving goddess

 Ptolemy Caesar (Caesarion) – Caesar living forever, beloved of Ptah and Isis

 Octavian – Autocrator ('ruler')

Acknowledgements

I would like to express my gratitude to John Ray, who patiently read through the first draft of *Cleopatra* and offered helpful advice. Any mistakes are, of course, my own. I would also like to thank Judith Corbelli and Steven Snape for their encouragement, advice and enthusiasm. At Profile, Peter Carson believed in this book, and Bohdan Buciak, Penny Daniel, Anna-Marie Fitzgerald, Lesley Levene and Nicola Taplin helped it to become a reality. In 2006 the Society of Authors generously awarded me a grant from the Author's Foundation, which allowed me to travel to Egypt in search of Cleopatra. I will always be grateful for their support.

My father, William Randolph Tyldesley, always wanted me to write about Cleopatra; sadly he died when this book was nearing completion. I wish that he could have read it.

Index